Giving
Hope and a Future

Bethany Christian Trust:
The First 25 Years

ANNE BERRY

CHRISTIAN
FOCUS

Rev. Alan Berry, a Baptist minister, founded the charity *Bethany Christian Trust* in 1983 in Edinburgh, Scotland. Its main mission has been to reach the needs of people in various situations. His wife, Anne, involved in the ministry from its inception until recently, has written this book recounting interesting anecdotes and testimonies from people involved in all aspects of the ministry.

Copyright© Anne Berry 2009

ISBN 978-1-84550-447-2

10 9 8 7 6 5 4 3 2 1

Published in 2009

by
Christian Focus Publications Ltd.,
Geanies House, Fearn, Ross-shire,
IV20 1TW, Scotland, Great Britain

www.christianfocus.com

Cover design by Daniel van Straaten
Printed by Bell and Bain, Ltd., Glasgow

o
Mixed Sources
Product group from well-managed
forests and other controlled sources
www.fsc.org Cert no. TT-COC-002769
© 1996 Forest Stewardship Council
FSC

CONTENTS

DEDICATION

To the memory of my dear friend, Margaret Rees,
with whom I shared many smiles and for whom I shed many
tears and whose latter years were testimony that by God's grace
there can be 'hope and a future'.

ACKNOWLEDGEMENTS

I would like to acknowledge the contribution of Les Bell, Eppie McClelland, Rev. J. R. G. Graham, and Rev. Tom Houston who read earlier drafts of the MSS and gave advice and helpful suggestions. The encouragement of former Bethany colleagues was greatly appreciated, especially that of James MacInnes whose fund of stories would have filled another book. I am grateful to Iona Molleson for allowing the use of her drawings at the head of several chapters. Most of the stories and testimonies included here have already appeared in previous Bethany publicity. I am grateful to those who have been willing to give permission for their inclusion here, but where I have not been able to contact people, names have either been omitted or changed and italicized to protect anonymity.

Finally I thank my husband, Alan, for the time he has given researching material, checking my facts, reading MSS, helping me to believe in the project and generally being a great support.

Key to *Bethany* locations

1. Bethany Shop Summerhall Place (1995)
2. Bethany Shop Hamilton Place (1st 1993, Replacement 2002)
3. Bethany Shop Gullane (1998)
4. Bethany Shop including Homemaker Haddington Place (1998)
   Bethany Homemaker Haddington Place (2001)
5. Bethany Hub and Workshop Jane Street (1998)
6. Bethany Shop Morningside Road (2000)
7. Bethany Home Farm Broxburn (1996)
   Matthew House on farm (2002)
8. Supported Housing Casselbank St (1988)
   Supported Housing now Bonnington Road (2007)
9. Bethany Christian Centre Casselbank Street (1983)
10. Bethany House Couper Street (1993)
11. Bethany Shop Dalry Road (2001)
12. Bethany Hall Jane Street (1994)
    Headquarters moved to Bonnington Road (2008)
13. Bethany Shop Duke Street (2002)
14. Bethany Shop Kirkcaldy (2007)
15. Martha House East Calder (2003)

16. Drop-in (Toastie Club) Dunfermline (1999)
    Floating Support Office West Fife Dunfermline (2003)
17. Drop-in (Toastie Club) Leven (2005)
    Floating Support Office East Fife (2003)
    New Methil Office (2008)
18. Bethany Shop Corstorphine (2001)

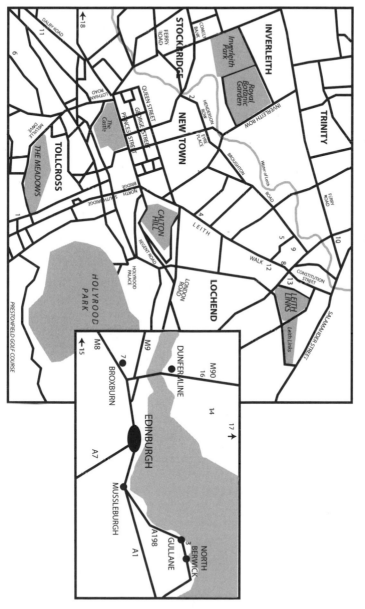

Maps of Edinburgh

INTRODUCTION

It could happen to you!

From time to time over the past few years several people have suggested that it would be a good idea to commit to print the beginnings of the Bethany story, before they become lost in the mists of time. Although I agreed with the sentiments, the thought of personally undertaking the task seemed overwhelming, and there were always more 'immediate' things clamouring for attention. Recently, however, two incidents occurred which prompted me to action. Firstly, in the period of transition from Tony Blair's premiership to that of Gordon Brown, I listened to a radio programme which advocated that the sooner Prime Ministers wrote their memoirs after retirement, the better. Having left Bethany employment six years ago, it seemed I had better make a start!

Secondly, I was encouraged by rereading the autobiography of Paul White, 'Jungle Doctor'. It was a story of his journey with God, told in his own style and from his heart, and therefore it became 'alive'. Whilst this 'Bethany' account is indeed about how the Trust was born and began to grow, it is not primarily about the facts and figures of homelessness. Rather it is a testimony of the faithfulness of God. Faithfulness which runs through all of what became known as Bethany's 'Seven Levels of Care,' through which the Trust sought to give an holistic response to the needs of homeless and vulnerable people. Because I want this story to 'live,' like the book I read, the parts of the Bethany journey in which I have been involved are of necessity told from my heart and in my own way. It is therefore more 'memoir' than straight historical record. Even while working for the Trust, there were many aspects in which I was never personally involved, and since I retired, the work has grown at such an amazing rate that it makes it difficult for those still employed to keep up with all that is going on, let alone someone no longer 'in the loop'.

Inevitably, then, I have drawn on articles that others have written in reports, newsletters, and annual reports. Indeed some staff, past and present, may well recognize their own words coming back to haunt or bless them! I am grateful for these contributions because they have been written by people to whom their particular experience or work has been meaningful and for whom, and through whom, God had done some wonderful things. But principally, this is the story of what can happen when an extraordinary God shares an idea with ordinary people who decide to act upon it. In a different context therefore IT COULD HAPPEN TO YOU.

Anne Berry
March 2008

CHAPTER 1

WRITE DOWN THE REVELATION (1981-86)

'Sunshine on Leith' is the title of a song made famous in the 1980s by the Scottish band, The Proclaimers. The sun however, does not always shine on Leith.

In the mid 1970s when Alan, myself and our two children arrived in Leith, where Alan was to minister in South Leith Baptist Church, there were clouds of unemployment, depopulation, and decline brooding over the area. Leith, the port area of Edinburgh had, until 1920, been a burgh in its own right. At that time it was merged with Edinburgh following an unofficial referendum in which the people of Leith voted by a ratio of five to one against the merger. Leith streets bearing the same names as streets in Edinburgh were changed and, according to the 'Leithers', Edinburgh claimed their trams. Despite being 'swallowed up' as Leithers perceived it, they still retained their proud and independent identity and lived out their motto – 'Persevere'.

Leith has a proud history. As the major port access to Edinburgh, it has served as the staging point for many of the significant events in Scottish history. Mary Queen of Scots' mother had her Court in Leith when she ruled Scotland as Regent for her daughter and about a century later it was both a battleground and ultimately headquarters for Oliver Cromwell's forces. Streets such as West Cromwell Street, Prince Regent Street, Wellington Place and Queen Charlotte Street link it to its past, while Admiralty Street, Madeira Street and Elbe Street reflect its former seafaring trade routes.

The docks at Leith underwent severe decline in the post-Second World War period with the area gaining a reputation for roughness and prostitution. Planners could not decide whether certain areas should be industrial or residential and so physically and emotionally the heart was knocked out of Leith as people were moved to outlying housing schemes. The disused railway station became a gathering point for 'down and outs' and a darker drug sub-culture flourished in a climate of deprivation.

South Leith Baptist Church

It is in this context that the Bethany story begins. Picture the Berry family in the late 1970s living in the South Leith Baptist Church manse. Alan has just finished yet another phone call from someone enquiring if we knew of any suitable accommodation for a student coming to Edinburgh. Picture the door of the South Leith Baptist Church opening after a Sunday morning service and several people asking to see the minister – not usually for spiritual help it has to be said, but often with regard to accommodation.

Little by little, week in, week out, the need for accommodation became increasingly evident, encompassing at one end of the spectrum the totally homeless person, and at the other end anxious parents of a teenager coming to study or work in the capital were telephoning to see if we could help and advise.

Many of the young people who came to the church door were being housed in very sub-standard conditions. In the main they were unemployed, from deprived backgrounds or with other social problems.

Some lived in cubicles which would be considered restrictive for animals. We met men who for years had shared a room with four or five others, with about one third of the space that Alan had had in the army, and a lot less privacy. We met young people who had been pushed from pillar to post all their lives because of their parents' marriage breakdown or death.

The need would not go away, nor would the conviction that somehow we were to be involved in the answering of our own prayers for this need. Alan was aware that while he was preaching about the love of God and the responsibility of Christians to demonstrate that love to others, there was often a gap between 'knowing the Word and doing it'. The challenge of the Parable of the Good Samaritan, Matthew chapter 25 and the letter of James took on a new significance.

In late 1979 he shared his vision for a Christian hostel with the congregation at South Leith and asked that they pray about whether this was the way forward, and if so whether they would be willing to help make it a reality.

Until that time there had been no suitable building available, but then one of ideal size and location came on the market – the former Burns Club, in Casselbank Street which was right across the road from the church. It had nine rooms and offers around £25,000 were invited. Alan believed that with very little modification this could fit the bill, but time was of the essence if another, maybe noisier, club was not to arrive opposite the church. Whilst sympathetic to the dream, the church felt unable to commit themselves to it and the opportunity to bid for the premises passed. It has been said that 'hindsight is the most exact science known to man' and, looking back, God's hand can be seen in this decision. If the vision had been that of just one church fellowship, it might well have stayed as such and probably not therefore have gone on eventually to be owned by the wider Christian public with support and staff being drawn from many denominations.

Alan and I approached Les Bell and David Belton, two people whose judgment and experience we respected, and they agreed to join us in seeking to make the vision a reality. With the help and advice of lawyers, Balfour & Manson, a trust was formed. The original trust document was comprehensive enough that it allowed for far-reaching ideas in relation to work with elderly folk, the unemployed, retired Christian workers etc., which could all be explored in the future if desired.

Initially the name 'Bethany' was probably chosen because in seeking to run the hostel as an 'extended Christian family,' it was hoped that it might be 'A Place of Quiet Rest'[1] like the home of Mary, Martha and Lazarus in Biblical Bethany, where Jesus was welcomed and made to feel at home. It was important to the trustees that 'Christian' should also be incorporated in the name of the Trust, for it was hoped that the work would be an expression of Christian love in action, and a response to alleviating the suffering of vulnerable people which is a cause close to God's heart.

However, finding a suitable property proved difficult. Buildings used as hostels or hotels, thus having the necessary planning permission and fire certificates, were expensive. Buildings which were otherwise suitable, but had not been used for multiple residence, required planning permission for change of use, and often owners were not willing to wait while such permission was obtained.

Les Bell, Alan Berry, Anne Berry, David Belton

The Trustees looked at the Old Convent beside St James' Episcopal Church in Leith, No. 70 Ferry Road, the YMCA building in 5 Casselbank Street and a flat at North Fort Street. It is interesting that in later years the latter two became part of the Bethany portfolio.

After several disappointments the former Burns Club building that had been looked at in 1981, was back on the market, albeit at a much increased price. In the meantime it had been used as a commercial hotel and thus already had a guest house

---

1.   I believe this is the meaning of the name Bethany.

licence and fire certificate and the owners were prepared to sell it fully equipped. Several people from South Leith Baptist helped prepare the hostel for occupancy, which if said quickly belies the amazing amount of work involved as the 'fully equipped' was a mixed blessing. The previous 'commercial hotel' had left mattresses that needed to be destroyed and all manner of unsavoury items that had to be binned. It was going be a step of faith at so many levels.

The accommodation was one amazing answer to prayer, but the next dilemma that was really going to stretch our faith was to see how a newly formed, unknown charitable trust could acquire financial support to establish itself and expand. Interest free loans and gifts from friends and individuals in South Leith and other local churches and grant-making trusts made up one third of the required amount. No Scottish bank would help but Berkeley Applegate, a firm from Torquay, was willing to service a mortgage for the other two-thirds of the initial capital costs, albeit at the current rate of 16%! All this made the early days possible, and the Trust will always be grateful for the confidence this firm showed in us, along with the faith of the first supporters.

But buildings and finance cannot operate without staff, and it has been said that an organization is only as good as its per-

sonnel. Rosemary Coiley, a young married woman, who was a member of South Leith Baptist Church, had caught the vision, and was sure God wanted her to be involved in bringing it into being. It was amazing how many details had to be sorted out but Rosemary and husband Mikki eventually moved into what was renamed Bethany Christian Centre. On 4th April 1983 it opened for business.

But what about the residents? The first ones included a young Christian man who had arrived in Edinburgh and was looking for a place to stay; two of the family of a local pastor who had been called to minister in another area; a mother and her son who were needing 'safe' accommodation; a sixteen-year-old who had recently left care but had been offered a place in a flat where drugs were being abused. And so the dream was becoming a reality.

By twelve noon on the official opening day of 7th May, the large upstairs lounge was crowded, with an overflow at the top of the stairs. The company was widely representative, with Edinburgh and Lothians Baptist Association officials, a local minister, the general secretary of the Edinburgh City Mission, members of South Leith Baptist Church, residents themselves and friends from Glasgow, Alan's home city, and Cowdenbeath in Fife, where Alan had had his first pastorate. Keith, one of the residents had painted the name of the Centre above the front door and made the 't' in Bethany in the form of a cross. It was to be a reminder of where the strength to carry out the work was to come from, and also the hope that for many coming through the door, it would become significant in their own lives.

Alan gave a brief resumé of how the Centre had come into being as a result of a vision of a few years' standing, saying he believed the Scripture verses in Habakkuk 2:2-3[2] were a promise from God. There had been setbacks and disappointments in relation to other properties, but 'Persevere', had become our motto too, and the promise had been confirmed in the purchase of No.6. Rev. A. Brunton Scott, vice-president of the Baptist Union of Scotland, spoke of a need being met, the Trustees' objective, and the faith necessary to bring such a project to birth. He said he was excited and pleased to be associated with it.

In expressing her gratitude for the opportunity of serving God and quoting from Psalm 16, Rosemary told those present how much their support had meant to her and her husband as they undertook the work. Refreshments were served; people had the opportunity to look round the lounge, dining area and one or two bedrooms, and so ended the first Bethany Open Day.

Being involved in the infancy of an enterprise has its excitements but it also brings its own pressure. In the beginning there was no rigid job specification other than trying to operate the hostel as an extended Christian family.

The job 'evolved,' with Rosemary being patient and flexible, but it was not easy for a young married couple living right in the middle of the job. Rosemary committed herself to both housekeeping duties and the comfort of the residents,

---

2.   'Write down the revelation and make it plain...it speaks of the end and will not prove false. Though it linger, wait for it, it will certainly come and will not delay'.

and went far beyond the call of duty. Although she was fluid as far as off-duty was concerned, providing this could sometimes be difficult. It would have been ideal if extra staff could have facilitated it, but the size of the operation wasn't really able to cover it on a full-time basis. Part-time volunteer help was sometimes available but there were often crises over who would cover days off and holidays.

During the first five months, the gas heating was overhauled, and a new stair carpet was laid. Early supporters of the Trust provided practical help in areas of cooking, cleaning and sewing, and saved some spending of our very limited resources by providing generous gifts of a new deep freezer, iron, toaster, second-hand linen, lamps and furniture.

But the work wasn't primarily about managing a house, but rather learning to build relationships with people. Lessons were being learned – sometimes the hard way. At the end of the first five months, six of the twelve places were still occupied by original residents, but it had become obvious how much care needed to be taken at the interview stage. The original vision had been solely to provide accommodation, but it was evident from the beginning that some residents needed a great deal of care, love and in some cases, supervision. Some potential residents had to be refused because it was not possible to meet their needs.

A supportive 'hands-on' management committee was formed comprising Magnus Flucker, Nan Shaw, Ina Taylor who, was an expert with a sewing needle, Irene Belton, and one trustee. They acted as back-up support for Rosemary as did the trustees and friends like Jeanette Wallace from South Leith Baptist, who became Rosemary's prayer partner. Whether or not Mr Tulloch, an elderly deacon of South Leith Baptist Church, had expertise with a needle we never knew, but he was a marvellous potato peeler and every Thursday morning presented himself and his peeler at the kitchen door of the Centre. Mrs Nancy Crichton, of South Leith, and Mr Sandy Logan, from Madeira St. Baptist, also came on board. For a considerable time they volunteered their respective bookkeeping and auditing skills. The only reward Nancy received for all her hard work was an annual bouquet presented by Les, in his capacity as hon. treasurer.

The service Rosemary rendered during those first eighteen months of the Trust's life was outstanding, but sadly after this time she had to leave due to ill health during a very difficult pregnancy. Happily a healthy baby girl arrived the next spring, born on 4th April, the Trust's anniversary!

Although our accommodation had much in its favour, it was a one hundred and fifty year-old Georgian building in the best Edinburgh New Town tradition. 'New Town' is rather a misnomer as such architecture dates from the eighteenth century but was certainly 'new' in comparison to the overcrowded, noisy and dirty 'old town.' The style was elegant and the large rooms were suitable for our communal activities but not for bedrooms as they were almost impossible to sub-divide. The fact that people often had to share a room was one of the biggest problem areas. Residents did not always appreciate the habits and behaviour of their roommates, or understandably just wanted their own space.

Rev. Ross Brown, Alan's successor as pastor at South Leith Baptist Church, often quoted 'there are no coincidences with God', and so perhaps we shouldn't have been surprised when the disused licensed Caley Club next door to the Centre came on the market after the owners got into financial difficulty. Imaginative dreaming saw that with work and finance this could be converted into single rooms for residents and staff accommodation. At a trustees' meeting a word of Scripture had been shared from Isaiah 54:2-3 which reads 'enlarge the place of your tent, stretch your tent curtains wide, do not hold back; lengthen your cords, strengthen your stakes. For you will spread out to the right and to the left.' At least one of the cautious trustees wanted to keep the focus on strengthening the stakes and consolidation, whereas Alan, ever the eternal optimist, was excited at the possibility of lengthening the cords and spreading out to the left, literally! But was it just *our* imaginations running on overtime, or was this the next step in God's plan?

Investigation began into the feasibility of the project. Whilst these deliberations were ongoing, Alan was still the minister of South Leith Baptist Church and as a couple we attended a leadership conference at Goldhill Baptist Church in Buckinghamshire, where Rev. Jim Graham was the senior pastor. Church elders gave hospitality to delegates and we accompanied our hosts to their evening house-group meeting. It was a memorable experience and at first a little overwhelming as it was certainly more exuberant and 'charismatic' than we were used to.

During the prayer time one young man said that God had given him a 'picture'. He knew nothing about us other than that we were visiting the conference and were from Scotland. However, he said he felt the picture was for us and went on to describe in detail Casselbank Street with Alan working on the derelict Caley Club, complete with yellow hard hat. Then he asked, 'does it mean anything to you?' Emotion made it difficult to answer that question!! It was such an encouragement and very precious. We had gone to the conference uncertain of the next step and here God had personally intervened to assure us that we were to go ahead. Ordering a safety helmet, colour yellow, was definitely on the agenda!

By May 1984 there was a verbal acceptance of our offer for the Caley Club. Provisional sketches were presented to our architect who in turn formalized them and presented them to the appropriate authorities.

And it was a time of change and growth in other ways. In December 1984 there was a dedication service for Miss Nan Shaw and Mrs Mary Stewart, who had replaced Rosemary and were working as joint wardens. Mary and husband Douglas had moved in and gave able assistance until February, and Nan started in November. When Nan became ill, Trevor Davies volunteered and later joined her on the staff.

In January 1985 we eventually took occupancy of the Caley Club after very protracted negotiations. The premises were in an appalling condition, with leaks and dry rot which meant only the shell was usable, and demolition work began. Was the whole thing really viable? Taken at face value it certainly made one wonder, but it had that all-important quality – potential – a word which has featured large in the Bethany story.

At the Bethany Open Day on 26th May 1985 supporters were able to view the building. Rev. David Black, from Bishopbriggs, was the speaker. He stood in the middle of the dereliction and praised God for the exciting new venture and committed all the plans to God. It definitely needed to be seen through the eyes of faith!

If the experience at the Buckinghamshire conference had been reassuring and uplifting, it was quickly followed by the reality of achieving the vision. The South Leith Baptist Church congregation was very generous and granted Alan three months, leave of absence. He still preached on a Sunday morning and did emergency visiting, but the rest of the time he was free to head up the building work. But it soon became evident that a three-month timetable was unrealistic and would need a miraculous element to make it possible. Again the church was generous and an enormous debt of gratitude was due to them for their understanding in extending the period of absence.

David Belton, one of the founding trustees had a fund of stories and witty sayings. One of these was very apt for this building project. In relation to assistance, he said 'the help of one boy equals one boy, two boys is half a boy and a group of boys is no boy at all!' Occasionally there was help forthcoming from Malta House, a Church of Scotland rehabilitation unit for men with addiction problems. The trouble was that many of the residents who came to help deemed themselves experts on every trade and spent a lot of time criticizing each other's work and 'doing their own thing', rather than listening to instructions and following the master plan. Sometimes a whole van-load would arrive and Alan would have to try and find meaningful employment for them all, and so was distracted from his own work. On other days he would plan jobs for a group and only one or two would arrive. It sounds churlish not to be grateful for such help, but it often added to the problems rather than relieving the pressure. However, it was a great learning curve in people management!

We did, however, have the services of an expert bricklayer called Eddie Crawford from Lochgelly, whose skill we had appreciated when the Cowdenbeath Baptist Church had built a new hall. Added to this, for two days every week, was the patient and careful joinery work of Alan's dad, Jim, and his friend, Ian Morrison. These two octogenarians had known each other for a lifetime. They worked well and steadily together and sacrificial giving of their talents was much appreciated. But it was slow work. Alan became increasingly exhausted and I became increasingly concerned for him. He said it was like looking down a long tunnel with no light at the end of it. It was definitely a stressful period. I could keep the rest of his life ticking along, but I didn't have the practical skills to help with the building – what else could I do? I could pray – and it became prayer bathed in tears. The answer to these prayers was God's miracle of provision for us and a salutary reminder that if God gives a task He will also give the equipping.

Alan's father had been at the Keswick Convention and met an old friend, John Begg, the father of Rev. Alastair Begg. He told him of his joinery activity on the Caley Club, or the 'extension,' as it had become known, and John Begg in turn told him of a man called Alan Yuille, from Golspie, a town on the north-east coast of Scotland. He had had his own joinery firm, but by that time was well retired. He had helped in various Christian projects, including building work in Asia. Maybe he would come and help? He did come, but when we saw him and realized all that was still to be done, we felt that although 'the spirit was willing,' it was a lot to ask of his 'flesh'. This sentiment was shared by his son, Walter, who 'just happened' to be an architect in Leith. Truly God's hand and timing was in all of this.

On a very memorable day, Walter Yuille visited Alan and greeted him with words that became famous – 'Mr. Berry, how would you like it, if, at no cost to yourself, I got in a team to finish off the part of the extension which has been designated as a manager's flat?' Walter's wife had been killed in an accident and he wanted to do something that would be a fitting memorial to her. Here was God's amazing answer, and Alan 'liked it' very much! The timing of God's provision was very precious, arriving when Alan's emotional and physical strength were at a low ebb as shown very graphically in a photo of him arriving home for his birthday tea looking as dirty as an old-fashioned chimney sweep and with weariness etched all over his face! Walter was true to his word and three journeyman joiners, plus apprentices, got to work with a will. It was like the story of Nehemiah when the wall was finished because everyone set to. It was an amazing gift, not only in the quality of the work, but in financial terms. Walter remarried, and Alan officiated at his wedding. It was with real sadness later on that he took Walter's funeral, when he too was killed in a car accident on the same stretch of road as his first wife.

Demolition work in the Caley Club had started in January 1985 and by November there was light beginning to show at the end of the tunnel. There was much for which to be grateful, not least safety during all the renovation work, voluntary labour and Berkley Applegate's agreement to provide a further loan based on two-thirds of the increased value of the property. After fifteen months' work by volunteers, staff and some outside contractors, the Bethany Christian Centre extension was in use under a temporary warrant.

The official opening took place on 31st May 1986 when the Scottish singer Alastair McDonald kindly came to share in a celebratory concert. He incorporated songs which had a caring message with his own testimony and some fun songs, such as 'The Wee Kirkcudbright Centipede' and 'The Jeely Piece Song', especially requested by our family. (Non-Scots readers may find the footnote helpful!)[3]

Supporters wanted to know where residents came from Some came direct from broken homes, others from prison, hospital, bedsit land or just roaming the streets.

Others wanted to know how they came. Some came through Housing Advice Centre, Supported Accommodation and Emergency Social Work teams, the Royal Edinburgh Hospital, and some were referred through churches. And where did they go to? Some just disappeared, quite often owing rent, others unfortunately ended up in prison, while some moved to rehabilitation centres or best of all, to their own flat or were reunited with their family.

There was obviously apprehension about going further into debt, but God seemed to have opened doors and we just had to trust Him to provide. We were very grateful to several churches who

---

3.   Kirkcudbright is a region in the south-west of Scotland. The song tells how the centipede walked along perfectly well until it began to think of which leg followed which! A jeely piece is a jam sandwich often thrown out of the window of a three-storey tenement building down to children playing in the back garden! This was much more difficult in a multi-storey flat.

gave their annual 'thank offerings' to Bethany and to Morningside Baptist Church, a local Edinburgh church, who 'adopted a room' in the extension by redirecting money they had been gifted.

 God had been faithful during the first year when over £15,000 had been given in donations and interest-free loans. He had been faithful too in providing another trustee, the Rev. Robert Gemmell. Bob had been director of the Baptist 'Elpis Centre' for girls in central Glasgow and had moved to minister in Duncan Street Baptist Church in Edinburgh. With his experience in ministry and social work he was to make a vital contribution to the life of the Trust, and his wife Marion later joined the staff team.

Legislation can work both ways. The government sought to prevent certain misuses of welfare money, and introduced a new 'four-week rule' which meant young people under twenty-six years had to move on after that time. Like so many rulings, genuine cases as well as the offenders were affected. Certain select suppliers of accommodation were exempt and granted 'hostel' status. When this was awarded to Bethany it ensured the necessary residential stability for younger people.

But it wasn't only the premises that had been extended. Over the months the vision had expanded too, for although originally the whole purpose of the Trust was to provide accommodation, it became increasingly evident that homelessness was often only the presenting problem, and many residents had other issues too. Staff had to be prepared to spend quality time with them and so God nudged the Trust towards its first tentative steps into 'informal rehabilitation'. Nan had a gift for homemaking and a great desire to emphasize the 'family' aspect of the work. She and Trevor sought to form supportive relationships with residents. Even after they, and some of the residents concerned, had left Bethany and moved to other areas, they continued to play a part in their lives by keeping in touch through letters and visits.

Maintaining twenty-four hour cover was often a balancing act and could be a logistical nightmare. Sometimes it involved a seventeen-hour day and sufficient off-duty periods were necessary to cope with the demands. Some of the pressure was alleviated by Peter Gibb's sacrificial help with catering. He did a power of work in the kitchen against immense odds before having to give up because of ill health.

The staff team also expanded with the arrival of Charles and Joyce Mathieson, who for a period of time worked alongside Nan and Trevor. Caring for people can be costly in terms of giving of oneself. Joy and sorrow, success and failure, wholeness and shattered lives, truth and lies, discipline and rule-breaking, love and hate ... these were all the contrasts with which these early staff, and indeed those who have followed them, had to grapple, day in, day out, with all the shades of experience in between.

And some of these struggles and the nature of the work were a concern to our neighbours in the street. The 'Not In My Back Yard' (NIMBY) factor was 'unofficially' alive and well for a time. However, there was a local residents' meeting already in existence and instead of waiting for them to make an 'official' representation about their anxieties, Alan decided to pre-empt this by going along to the meeting. He was able to allay some of the worries and at least if there were concerns they were aired in an appropriate place rather than becoming a whispering campaign behind closed doors.

And so the vision had started to become a reality. But was there more to follow?

I think our sentiments at that time were similar to those expressed in Churchill's famous statement, 'this is not the end ... it is not even the beginning of the end ... but it is perhaps the end of the beginning.'

CHAPTER 2

GROWING PAINS
(1987-91)

Come back again to the South Leith manse on a Sunday evening. Alan has just returned from the evening service. He is struggling with the implications of what he feels God is saying. Indeed, he has struggled like this every Sunday evening for a while. He has been getting more involved in the work of the Trust and it is taking its toll, both physically and emotionally. He knows God called him into the ministry; he feels a responsibility to his congregation, and indeed that it would seem wrong to leave them when he had only been back with them full-time for a year, yet he can't shut out the Voice. Is he turning his back on his calling, or is this a new calling? As a respected mentor and friend, Rev. Tom Houston, who had been Alan's pastor in Nairobi when Alan was stationed there during his National Service, pointedly asked 'What is this doing to your ministry, Alan?'

But then there was the trustees' meeting at which they asked Alan if he would consider working full-time with the Trust. I knew the verses from Joel about old men dreaming dreams and young men seeing visions, but this wife was having nightmares! Where did I fit in and what about our family? It was fine me visiting Bethany, giving, praying but going to live there was quite another thing. And then I was happy being a minister's wife. I liked being a minister's wife and I even argued with God that I thought I fulfilled that role pretty well! But neither did I want a husband who was torn in two – and he couldn't do two jobs.

Alan decided to go to visit two Christian leaders, Rev. Jim Graham and Rev. Selwyn Hughes, whom he greatly respected, knew personally, and felt he could trust to give him godly advice. I was sure I knew what the outcome would be before he went, but prayed I would be able to happily accept the inevitable! After all the verse we were given on the occasion of our marriage was 'Workers *together* with Christ'. As Alan shared the things on his heart, they each said to him, 'Listen to yourself, Alan, *'you can't not do it*, the passion is from God.' And so Alan came home knowing that God would provide another pastor for South Leith but this was to be his new ministry. He resigned from the church in January 1987, worked part-time in both jobs for three months and then became full-time director of the Trust.

The term 'director' was a good description because besides working with Nan and Trevor as manager of the Centre, it allowed him to explore the possibility of being involved in new projects. There was a vision for helping the unemployed, those with addiction issues and providing a rural agricultural/horticultural rehabilitation centre. The new post would also give him the opportunity to visit various projects around the country and see what was being done in the areas of alcoholism, drug abuse and other social problems.

There were other changes too. Norman, Alan's brother, replaced David Belton as a trustee. Alan was particularly pleased that Norman was willing to be involved as he greatly respected his 'sanctified common sense' and felt his insights would be a real benefit to the Trust.

In March 1987 a prayer meeting for those who wanted to see the Lord working through Bethany, was started at lunchtime on the first and third Tuesdays of the month. One of the prayer requests was for a couple of mature Christians who would be willing to come to stay at Bethany and make it their home, and thus be an influence for God and for good. That prayer was answered, and Jim, Sheena and John all came for a while and were a great encouragement. The fourth anniversary of the Trust was celebrated with the lounge in the Centre being decorated, courtesy of the Edinburgh & Lothian Baptist Association Women's Auxiliaries.

After nearly three years of valiant service, both Nan Shaw and Trevor Davies felt God prompting them to leave the work of Bethany. We were deeply grateful for all their dedicated labour, especially at times when Nan had been very unwell. There was much rejoicing in Madeira Street Baptist Church when they later married, and Alan was privileged to act as best man. The marriage service was even delayed for a minute or two while Nan got her breath back after letting out an audible gasp at being confronted with her English bridegroom resplendent in full Highland dress!

It seemed with Nan and Trevor leaving there would again be a staffing crisis, but God was faithful. Trevor finished on a Friday and David Belton, our ex-trustee, offered to commence full-time on the following Monday. Emma Pendry arrived as the first Careforce[1] worker, and April Newlands and Margaret Thomson helped as volunteers. David's appointment was only to be temporary, but he came with a wide experience of working in a hostel environment and his enthusiasm and spiritual insight were greatly appreciated. The 'kitchen' incident was typical of his commitment. The room needed painting, but it was such a busy place to have out of commission; how could it be done? Late one evening David locked the door, painted right through the night and was open again for business in the morning!

In September 1987 we, as a family, moved from the manse to the manager's flat at 48 Kirk Street. There was just one door that divided it from the rest of the hostel. Living on the job was a sharp learning curve. It was difficult to be off-duty, even when you were! For the two teenagers who had homework to do, to

---

1. Careforce is a Christian organization which seeks to give young people the opportunity to volunteer for a year in a church or 'caring' context. Bethany has been greatly blessed over the years through such volunteers and more is said about this in Chapter 18.

be surrounded by much more exciting diversions like a snooker game or the chance of a gossip, it was quite a challenge.

On one particular evening, while my mother was visiting from Nottingham, the adjoining door was knocked fifty-six times! Requests from residents ranged from pleas for Elizabeth and Stephen to go swimming, to the loan of a needle and thread. What the constant interruptions really signified was that people just wanted to know someone was there – and sometimes I wished it wasn't us they wanted!

Both our children were in the school band and there were sometimes school exchanges in connection with this. On one occasion we had two very pretty Danish girls staying with us in the flat. The adjoining door was knocked continually while they were visiting!

The friends of the children were always welcome, and they did visit, but they were no longer just round the corner from them as had been the case in the manse. Now we were living in an environment where many residents had a history of drink and drug abuse, and both our children were at an impressionable age. We had not been prepared for the pressure under which our changed circumstances put them, nor indeed at times the moral dangers. When Elizabeth sat her Higher English exam, she told us that one of the essay choices asked for an appraisal of how the candidate felt about 'circumstances over which they had had no control but which had changed their life'. It was not difficult to guess which question she had chosen and it would have made an interesting read!

But she thrived on the rush and bustle of the place and during her first year at college gave us some much-needed breathing space by cooking breakfast for the residents on Saturday mornings and manning the office for a while. The young men by and large saw her as a sister and were quick to protect or defend her if anyone should step out of line. But she was an attractive girl, and Alan spent some nights walking the floor and praying hard as some relationships began to give cause for concern.

One of the difficulties she had to contend with when we first moved was that two of the residents were actually at her school. Going to school was no problem for her, but to go with them was certainly not an option. However, for one of the young men, although intelligent, school attendance was not a high priority. He would always leave in time but didn't often manage to actually make it. The 5th/6th year guidance teacher was regularly on the phone enquiring after his invisible pupil. One day the young man did actually get knocked down on the way to school. Before Alan could explain what had happened, the long-suffering teacher said 'Don't tell me Mr Berry, he's been attacked by a man-eating tiger in Craighall Road!' You couldn't blame him, after all his pupil had used up every other excuse.

One of my concerns was having enough food when the residents queued up for meals. I hadn't been used to catering for twenty-six and was anxious when about eighteen people had been served in case there wouldn't be sufficient for the rest. Peeling potatoes for such a large number may sound like a chore, but it was wonderfully therapeutic. No matter how stressed one felt, it was amazing how much frustration could be worked off with a potato peeler. One just grabbed the potato, scraped away and it never said a word! Sometimes, if residents failed to surface in time for breakfast there was *too much* food, but Perro the dog was always glad when this happened, as she was particularly partial to black pudding. Over the years 'ex-chef residents' such as Jim, John and David were responsible for some wonderful food.

When we were on kitchen duty, we had meals with the residents. Often Saturday teatimes could be difficult as residents who supported rival football clubs would get aggressive with each other depending on the score, or if they had had a drink. Bad language was something that was not tolerated in the dining room, but residents could also be abusive to staff if they were confronted about this. This impinged on the family too. Stephen especially did not like me addressed in a belligerent tone, and would jump to my defence. Christmas too was not a holiday for us and it was not easy for two teenagers to have to share their lives, their parents and even Christmas Day with many others, all of whom seemed very demanding at times.

On one occasion a resident who wished us to 'adopt' him decided he wanted to come with us on holiday, and hid in the caravan we were taking. It was essential we had a 'family-only' holiday, and that meant the four of us and no more, but it was difficult explaining that to the resident who only wanted to feel part of a family. It was a bitter disappointment to him, but as our family said on that occasion – 'if he's going, we're not!'

It was the policy in the early days to have both male and female residents in the unit. One lady came to us from Cornton

Vale prison and was obviously greatly disturbed mentally. She had a sad history of being abused by her father, resulting in a hatred of men. It was a delicate situation and in those days we had little or no formal training in dealing with such problems. She felt disorientated and insecure being out of prison and had smashed shop windows in Leith, hoping to be rearrested and taken back to the 'safety' of prison. The Centre, plus extension, was fully occupied and Careforce worker, David Brown, had given up his room for her, and was occupying a caravan at the back door of the Centre. The lady was muttering, cursing and screaming to herself in the room, and it was one of the occasions when I *felt* the presence of evil and that demon possession was a reality. In that condition, and with her antipathy to men, it was not safe for David to enter the room, and I was too scared, so we sat outside and prayed earnestly. Suddenly, there was the most terrific crash, as she hurled David's TV through the first-floor window into the street.

Obviously the commotion had an electrifying effect on the rest of the house, and where I thought was my teenage family in all this? They were doing sterling service. Elizabeth had escorted our blind female resident to the safety of the lounge, was quietening another female who was prone to 'hyperventilate to order,' and Stephen was out in the street with brush and shovel sweeping up broken glass!

But it wasn't only TVs that came through windows. There was a memorable occasion when Alan was in a first-floor bedroom speaking to a resident, whose surname began with 'Mac', and who was under the influence of drink. Alan turned away for a moment and when he turned back, the resident had disappeared, but not through the door. In his inebriated state he thought he could fly and had taken off through the open window. The residents in the dining room downstairs were amazed when they went outside to find him shaken but unharmed. 'Is it a bird, is it a plane, no, it's Superman' took on a whole new meaning and for a long time afterwards this extraordinary feat was known as the 'Mac … factor'. (Name withheld for obvious reasons!)

On another occasion we were rejoicing that several residents seemed to be making real progress and some had trusted the Lord. Then a few weeks later, one of them was dismissed from work for dishonesty and another two had started drinking again. Were we getting anywhere we asked ourselves? Was it worth all the hard work and what seemed like constant hassle? David Brown and I were in the kitchen feeling dispirited because of these circumstances when in burst Danny Rogan resembling a walking Harvest Festival. Danny, a retired man, was a supporter of the Trust and had family in the greengrocery business. He was laden with sacks of potatoes, vegetables and fruit. This was so generous, but more than that we felt God had used him to bring that 'special' touch when he produced a bouquet of flowers for me in honour of it being St Valentine's Day. It was just as God promised in Psalm 145 verse 14, 'The Lord lifts up all who are bowed down'.

Discouragements can come in many shapes and forms. While we still lived in the manse we sometimes got phone calls from friends of alcoholics ringing on their behalf to tell us how well-off we must be and how our children would be 'set up for life'. They had seen in the newspaper that this or that firm had given a gift for the work of Bethany. They obviously thought it was going straight into our bank account! This distressed me, but Alan was much more philosophical about it and I learned to leave such comments with the Lord and not to try to always want to justify ourselves.

There *was* hurt, though, when we returned from holiday to find a lot of our tools had been stolen, and the occasion when my watch disappeared from the kitchen in the Centre. I had been peeling potatoes and had gone to answer the phone. When I returned the watch was missing. It was not the monetary value of such articles but the feeling that residents, whom we were seeking to help, would do that. Another learning curve. After all, I had always lived with people who spoke the truth and dealt honestly with each other. Many of our residents had never had that privilege and I had to learn that such incidents were not meant as personal attacks, but 'making the most of opportunities' in their book. I had to learn too that not all situations were as they seemed. There were frequent times when I would be seeking to comfort a resident because of circumstances which I just took to be the case as reported, only to find that I had been well and truly 'conned' and had 'green' written all over me. However, I prayed, as I am sure many others have done, that I might never go to the other extreme and get to the stage where I didn't believe *anything* I was told and fall prey to cynicism.

With a small staff team and a lot of residents, many of whom were far more worldly-wise than staff, who were learning 'on the job', crises of differing magnitudes could be a daily occurrence. 'How did residents manage to get out of the office with their benefits cheque, and do a runner?' asked one of the trustees in amazement. Short of tying them up in the office or having eyes in the back of one's head, it was almost impossible to prevent such things. 'And what about the office?' 'Yes, it was securely locked up as usual one night but that didn't prevent some of the "experienced" residents breaking into it, and the safe!'

But even some of those who considered themselves 'hard men', and had a history of literally fighting their way out of situations, had their own vulnerabilities. I entered the lounge one evening to find one such resident in abject misery suffering from toothache. He was petrified about going to get treatment but, as I reasoned with him, it couldn't be worse than the pain he was already experiencing. Eventually, a very nervous, miserable young man finally agreed to accompany me to the emergency dental department at the Western General Hospital. There were a lot of patients anxiously waiting, and no-one said a word. My friend had taken painkillers and was beginning to feel drowsy. Before his turn came, he had fallen asleep with his head on my shoulder, looking like a lost little boy. When he finally came out from seeing the dentist he was smiling and proudly announced, 'the dentist said I was very good and brave!'

One discouragement, with which all those who regularly do housework will readily identify, is the frustration of seeing a place, which has just been tidied, immediately messed up. In my case it involved the downstairs lounge in Bethany Christian Centre. I am not the tidiest person in the world, and have been known to push things haphazardly into cupboards out of sight, but I do like a place tidy to the eye. How discouraging it was to clean the lounge only to find it the next morning scattered with discarded chip papers, Coke cans, and sometimes unmentionable objects. And so it got cleaned again – until one day patience snapped. I announced to the crowded room that I had had enough of their disgusting habits and threw an empty Coke can into the air. I hasten to add that it was not aimed at anyone, but merely a gesture of frustration. I swept out of the room and went down to our bedroom in the flat.

There remorse overtook me. Was I not supposed to be a Christian setting an example? What would residents think of my outburst? But surely, I justified myself, we were supposed to be running this Centre like an extended Christian family and my frustration was just the reaction that any parent would feel if these circumstances were happening in their own home. They, the residents were like children who needed to learn! Having explained my case to another staff member, and shed copious tears, I thought I had better go back and apologize. There were renovations taking place in the Centre, and to my great embarrassment every resident I met on my way back to the lounge was wearing a safety helmet, and a prominent notice had been pinned up with the incriminating message 'Hard hats will be worn when Anne Berry is around!'. Point taken, lesson beginning to be learned! But happily, at least for about five days, my point was also taken and the lounge remained tidy. Some time later when Gordon Weir asked if I would like to train to become a project worker, I declined, knowing my own limitations and only half jokingly replying that I thought he might have as much trouble with me as with any resident.

Going up to the top floor at the Centre could be quite an effort first thing in the morning, especially if one was trying to prepare a cooked breakfast for twenty-seven people. But if one member of this 'extended Christian family' had difficulty getting up, it was part of one's remit to encourage them to do so. A certain young man loved his bed. So much so that most mornings his boss was on the phone asking if he was out of it, as he had again not appeared at work for the early shift. So began the long ascent to the top of the building. After the third time, one became short of both patience and puff. Another young man who slept up there had no difficulty in getting up in the morning. He had started work at the zoo and was very enthusiastic both about the job and his bright orange work clothes – so much so that he went to bed in them and was ready for the next day immediately he was out of bed! But there was one ascent, albeit only to the first floor, that highlighted some of the more devastating circumstances that can occur when a house is full of people all needing some level of support.

During the week in question, Alan had had conversations with one young resident whose father was dead, his mother an alcoholic, and who himself had been in foster care. He had been brought up in the Catholic faith and was searching for meaning in life, and contemplating going back to church. He was a fitness fanatic, and as far as we knew had never taken drugs. Sadly, he was offered some and must have thought he would experiment. He didn't come down to tea and we realized we hadn't seen him for several hours. I went up to knock on his door and had a terrible premonition which turned out to be all too true. He was lying peacefully on the bed, but was dead. In my mind's eye I can still see his face. It was such a waste of a young life and it had a sobering effect on the house. The heartfelt devastation experienced by residents and staff alike was compounded by the attitude of the senior policeman who came to investigate and displayed a completely insensitive attitude. It was obvious he needed to have the run of the house to do his job properly, but it was the rudeness and arrogance that accompanied this that made a difficult time even more so. Fortunately, someone came to take a group of residents out in a minibus to get them away for a while and a young policeman was assigned to take statements from the staff. He was so different and sympathetic and told us he was a Christian too. We felt God had definitely arranged for him to be on duty that evening and his attitude went a long way to alleviate the hurt, and indeed resentment, caused by his superior officer.

Sadly, over the years there have been others whose lifestyle has eaten away at their bodies and shortened their lives, and some, who in despair, have taken their own lives. Often it was after they had left Bethany and found being out in the community hard to deal with. Such occasions are always difficult times for staff, who have previously or who are currently giving some level of support. Questions flood in – 'could we have done more, what if, what if?'. But ultimately people are responsible for their own choices and staff would cease to function if they took all the burden on themselves.

Sometimes, even when the behaviour of residents left much to be desired, it also caused smiles, as the following story shows. Our family accommodation was on the ground floor, with a window looking out on to Casselbank Street. One night we had an unexpected visitor, and he didn't come to the door. Rather, our living room window suddenly opened and an inebriated John Rodgers rolled through it on to the floor. He was aware that if he had gone to the front door of the Centre he would have had to face the consequences, so he thought he would come through the window of another resident's room. Unfortunately for him, his counting of windows let him down, and it is difficult to say who was the more surprised when he encountered Alan sitting at our dining room table.

But others did use the front door, and most, like Brian, a Leith community policeman, were welcome. He made a point of dropping in periodically, usually when there was a football or rugby match on the television. Wearing his uniform, he sat in the downstairs lounge among the residents and watched the games and chatted. Most of the residents had had brushes with the police and weren't exactly members of their fan club, and Brian did a great deal to bridge the gap. He became accepted by the residents, who began to realize that a policeman's presence did not automatically have to be threatening.

Other visitors could be less welcome. On one occasion the irate parents of a resident, who were themselves drunk, were causing problems at the front door. They were shouting at a female staff member and when I went to investigate they shouted back at me 'Mrs Berry, we'll "bury" you!' Suddenly a voice behind them said, 'Is there a problem here?' Ross Brown was standing behind them. He had been at the church door opposite when he heard the commotion and came across to offer help. The couple, who were small in stature, turned, to be confronted by Ross who is tall – 6ft 5in. tall! They had obviously heard the maxim, 'never take on a fight unless you think you can win it'. They decided discretion was the better part of valour and disappeared! Again, God's timing was perfect.

Life was many things, but never dull and often challenging. Sometimes this took the form of dealing with aggressive behaviour due to substance abuse. Several residents suffered from mental illness which could manifest itself through erratic or obsessional behaviour. Two female residents had an obsession with dialling 999 and this, much to our embarrassment, resulted in unscheduled visits from the fire brigade, until severe warnings were issued to dissuade them. Another resident collected and hoarded paper and cardboard in his room. He might have received the approval of the recycling lobby, but certainly not the health and safety officer.

One young man was constantly concerned about the possibility of gas leaks and maintenance of equipment, and again we found ourselves trying to explain to the representatives from the Gas Board and Rentokil etc., that they had not been 'officially' called, and we did not require their services.

Cleanliness was the obsession of another resident. Everything was sanitized. Chairs were wiped before being sat on, plates were rewashed before being used, cord pulls in the bathrooms were covered in tissue paper, and the serving of food and medication had to follow strict

Marion Gemmell

guidelines. Marion Gemmell was the key worker for several residents who had special needs and I was impressed by her patience and understanding.

More changes came in 1988. Planning permission was sought to convert the two large attic rooms in the main house into six single bedrooms. In October of that year the Trust was registered under the Government training scheme. This meant it was accepted as a suitable placement for one or two people aged between twenty and sixty years who had been unemployed for at least six months. Because we wanted them to live in they did not need to come from the Edinburgh area.

That month too saw the arrival of Fiona Weir to work as Alan's deputy. Fiona had had a great deal of experience working in

a Church of Scotland rehabilitation centre, and had to leave her post when she married Gordon as the Church of Scotland had a policy which debarred married couples from working together in such units. Their loss was the Trust's gain, and Fiona's contri-

Fiona and Gordon Weir

bution to the life of the Trust, both at that time as a project worker and later in administration and church liaison work was very significant.

At the end of the year there were visits each Thursday from Charlie Malone of the Stauros Foundation in Glasgow. 'Stauros' is the Greek word for 'cross', and the organization sought to bring a message of freedom from addiction through the power of the gospel. Charlie made himself available to anyone who wanted to chat and had many good conversations. After tea on these days residents were invited to a time of praise and a sharing session. This was purely voluntary but proved to be well attended and was the forerunner of a regular Praise Night. One such was particularly significant. Arthur Williams of Stauros was speaking and it was on that night that John Rodgers (of climbing through windows fame), felt he could no longer put off getting his life sorted out. He spoke to Fiona in the office and realized he had to make a commitment to the Lord because he had run out of options and had nowhere else to run.

By December 1988 the Centre was bulging with twenty-seven residents. One of the areas of concern was what was best for residents when their stay in the Centre came to an end. Often they still needed a level of support and were not ready for an independent tenancy of their own. If such help was not available it was easy to return to old ways and chaotic lifestyles. Self-catering accommodation with some level of support seemed desirable, but where and how could this be provided? Again the Isaiah verses came to challenge, 'Enlarge the place of your tent, stretch your tent curtains wide, do not hold back; lengthen your cords, strengthen your stakes. For you will spread out to the right and to the left; your descendants will dispossess nations and settle in their desolate cities.' This time it wasn't right and left that was available, but right across the road at No. 5 Casselbank Street and next door to the church.

The building had been the headquarters of Y.W.C.A. of Scotland and negotiations with Christian Alliance (their new name) resulted in it being purchased for staff and self-catering accommodation.

Originally, before Leith became part of Edinburgh, Casselbank Street had been called Hope Street and No.5 had been Hope House. The Y.W.C.A. had called No. 5 the 'New Hope Centre' – we thought we'd bring back the name! It seemed very appropriate, and Alan Palmer-Hudson, our potter friend, and David Brown's foster-father, created a lovely plaque bearing that name to put above the front door. There was a rumour at this time that people in Casselbank Street who were thinking of selling their property, might feel they should give Bethany first refusal as we seemed to be intent on buying up the whole street!

There was dry rot in the building which cost £1,500 to treat, but a sponsored walk along the Water of Leith raised just the right amount. With the buying of No. 5 our indebtedness increased to £99,000 and we gulped. Shortly after this at the staff prayer time David Brown said God was giving him a 'picture' of a mountain, but the mountain was gradually getting smaller. We held on to that promise and were grateful for a generous gift from the Scottish Telethon appeal. After just eight months, the debt had decreased to £46,000 and the Trust owned two-thirds of their property – truly amazing after just over six years.

As a family we moved across to the top floor of No. 5 just before Christmas 1988 – not a time to be recommended for a removal, but despite the chaos, we did manage to put up a Christmas tree! Our move released No. 48 Kirk Street to be the first self-catering flat and so what was later to grow into the Supported Housing Division came into being. Permission to convert the attic rooms in the Centre was granted but that job had to be put on hold until Hope House was finished and the financial position re-examined. After ten months of waiting, a building warrant was granted to carry out the work on 5 Casselbank St in order to make the whole building suitable for multiple occupancy. In the meantime, John Rodgers lived in a virtual building site downstairs, and one room was occupied by David Brown and the next one by a lady resident. John and David were a lethal combination and always up to tricks, one of which was to listen through the wall to the lady resident's 'talking scales' and then mimic them! Dorothy had visual impairment and so the scales were a great help to her. She had a very trim figure and didn't need to worry about her weight, but the boys teased her terribly and it was to her credit that she took it all in good part.

Then someone else came to live with us in No. 5, and she was the subject of an interesting rumour. The dictionary defines 'rumour' as a 'currently circulating story or report of unverified or doubtful truth'. Such rumours are not unknown even in Bethany, where half a story is heard and the listener surmises the rest! Such was the case regarding the origins of Perro, our cross-collie dog. Bethany staff and residents arrive at the Trust at different stages in their lives, but she was actually born on the premises. Such was the truth of the case and she had been spoiled, loved and cosseted since the day of her birth in No.5. The rumour was much more interesting, and I was made aware of it when Perro was a few years old. I was met one day by a resident who thought it rather wonderful that Bethany had not only provided accommodation for homeless *people*, but even a homeless *dog* which had been ill-treated and abused, rescued by us and given a new, safe and secure future within the sanctuary of our family! A lovely story, and much more romantic than the truth!

Perro's mum, Star, belonged to Emma Pendry. While Emma worked her Careforce year, Star was left in the care of friends, but later when Emma decided to extend her time with the Trust and had her own accommodation, Star joined her in Edinburgh. Unknown to Emma, Star was in pup when she arrived and not long after had a busy Sunday morning producing ten pups. Star was not a big dog but coped valiantly, although ten was just a bit too much and, despite our trying to bottle-feed the two smallest pups, they didn't survive. Two small balls of brown fur bore some resemblance to their mother, but six pups definitely pointed to dad being a variety of collie. We had always said that while living on the premises, and especially at No.5 with no garden, pet dogs were not an option.

However, with Perro cradled in the hand of one of our children and the other saying 'Oh, dad, just look – please, please, please – it's not surprising that at least one pup soon found a home. Perro, like her mother, proved to be very obedient, docile and affectionate and she became much more than the family pet.

She was a Bethany dog from the start. She never managed an SVQ in Care, but in her own way influenced many lives for good. She gave affection, comfort and a listening ear to many residents who shared their troubles with her and she never betrayed confidences. She had one special friend, Jim MacNab. They had a mutual understanding and strolled round Pilrig Park together, no doubt with Jim giving Perro the benefit of his philosophizing!

Residents were warned that Perro did not approve of going into pubs. However, on one occasion a resident asked if he could take

Perro to the park. Quite a while later a phone call was received from the manager of a hotel on the other side of Edinburgh saying that they had an extremely inebriated customer sitting outside accompanied by a very dejected-looking dog who was wearing a name tag on which was the Trust's telephone number. Fiona Weir went off to retrieve them but to our family's amazement the resident was back at our door the next day asking if he could take Perro for another walk. 'You must be joking' was the answer!

It is not uncommon to see people begging on the streets, and Edinburgh is no exception, but another 'walk' with a resident involved Perro being taken to Princes Street, where the resident found a begging pitch, and he and Perro made themselves comfortable. When the incident finally came to light, we just hoped that nobody had recognized her!

Enough about Perro! When the renovation work at Hope House was completed, the first floor was to be used as a self-catering flat. The decorating of the stairs was a massive job but we became the recipient of a tremendous benefit under the Government Employment Training Scheme. Cobalt Training redecorated the complete stairway. For three weeks' work of a four-man team, only a very small sum was asked towards overheads. They did an excellent job and were willing to do more work in what was always going to be on ongoing task, like the painting of the Forth Rail Bridge.

Work was done on the top-floor kitchen and bathroom and was finally finished in December 1990 – just in time for us to be looking to purchase our own accommodation! We moved into North Fort Street in March 1991 and were ably assisted by several residents whom, I am sure, would never again volunteer to haul a piano up three flights of stairs.

All the Bethany premises required furnishings and the Trust had kindly been allowed to store furniture in Bellevue Baptist Church, which had a huge suite of buildings. The fellowship there were moving and the building was to be sold, and other storage accommodation was needed quickly. Again God was faithful and just at the right time Lockhart Memorial church building was made available to us.

And so the years of the late 80s, early 90s were ones of growth, with the premises constantly full, making life both exciting and tiring.

The two attic rooms in the original hostel were made into six single rooms. Various firms came to look at the job, but because it was a listed building and the Council's planning department had insisted on a rounded dormer window, the estimates were complicated and expensive. God had other plans. Alan Palmer-Hudson, David Brown's foster-father, gave up seven weeks to come and head up the building work – all free of charge. Alan agreed that if David went home to Margate for a few weeks to help his mum with their pottery business he would come and oversee the Bethany renovation. What a gift that was – not only his theoretical expertise, but his practical skill and tireless energy. He worked alongside Alan Berry and one or two residents, particularly Lewis who was anxious to be involved. Two rooms were out of use and the hostel was overflowing, with the large lounge turned into a bedroom and the dining room into a lounge – all this added extra strain to situations that could be volatile in themselves. However, when the windows were installed and the dividing walls inserted the improvement was so vast it was hard to visualize what they had been like; and the Lord was good in that the weather was wonderful all the time the roof was off.

But growing can be painful too, and these were also days of steep learning curves. As a Trust we had always tried to carry out the work God had given us to do to the very best of our abilities. The staff comprising Alan, Fiona, David Brown, volunteers Jason and myself were dedicated, committed and enthusiastic. Even with these advantages there was always room for improvement and change came about through circumstances which for a while became very uncomfortable.

However, before that, we were given an awesome reminder of God's faithfulness. The sponsored walk in 1989 was a misnomer – it was definitely a climb, and that right up Ben Lomond! The day was windy with the usual mixture of Scottish weather. Not long before we reached the summit, the most amazing rainbow appeared arching right over the top of the mountain. We felt we could reach up and touch it. We stopped, marvelled and took fresh strength. We did make it to the top, but the memory of that rainbow was an encouragement to hang onto in the difficult days that were to follow as we climbed mountains of another kind.

Up to the end of 1989 Bethany was an accommodation agency taking twenty-six people. But it was reeling under the Government's restriction of benefits to such establishments. In October 1989 the Trust began to face a real economic crisis. All new residents were on much reduced benefits. What was called 'transitional protection' was accorded to those already in residence. This meant that the previous rent would be paid, albeit from three sources. All new residents received only housing benefit at the rent officer's agreed rate, plus a standard allowance based on their age. These payments were quite inadequate and we thus faced staff reductions and a curtailing of the services offered. Many hostels, commercial hotels and bed-and-breakfasts faced closure.

In addition to this it came to the Trust's notice that it probably should have been paying VAT over the previous three years at least. In our innocence we thought charities were exempt. A large bill, not to mention an immense accounting task, lay ahead. God used this revelation to point us in a new direction down the 'registration road' because Social Work Registered Units were exempt from VAT. With this in mind we began actively approaching the subject of registration of the unit. It involved us in defining our client group, our care package and assuring the powers that be that the buildings were in an acceptable state for environmental health and fire authorities. We needed to convince them that we were going to approach the task in a thoroughly professional way. If registration was granted we would also be eligible for a higher allowance from the Department of Health and Social Security. Both Fiona and Gordon Weir, who was in the process of finishing his social work qualification, were a tremendous help in these preparations.

On 22nd February 1990 Bethany was indeed registered under section 61 of the Social Work Scotland Act as a care unit for people who were homeless and had special needs. It affected the Trust in areas of staffing, accommodation and the care package offered.

Each resident was assigned a key worker from the staff team with reviews being held every six weeks and involved outside agencies, including social worker and minister where applicable. With more staff, and drawing on the lessons learned, we were able to give a greater level of care to help each resident think through the issues around them, and look for and work towards answers.

Improvements had to be made in the accommodation too. Sadly the work on the top floor, which had been carried out only the previous year, had to be modified because the rooms were too small. Some of the double rooms in the extension became singles, and radical changes were made to the office and laundry facilities. All this meant that only eighteen people could be accommodated instead of twenty-six, but it had to be admitted that when twenty-six, plus friends, plus staff were at home together, the crowd effect could be far from helpful.

The Trust could no longer charge a rent as such, but the Government set a care allowance figure for services offered, and this was higher than the old hostel rate and was to be reviewed regularly.

We were particularly glad that the Social Work Department made no effort to curtail the Christian nature of the work as long as this was not forced upon residents. They respected the position and motivation of the Trust and our stand that all staff should be practising Christians.

All this led to better care inside the Centre and the appointment of Gordon Weir as the first field worker in June 1990. He was to give support to those who had left the main unit and were either living in Bethany's self-catering flats or those supplied by the District Council. What it did do, however, was leave a gap. The Centre had become a rehabilitation unit for homeless people with special needs, mostly addiction, but this meant Bethany was without an immediate access hostel and this was an urgent need. One possibility was to relocate the care unit, perhaps to a rural setting and re-establish 6 Casselbank Street as a direct access unit.

Added to this, Gordon reported that it had been a difficult time managing the two self-catering units. This brought to light some weaknesses. Through these experiences the Trust moved steadily with a clearer vision and a better framework.

There had been no tenancy agreements, nor did we know the provisions of the Rent Act, for it made no reference to hostels. Both of these omissions had to be rectified quickly. With the help of the lawyers, proper short term assured tenancy agreements for six months were put in place with each tenant. These could be renewed on a monthly basis by what was known as 'tacit relocation'.

Further purchasing of flats for straight rental was delayed and the possibility of leasing mainstream housing investigated. The hope was to furnish these and give a level of ongoing support which did not encourage a dependency syndrome. There were discussions with the Social Work Department with a view to using part of the accommodation we already owned as a registered unit for those with learning difficulties.

People who had moved out into council flats continued to be supported and sometimes furniture and carpets were supplied.

A van, furniture and porters were available but the services of a driver were required. Here was the embryo of what would grow into Bethany Homemaker.

After much thought, deliberation and prayer, it was decided to appoint Gordon Weir as officer in charge of the hostel. Gordon came to the post with several years' experience as officer in charge

Joe Kirkhouse

of Malta House rehabilitation unit and was able to use his newly acquired social work skills to refine the care package. Halfway through 1991 Joe Kirkhouse joined the Trust as field worker, bringing with him tremendous drive and enthusiasm, and the housing portfolio increased with the leasing of a double-upper flat with eight rooms, a kitchen and two bathrooms in Leith Walk. This was to house Careforce volunteers. Its location offered convenience for work whilst being far enough away from the main unit to allow for relaxation and privacy in a pleasant environment. Three flats in Henderson Street in Leith were also purchased to accommodate residents 'moving on'. These too had 'potential,' which in Bethany terms meant they were in need of a great deal of renovation! All this freed up the director to spend more time on areas of advance and dream more dreams!

The purchase and renovation of these single-bedroom flats, work at Leith Walk and in the main Centre, all cost money. Yet Bethany was still 'in the black', demonstrating again God's continued faithfulness Eighteen months previously, the Lord challenged the trustees that the 'labourer was worthy of his/her hire'. All the way through the early days of Bethany there were people who had been willing to work for accommodation, plus a very small stipend. Such sacrificial service was much appreciated, but on registration with the Social Work Department we realized that this should not and could not continue. In the year in which Bethany started to pay National Joint Council rates for the job it moved from owing £12,000 on buildings purchased to an end balance of £55,000, a swing of £67,000 in one financial year. We praised God and recorded our thanks for the good housekeeping and many gifts both great and small from individuals, churches and trusts, which made this possible. We believe God honoured the policy decision which made this possible and we were able to pay cash to Scotmid for the three flats costing £17,000, £17,000 and £19,000 respectively.

In 1991 Gordon Weir and Alan were prayerfully considering the future of the Trust's work. They felt God prompted them to put down in the form of a flow diagram what they would like to see the Trust accomplish in the next few years. Initially it was on the back of an envelope and then presented to the trustees. The vision was as follows:

1) Care Caravan for Street Work
2) Emergency Hostel – at that time the missing link
3) Care Units for people with special needs
4) Shared self-catering accommodation
5) Single-bedroom flats
6) Homemaking Support

The trustees accepted the plan in principle. Thus, the first six rungs on the 'ladder' of what was to become known as Bethany's 'Seven Levels of Care' were agreed as the way forward.

As has been shown, until this time Bethany Christian Centre had been the principal focus of the Trust's work and had moved from being a direct access hostel to become a rehabilitation unit for people with special needs, usually of an addiction nature. The chapter has also shown how being 'needs-led' the work began to expand into the areas of Supported Housing and Homemaking services.

The next few years were exceedingly exciting and busy as these sections of the work continued to grow. Alongside these, the other 'Seven Levels of Care' became a reality. The Care Van Ministry was Level 1; Bethany House, the Direct Access hostel provided the missing link at Level 2; Level 6 expanded with the creation of the Bethany Shops; and Level 7, the new Training and

Work Creation section was formed which sought to equip clients for meaningful employment.

By God's grace, a lot of hard work, understanding and increasing professionalism on the part of staff, there were those who used what Alan called Bethany's 'ladder out of the pit of homelessness'. One of the great encouragements today is to look round the Trust and see those in managerial positions whose first actual contact with Bethany was as service users themselves. For example, John, Paul, Colin and Gavin are all following the Lord and seeking to express their faith and love through serving others in various responsible capacities throughout the Trust. They will reappear in the pages of this story for they have played an integral part in its growth.

Because so much was happening in rapid succession, and in different directions in the early 1990s, it is difficult to try to continue to tell the story chronologically. Indeed, just to complicate matters, the numbers given to the 'Levels' correspond to how Bethany saw its work as a 'continuum of care,' and not to the chronological order in which they came about.

Some of the following chapters therefore give an account of the growth of the different levels from their beginning until the present. Others take a thematic approach, dealing with different general aspects of the work such as finance, public relations, the vital contribution of churches and volunteers, and caring for the staff. Running through the whole, however, even the disappointments, is the faithfulness of God.

Seven Levels of Care

Bethany Christian Trust

Level 1   Care Van

Level 2   Emergency Unit

Level 3   Rehabilitation Unit

Level 4   Shared Supported Housing

Level 5   Single Supported Housing

Level 6   Homemaker Furniture Unit & Charity Shops

Level 7   Work Creation & Training

CHAPTER 3

COME IN FROM THE COLD
CARE VAN AND CARE SHELTER
(LEVEL 1)

THE CARE VAN

The reasons why people find themselves homeless and on the streets are complex. Most of them have suffered traumatic incidents, involving perhaps addiction to alcohol or drugs, crime, family breakdown or mental illness. These in turn have led to loss of tenancy or home, resulting in nowhere to live – sleeping rough may become the only option. One person who experienced this, saw life on the streets not 'as black and white', but 'grey'. He described himself 'standing in shadows on corners, closes and doorways – sitting, pacing, moving around, keeping warm. Asking for help, looking for suitable accommodation – guessing the unheard conversation of people passing by – watching, anxiously waiting, wandering, despairing'. For him each day was largely unpredictable, but he knew that every night of the year at the same time the Care Van arrived at Waverley Bridge – and that wasn't grey, but white.

The Care Van provides an immediate response to the needs of men and women on the streets of Edinburgh, acting as a gathering point in the heart of the city for individuals in need and without secure accommodation. Many appreciate the hot soup and buttered rolls, the information and advice including the booklet 'Where can I find help?', the warm blankets and the opportunity to escape the cold. Even if it is a summer's evening, there can still be the chill of despair, and the friendly smile, the ready accept-ance, the genuine concern and real personal interest have been valued by those who come to the van looking for assistance.

This aspect of the Bethany story began in 1990 when Bethany nego-tiated a formal arrangement with Edinburgh City Mission to work together to regularly help the homeless where they were in the city. The plan was to have the scheme up and running before Christmas of that year. It was rather like the idea of the old soup kitchen but 'on wheels'. The enterprise initially involved collecting a caravan each Friday and Saturday evening. From 11.30 p.m. to 2.00 a.m. it was stationed at Waverley Bridge and then taken on to 'closes' and courtyards where it was thought people might be sleeping rough. Graveyards too, where elaborate old tombs gave some shelter from the elements, were favourite places, though these offer less refuge now that the city 'Ghost Tours' have taken over.

Gordon Weir, reflecting on the first time that Alan and he, along with Bill Chalmers and Ian McNeill of ECM went out, said, 'we towed an old caravan around the city 'kerb crawling' – on the lookout for people sleeping rough. In the van there were about two hundred bread rolls and about ten gallons of soup. Every so often Alan would give a shout, pull the caravan over, leap out the driver's door and disappear over a cemetery wall or down a darkened alley, indicating that we should follow, bearing rolls and soup for any unfortunate soul encountered. After hours of cruising the streets we met only one elderly, homeless man. He was left with his heavy overcoat bulging with rolls and a cup of soup in both hands. He had a bemused expression on his face as we drove off into the night. We congratulated ourselves on the success of the mission and rationalized that the next time there certainly would be more people!'

Persistence did begin to produce results. By April 1991 over twenty churches had supplied team members. Because homeless people were so widely dispersed throughout the city the teams had varying success in finding them but many worthwhile conversations took place and the soup etc. seemed to be greatly appreciated. Depending on the availability and willingness of drivers with tow-bars on their cars and further volunteer teams, it was proposed to extend the provision to other nights of the week. By late 1991, the caravan was out three nights a week, with a fourth night being covered by the Salvation Army with their minibus. In these early days the 'Breadwinner' shop in Bruntsfield kindly donated a regular supply of rolls.

Photograph by D. Edmonston

After fourteen months of using the caravan, a significant step was taken and the work moved to the Sailor's Ark in New Street. It was open from 9-11 p.m. each night, with up to fifty using the facility. However, after two or three months there were major areas of concern. It was necessary to rely heavily on a few supervisors, and more were needed for security and leadership. Discipline was an issue; drink, with its accompanying belligerent and violent behaviour, was a major problem. The lease on the Ark was on a trial period and there was nowhere to move to if it was not renewed.

Violence did increase, as did local complaints, and the facility had to be withdrawn and reconsidered. It was back on the streets, but plans were put in hand to purchase a mobile shop-type of vehicle if and when one could be located. By September 1992 such a vehicle had been purchased, painted and clearly marked for service on the 'soup run'.

In addition to the volunteer teams who have done such sterling work over the years, the Steering Committee worked hard behind the scenes. Rita Sutherland organized the cleaning of the van, and David Murray kept the electrics in order.

Care Van volunteers never know whom they will meet, and one evening produced a big surprise. It was the Five Nations rugby season and Wales were playing Scotland at Murrayfield. Many Welsh rugby fans don't just travel north for the game but make a holiday of the event and red-and-white scarves can be seen up and down Princes Street for days preceding the match. There is always a spirit of camaraderie and regardless of who wins, the fans mostly manage to stay on friendly terms. This particular Saturday, Scotland had won and a group of Welsh rugby fans were commiserating with each other as they approached Waverley Bridge. They had consumed quite a lot of drink, but it had made them mellow rather than belligerent and seeing a mobile soup van they decided that hot soup and rolls were just what they needed. They were made welcome, served soup, told about the purpose of the van and left after giving a handsome donation to its work!

In 1997 one volunteer told of some of the people she had met and what the experience meant to her ... 'Angus is a charming, gentle-spoken man, well-educated with an air of authority. He saw service in North Africa during the Second World War, so he is not young. His trademark is the umbrella over his arm. Doug is rough, aggressive and unpredictable; his life and his mind ruined by drink. Neverthe-less he is kind-hearted. Two more diverse people would be hard to find, yet we meet them regularly on the Care Van. There are many more like them – young people too. All have the same need of com-fort, the need to be recognized as a person in their own right. Care Van volunteers have come to know the "regulars" and to appreciate them as individuals, viewing many of them with affection, but we are aware that anyone who comes to the van has a need, young or old. Some youngsters are afraid, some brash, some are a nuisance, out for a laugh perhaps, but their need for recognition is the same. The Care Van is there as a ministry to people in need.'

Eighteen years on, volunteers are still giving out the message to those who come to the van that things can change, that they are worth something and are of value. They are not just giving out tea, coffee and blankets but seeking to show that Jesus cares and so do they.

The first Care Van did valiant service, but in 2001 it was replaced by an 'R' registered Mercedes-Benz 'Sprinter'. The new van had a side-serving facility as well as an inside counter, making the task of the teams easier in providing soup, rolls, clothing, etc. The new  features and the van's reliability were much appreciated by the volunteer teams. Welcome donations from churches and individuals and one incredibly generous anonymous donation from a city businessman made the purchase possible. The lettering on the van was a gift from another caring supporter. During the year 2004/5 the layout of the Care Van was again developed. The limited seating was removed, making it easier to serve the group that gathered in anticipation of the team's arrival each night. Also during that year, a programme of training commenced to develop the team of over five hundred volunteers who among them had served more than 10, 500 cups of soup that year.

THE NIGHT SHELTER[1]

The problems of sleeping rough increase over the winter months when temperatures can become dangerously low, so in December 1996 the Trust joined with Edinburgh City Mission to run a two-week temporary night shelter for Edinburgh rough sleepers. Over the Christmas period, the pilot scheme used five church halls and teams of volunteers from local churches to provide overnight accommodation and a hot meal.

---

1.   There is an interesting chapter on the Care Shelter in Harry Reid's book *An Old Kirk in a New Scotland* (Edinburgh: St Andrew Press, 2002).

Following its success, nineteen church teams and seventeen churches offered comfort, hot meals and overnight accommodation between December 1997 and March 1998, the project being part-funded by Crisis and Shelter. Initially only one worker was provided by Bethany. Church volunteer teams gave additional cover by either remaining in the venue all night, or in some cases working shifts. This was the situation for the first three winters but it became increasingly clear that a more consistent team was required as a large strain was being placed upon the volunteer teams who often had to go to their own place of employment the following day or take an annual leave day in order to recover.

Staff made up the beds of mattresses and blankets, and dimmed the lights, making the venue seem homely as they felt it was important to get the right atmosphere. They and the volunteers then had devotions before the clients arrived.

Writing a few weeks after the first three-month Care Shelter,  project worker Paul Oliver said that he found himself somewhat shell-shocked for a while after the venture finished. He felt the project immensely worthwhile with many good conversations and times of laughter with those who used the Shelter. It was not so much 'staff' and 'client' relationships but rather person to person. It was rewarding to assist people in finding more secure accommodation but also to help others with addiction problems.

However, the reality was that many of the people were carrying extremely heavy burdens. Burdens of pain, confusion, loneliness and fear, and the lives and conditions of some who used the Shelter could only be described as tragic. Paul felt it was impossible to spend nearly three months of one's working life in the midst of such brokenness and tragedy and remain unaffected. One of the things that struck him was how thin the line was between 'them' and 'us' – in different circumstances it could so easily have been him in a similar situation.

Often a first name is all staff get to know of someone using the Shelter for the first time. There is no obligation on them to provide even as much as a surname. People use the shelter for different reasons. For some on the streets of Edinburgh there is suspicion, unease and frustration about dealing with 'the system'. Many have no desire to become involved and again have to disclose the details and the circumstances that resulted in the pain and disappointment of homelessness. Others think it is pointless as nothing is going to change. So although the Shelter is not ideal, the caring unquestioning environment that it provides along with a hot meal and a night between two warm blankets in a church hall with up to thirty others, is a much better option than trying to huddle up to keep warm outside on a freezing night.

It is unknown how many men and women will be waiting on Waverley Bridge when the minibus arrives to collect them each night at 9.30 p.m. Over a seven-day period in the winter of 2002/3 fifty-two different people used the Shelter for the first time. Jean Dallas who worked there over four winter sessions said although it helped initially to provide one night's food and rest, she believed the Shelter had kept hundreds of people alive over the years by doing this. It opened the door to many more opportunities, and relationships and trust were able to be built up. Jean said there were many success stories of people who had been able to move on into their own flats and start work, and she was still in touch with some of them. During her first year, she found the smell of people's feet hard to cope with, so the staff got a basin and soap and offered clean socks. The clients liked the fact that they could get themselves clean. The following year earplugs were introduced to help people sleep through snoring! Jean felt each year was better than the last, but had an awful feeling when the Shelter was closed until the next winter.

For some Shelter users, the priority is setting out a bed for the night and trying to get as close to a radiator as possible. As the venue changes each evening, it is first come, first served and no-one has an established pitch. Often the more withdrawn do not wish to compete in the scramble, and eat first and then gather their blankets in any space that has been left. The hot and wholesome meal provided by the church catering team is always appreciated.

It can be noisy at times and is generally boisterous as people interact with each other and with the staff team; the latter practised in the art of being able to participate in two or three conversations at any one time! As individuals become familiar with the Shelter and the Bethany workers who are there each night, there is often more of a willingness to open up and talk.

A significant number of those using the Shelter have serious drug problems and each year the clientele appears to be younger, with noticeably more young women using the service. Emotions can run high in the sometimes tense environment where Bethany workers need to be ready to deal with a wide range of situations. Positive peer pressure among the Shelter users, however, also ensures that situations do not get out of hand and there is a level of quiet after the meal and lights-out at 11 p.m. The vast majority want simply to 'get the head down' in preparation for the following day which begins with breakfast at 6:30 a.m.

There are ongoing issues that face staff. One is the request for service users to bring their dogs into the Shelter. Another is the early 'waking time'. At present lights are on at 6:30 a.m. and service users are expected to rise, have breakfast and leave by 7 a.m. The time frame allows for workers to clear the venue, clean and tidy, and return to their base by 8 a.m. when the shift finishes. A later waking time would have a knock-on effect. Although unpopular, a change has been observed among regular service users who have adapted to a regular sleeping pattern; going to bed earlier than they might do otherwise. A later waking time might discourage them from settling down at night, which could create management problems.

Some nights can be particularly challenging. One February evening in 2005 was summed up by staff as 'Oh What A Night'. It involved one girl who was in the early stages of pregnancy and had been found begging outside a coffee shop. She had been brought to the shelter by two members of the public but it transpired she did have accommodation; she left after food, returned about 1:30 a.m. and left again with another service user. One young man accused another of pricking him with a needle. Whilst that was being investigated, another person presented with serious detox tremors. He had been prescribed anti-psychotic medication but had not been taking it. NHS 24 was contacted and an ambulance organized. Another young man who had been involved in an 'incident' earlier in the week was told that he would be banned for a further three nights but was welcome to return after that. He took this news very well and walked away. One staff member had to unscramble a story about a 'stolen' bottle of vodka. The police arrived at 2:15 a.m. with a young lady who had been assaulted by her partner and again at 3:20 a.m. with a young man who had been found walking the streets slightly intoxicated. Early in the morning another Centre phoned regarding a girl who had lost her accommodation and were given the assurance that she would be welcome at the Care Shelter.

Sometimes it is the users of the Shelter who cannot get to sleep because of noise outside! On one occasion when they were tucked up in bed at a church in central Edinburgh they were disturbed at regular intervals into the early hours of the morning as groups of mainly young professionals left the nearby pubs and clubs.

The Care Shelter is an expensive enterprise, but the generosity of churches and teams in providing accommodation and food cannot be overemphasized. There is sincere gratitude too for the involvement of the City of Edinburgh Council. In 2000 they re-directed £32,000 from Rough Sleepers Initiative slippage money to pay for staffing the Shelter. In the winter of 2002/3 public grants were not available but Bethany still provided the service in the belief that it met a real need.

In 2004/5 the Shelter was extended to run for an additional two months. This meant a bigger commitment from churches to provide venues, a bigger financial commitment from the Trust and an even bigger emotional, physical and spiritual commit-ment from staff. Indeed after the 155 days of the 2006/7 winter, the staff were exhausted but another five hundred people had been safely seen through a Scottish winter. No-one knew who would turn up each night, whether regulars would return, or if new faces to the streets of Edinburgh would come looking for help. There had been many challenging times when service users had been difficult or despondent, unwilling to face up to the reality of their situation. This is crisis intervention and not a lasting solution, but there were encouraging tales of those for whom his or her time in the Shelter has been the beginning of recovery.

Neil was one who said 'I found the Care Shelter very helpful, as it was more relaxed than a hostel, and I was given help there to look at my alcohol and drug addiction. I was also helped to find other accommodation'.

One of the 2006 service users said she had lived on the streets for ten years since the age of twelve. She had her 'pitch' for begging in the centre of the town. That day three people had spoken to her. One was the Catholic priest who gave her a cup of tea. Then a lady chatted and took her to the kiosk round the corner for a coffee. She also bought her a craft pack and she made a greetings card for her mum. Later a businessman spoke to her and said he wanted to take her to his home, but she was wary of this because she felt something bad could happen to her. She told the man she didn't want to go, and he gave her £2 and left.

She had been at the Care Van that night, knew the Shelter was opening again and arrived on the minibus. She had used it in previous years and liked it because people were friendly, listened to her and didn't judge, which she found really important. On arrival she went straight to pick out a bedspace for herself and a girl she was 'looking out' for who had been on the streets for six weeks. She got something to eat and the staff helped her sponge her jacket as soup had been thrown over her during an argument at the Care Van.

She had used heroin but was on methadone instead. She was glad that she didn't have to go looking for drugs any more. She felt she had friends at the Shelter, and also felt part of a community on the streets. She would have liked a home of her own, although she recognized she would need help to live in it. She felt she knew how to act in other people's houses, but wouldn't know how to act behind her own closed doors.

One man who phoned the Council in desperation was referred to the Shelter for the night and was met with a warm welcome. He said afterwards: 'The volunteers were so nice to me; it had been such a long time since anyone had been nice to me. It was a new experience'. He was later given a place in Bethany House and found work. He said his life had changed so much that sometimes he didn't believe it. He hadn't drunk since he had entered the doors of Bethany. His thoughts were on better things and how to live his life.

And Stephen, who had used the Shelter in 2003/4, wrote that he was delighted that he didn't need its services the next year. He had been interviewed and accepted by Bethany Christian Centre who had given him 'the opportunity to seek a new way of life which had been beyond anything he could have imagined'.

The Care Van and Care Shelter projects give the opportunity for many individuals to serve others and for churches to express their Christian love and concern through financial giving, making their premises available and enjoying fellowship and working alongside others who share their faith and commitment. Bethany's 2006/7 annual report stated that hardworking volunteers at the Care Van gave out more than 13,400 hot drinks over the year to around thirty-seven people each night. Currently thirty two church teams and two composite teams are involved. At the Care Shelter 754 individuals were saved from a night sleeping rough and given shelter in no fewer than twenty-five venues. Hot food had been served by forty-six different catering teams and advice given when this was requested.

On Christmas Eve 2007 the venue was the Edinburgh City Mission Hall. The team had to gather extra supplies of bedding because a record fifty-two people arrived. Nineteen left after having something to eat and thirty-three stayed over. They even had a surprise visitor – a volunteer from Edinburgh City Mission dressed as Santa whose appearance and gifts, provided by an Edinburgh financial services company, were greatly appreciated – another example of seeking to 'warm' the hearts of those who have come in from the cold.

Recognizing the difficult circumstances faced by the many people helped by the Care Van and Shelter it is not surprising that many clients choose not to return after one visit. Neither the willing workers who volunteer each evening nor the Trust are able to accurately measure the overall impact that Bethany's vital services make in the lives of literally hundreds of different people each year. Instead, there is the confidence that precious seeds of hope are being planted as people continue to care both by day and night and invite others to 'come in from the cold'.

CHAPTER 4

TOWARDS INDEPENDENCE
SUPPORTED HOUSING ACCOMMODATION
(LEVELS 4 & 5)

Hope House

In 1991 the Field Work became known as the Supported Housing section and showed considerable expansion. Our move as a family from No.5 Casselbank Street released the self-contained flat and gave another four spaces, making a total of ten single bedrooms near the Centre. This provision for 'moving on' was vital in preventing the Centre from becoming a bottleneck and in creating stepping stones from the Centre towards independent living.

Newly appointed field worker, Joe Kirkhouse, continued regular house meetings and consultations with tenants who were already settled, but much of the growth in Levels 4 and 5 was new. In July 1991 the Trust received the keys for three single-bedroom flats in Henderson Street. They needed an immense amount of work as none of them had either a bath or shower. Alan and Joe did some of the renovation work, and as Alan said, 'it was a good job Joe liked practical work!'

The housing committee of the District Council agreed in principle that four council houses could be allocated to Bethany with the Trust acting as the landlord. Consequently in 1991 the missive was signed for a completely renovated flat in the Royston area and a delighted new tenant moved in. A second allocation was on the third floor of a medium-rise block of flats. This was registered with the Social Work Department so that the tenant could receive an appropriate level of support resulting in daily visits being made by Marion Gemmell. As she had done in the Centre, Marion demonstrated amazing patience, perseverance and good humour, in a stressful situation.

The third house was in Pilton housing scheme and by January 1993 the two flats in Kirk Street, which operated as satellite units from Bethany Christian Centre, had been accepted for registration and were occupied. The tenants received regular visits and advice from support workers. The extra accommodation meant that, while priority was still given to those moving from the Centre, it was also possible to offer accommodation to people directly after their needs had been carefully assessed.

These additional flats were an exciting fulfilment of the dream that people should have their own home with a level of support that did not encourage dependency. The hope was that the level of housing stock would rise steadily, thus making a significant contribution to alleviating homelessness. The service and advice provided within a tenant's home, covering a wide range of issues such as budgeting, household management, benefits and life skills, would hopefully enable them to develop their own ability to maintain a tenancy and to live independently within society.

During the years 1992/3 the Trust assisted a number of people in emergency situations including two involving mothers and children. Sometimes people moved on more quickly than staff would have wanted due to their reluctance to accept the support offered. However, a number of people who had been in shared accommodation felt ready to move on to a single tenancy, and demand increased. In 1993 Joe left the Trust to become a full-time house father and his successor, Diane Williams, set herself and the team

– which by this time comprised Marion, Elaine Harley and Ronnie Mill – the task of doubling the housing stock during 1994/5.

Although the work was often difficult, there were encouragements. In the 1994/5 annual report one tenant said that he first heard about the Trust when he was due out of prison. He had nowhere to go on his release on parole. He was given a room in shared accommodation at No. 5 which gave him the chance to get himself sorted out and try to reintegrate into society. He received a lot of support, stayed in the flat for nine months and then moved into one of Bethany's single-bedroom flats. He appreciated the fact that he could still get support if and when he needed it, and felt if it hadn't been for the Trust's help he would have been on the streets or back in prison.

Another early tenant was Graham. In 1990 after his mother died he had to move out of the home they had shared in Musselburgh. He managed to get a flat in Greendykes but, not long after moving in, had a very difficult time due to neighbours' antisocial behaviour. His minister, Rev. Harry Telfer, and friends in Duncan Street Baptist Church were very supportive, and he said he was praying for help. His prayers were answered when he was allocated a Bethany single-bedroom flat in Leith. Later, when his health deteriorated, he moved to a specially adapted flat, where he still lives, and is grateful for the assistance of good home helps, his GP, nurse and Bethany's support workers.

By November 1994 the housing stock included flats in Kirk St, Eyre Place, Easter Drylaw, and one owned by Castle Rock Housing Association. Another flat was in a stair which was reserved for 'women only', and a mother and her two children were Bethany's tenants there. In 1995 a generous grant of £5,000 from Abbey National Charitable Trust was earmarked for the expansion of the supported housing stock.

Over the years central Government has made funds available to improve sub-standard flats and in 1998 Bethany began to benefit from the Empty Homes Initiative. A successful bid to Edinburgh City Council released a total of £165,000 which eventually allowed the Trust to house nine more people in single-bedroom flats around Edinburgh. The first six properties were already owned by the Council but were in a state of disrepair.

The Council spent £120,000 of the grant total renovating the properties, which were then rented to the Trust. Bethany used the final £45,000 to renovate the remaining three properties which they then bought from the Council.

However, one of the real problems for many tenants who move into a single-bedroom flat is loneliness. The transition from a hostel environment, or even a shared tenancy can be difficult. The Supported Housing team has sought to encourage tenants to take advantage of activities and groups that help alleviate the sense of isolation and enrich life.

During 1996, when Gillian Porter took up the post as manager of the Supported Housing team, three tenants responded to the challenge to 'do something completely different'. They completed weekend residential courses in conservation and outdoor activities with Venture Scotland and this led on to involvement in further conservation activities on a local scale.

Supported Housing staff

A 'befriending scheme' was developed to offer informal support to those living in Bethany flats and to help them feel at home in the community. 'Tenant Jim' and 'befriender John' were two who were involved in this scheme. After a brief induction and training period John was introduced to Jim. When the scheme was suggested to Jim he decided that he had nothing to lose, although he confessed he didn't think it would work out and wondered 'how many times a week must I see this bloke?'! But it wasn't like that at all. John was busy and did his own things, and so they had fortnightly visits. They were usually connected to their mutual interest in Scottish history and became enriching experiences.

Such friendships are important to tenants, who in seeking to steer their life in a different direction, feel no longer able to visit some of their old haunts or socialize with former friends.

A shared meal for tenants has become a feature of Christmas celebrations and in 2000 the entertainment was provided by a group of Russian musicians who had been staying in Hope House.

A client group from Supported Housing, called Sunshine on Leith Action Group (SOLAG), was formed. It was set up to serve as a forum of Bethany's clients to feed back to the management about the service. Some of the service users wanted to fundraise after the Tsunami and the group evolved into a social group who met together on a weekly basis to fundraise, serve the community and visit places of interest such as the local fire station. Later the Community Education department became involved with some of the activities and Supported Housing organized monthly outings for the clients, all of which have helped to dispel feelings of isolation and loneliness.

Later Supported Housing team

Holidays are a great way to get to know others. In 2007, about a dozen tenants went on a week's holiday to the Windmill Christian Centre in Arbroath and new friendships were formed. They visited a local country park, Scott of the Antarctic's famous ship the *Discovery*, the town of St Andrews and went sea fishing. The group caught a very respectable number of fish and the evening's menu was quickly changed from stew to cod in lemon with new potatoes, which was pronounced 'absolutely yummy'! The group had a walk along the clifftop path one morning. For a while they wondered if they were about to lose two support workers in one go because the latter had chosen to walk at the bottom of the cliffs and the tide was slowly coming in. However, they did eventually make their way back safely. Everyone greatly enjoyed the holiday and the Centre often echoed with the sound of laughter.

WOMEN

The Supported Housing section does not only support men. From October 1998 to January 2000, No. 48 Kirk Street, the flat adjacent to the Centre, accommodated four women in a community flat. They received external support and a volunteer stayed overnight.

One of these tenants initially arrived at Bethany House, the direct access hostel, where she told staff members Liz and Gavin that all she needed was a plug socket for her alarm so that she could get up for work, and a roof over her head. She was used to bushes for walls, tarpaulin for a blanket, with carpet and pallet board for a bed. At the House she appreciated the organized activities and the pre-employment course with trainer Alex McGowan. There were lots of caring staff with big shoulders who helped her pick herself back up and eventually move on to the women's community flat. Here she built up to independence and got ready for a flat of her own. Looking back she didn't think she could have made it on her own. She thought she would still have been in the same mess. She felt God had shown her the way to Bethany, taken her off the streets and shown her what it was to be loved and wanted again.

Jacqui Bain had always had a heart for the work of the Trust, and with her family grown up she felt free to do voluntary work. She had already met this lady at Bethany House and when the women's flat opened Jacqui volunteered to do overnight cover once a fortnight. She drove round about 8:00 p.m. spent time with the girls, chatting, watching TV, and on one occasion having a bash at a puzzle that they had produced. Sometimes the girls were out or had their own friends visiting, but all in all it was a very comfortable time. They each had their own bedroom and in the morning Jacqui just slipped out and set off to her own workplace. She thanked God that He had shown her something practical she could do, as she was quite a home bird and was happy to share time with others in their home environment. She found the best way to have a friend was to be one.

Support has been provided for single parents since 1994. Provision for single mothers was seen as part of a wider move within Bethany to provide more services for women. Many single parents simply appreciate the opportunity to spend time with another adult, and talk through some of the difficulties and pressures of raising a child alone.

Such was the experience of one tenant who had had a child when she was twenty years old and felt her life had changed so fast. She started to move around from place to place living with family members or friends for a few weeks or sometimes months in one place. On one occasion because of a failed relationship she was forced to leave her home and move into temporary accommodation. Her son was three months old at the time and she found it hard to manage as a single parent. She simply didn't know how to be a mum, and her son was taken into care for six weeks.

During this time she heard about Bethany Christian Trust. She met with staff and realized the whole set-up was totally different from what she had imagined. Because she knew it 'was run by Christians,' her first thoughts had been, 'they'd better not preach the Bible to me'!

When she first moved into Bethany accommodation, she found it very hard. Her child was returned to her but the flat didn't feel like home. When her support worker showed her how to manage her money and work on housekeeping skills, she was able to set goals. When she reached them, she felt great. She thought that without Bethany's support she would probably still have been moving from place to place and trying to cope with her child on her own.

It was still hard to manage but she was able to buy things for her flat. She was settled and her child was happy and knew where home was. If she had problems she wanted to discuss she only had to phone her support worker who would be there when needed. Her son went to nursery five days a week and she coped better with him because she had people to help her, and had made friends with other mums through the nursery and groups at the local community centre.

In March of the same year another tenant wrote a letter of thanks to various Bethany staff members. She said 'I felt I had to put pen to paper and give thanks to several individuals within Supported Housing for the hope and love you have all shown/ given to me throughout the years. Having been nearly six years in Bethany Supported Accommodation, I've known staff past and present who have supported me, cared, stuck by me through the good and bad times and I've appreciated the listening, talking, understanding and debating of addiction worker Denise. But now I am looking forward, after nine years in various homeless projects/supported accommodation. I have two beautiful children, my lifestyle is more focused, more stable and I have secured my own tenancy. I am so thankful that you have all been there for me and my children. I feel that I owe it all to Bethany and God, that eventually and finally I am where I am, and that is somewhere positive and challenging.'

With the 'Levels of Care' being separated into different chapters in this Bethany story, the impression might be given that they are self-contained sections. In one sense this is true, but they are also part of a whole which seeks to provide an holistic response to homelessness and so they support and complement each other. In this respect during the year 2003/4 the Supported Housing team was encouraged to see tenants becoming involved with Bethany's Community Education programmes and benefiting from developing their social skills whilst gaining qualifications.

After ten years with the Trust, Gillian moved on and for a while, Elaine Harley succeeded her as Supported Housing manager. Those years were also significant in other respects. Because the number of Supported Housing staff had doubled, they were able to accommodate people with greater support needs. However, their offices were no longer able to accommodate *them*, and the team moved to larger premises at 65 Bonnington Road where the extra space was greatly beneficial. In that year too Bethany began new partnerships with Rock Trust and The Ark, offering accommodation and support to asylum seekers.

DUMFRIES

Besides widening the level of support, the work expanded to new locations. During the years 2001/2 planning and preparation took place for an initiative in Dumfries in south-west Scotland. Christian Care for the Homeless (CCH), an umbrella group comprising most of the churches in the Dumfries area, had a concern for helping homeless people. It had already started a small furniture project and was in the process of buying premises in the Whitesands. CCH invited Bethany to provide supported flats, and Dumfries and Galloway Council were approached.

By the following year a total of twelve supported places in eight flats were provided for the first time. This gave opportunities for single men and women from homeless and vulnerable backgrounds and ex-offenders to have their own tenancies backed up by Bethany support worker Lizzy Robertson and James MacInnes, the latter being redeployed to act as Senior Support worker in the formative stages of the work. With many supported tenants from an addiction background it was interesting that the Bethany Supported Housing office was at 26b Brewery Street in central Dumfries!!

First Dumfries Team

Some difficulty was experienced with the two-bedroom flats because there was often a problem finding compatible flatmates, and in 2006 two of these flats were handed back to the Dumfries and Galloway Housing Partnership. However by the following April a new referral relationship with the Council's homelessness team began and is progressing well. Two one-bedroom replacement flats were handed over to Bethany in August and September 2007 and the Dumfries and Galloway Supporting People team review of the service was satisfied with the quality of support delivered by Mike Pudsey and team, and strongly desired that it should continue.

The Dumfries staff are a long way from their colleagues in Edinburgh and must at times feel rather isolated and 'out of the loop'. They, perhaps of all the support workers, need to know they are remembered in prayer and not forgotten, tucked away in their own corner of the country.

Fife

In 2003, the local Council invited Bethany to establish a new housing support service for vulnerable adults in Fife. With the support of Bethany's Training and Addiction teams, the service covered Dunfermline and West Fife. It assisted individuals living in Council and Housing Association tenancies in all aspects of managing and sustaining them. This included help with shopping, cooking and cleaning, as well as financial matters. It was hoped that the comprehensive and flexible support structure would encourage personal development and allow clients to learn new skills leading to independent living.

Not all of the Fife tenants had actually been homeless but it is fair to say that many of them could have become so but for the support they received. Some may best be described as being 'homeless at home'. Whilst they had a fixed address, their life was unsettled and transient, and some struggled with alcohol/drug-related issues. They faced many of the same challenges as a person on the street or in a hostel. Having a house is not the same as having a home.

Amongst early clients was a young family caught up in the midst of addiction. After a few weeks of support the father recognized that he needed intensive help and moved into Bethany Christian Centre. Additional support was given to the mother, who understandably required extra input at that time.

Another service user was living with her nine-year-old son Neil (not his real name). She had issues with alcohol and this was a significant factor in a dysfunctional house and home. Neil was sleeping on a mattress on the floor, using a duvet without covers or sheets. Budgeting was an issue as a lot of money was spent on alcohol and crisis management of debts. In addition to the housing support she received, she met with addiction worker, Cath. She wanted to provide a bed for Neil but was unable to accommodate this in her budgeting. The support staff agreed to supply a splendid 'good-as-new', metal-framed cabin bed through Fife Homemaker and they set the price, gave her a 50% discount, and then arranged to match her pound for pound as she saved for it. After a couple of weeks she paid what she was due and the bed was delivered.

At the next visit the Support worker commented on the lavish bunch of flowers in the living room and she was told these had been a gift from the triumphant Neil, as was the second huge bunch that decorated the kitchen. Awkwardly and with a degree of reluctance mixed with an obvious pleasure and pride, she admitted that Neil had pilfered these from the Council display roundabout at the top of the road as a thank-you for the bed!

The following year, Fife Council requested that Bethany's service be increased four fold so that it might also take in the area around Leven. This resulted in an additional office base in Leven and an increase in the size of the support team.

The experience of a Fife lady, Roberta, highlighted in the 2005/6 annual report is an example of how tenants, support workers and other agencies, including churches, can work together to bring about real change, so much so that a support worker can actually find themselves redundant! Roberta's friend tells the story – 'I met her at Remploy which is supported employment for disabled people. A few years ago she asked me for help because her toilet in the flat needed fixing, so we arranged for a housing inspector to call. He realized Roberta wasn't coping; she simply did not have the skills she needed to look after the property. The housing inspector arranged for the Council to treat the damp and the walls, repaint the place, and she was referred to Bethany.

'The first thing they did was help Roberta with budgeting so she was able to get some new furniture. Then, week by week, she was shown how to look after herself properly, then taught how to compile a recipe file and to bake and make scones. Someone took her out for coffee and shopping every Friday, and she learnt how to do the necessary household tasks. The support workers used a noticeboard in her kitchen to remind her of what to do, and when.

'Community became a huge part of Roberta's life. Before her contact with Bethany she had no social life, but she was encouraged to get involved in her local community and began regularly attending the parish church and guild. She made friends, invited people from work to her house, and even went for a holiday in Majorca with three of them. Roberta received help from Bethany for around two years but the time came when she no longer needed it, as she was able to look after herself'.

Another client who, when the team first began to offer support, was sometimes eating food from out of the bins behind cafés and shops, began to establish good routines and even explore a little beyond the

ASDA savers' tins of ready-made food! His house, which had been bare except for a battered sofa, was furnished by Homemaker. For a number of months he used the Toastie Club Drop-In which helped develop his confidence. While doing a regular fortnightly shop with his support worker, he asked to add 'wee white paper cake things' to his list of messages – 'and chocolate and a box of crispies'. This was done, and the following day he presented a staff member with a bag of chocolate crispies, with chocolate so thick that it could have broken a new set of dentures!

In 2007 between the two locations in Fife, the Housing Support team had a contract to provide 210 hours of support to an average number of sixty-two service users each week and was continuing to develop relationships with the Council and other service providers. Fife Council undertook a review of their Supporting People funded services with a view to bringing their budget for this initiative into line with that required by the Scottish Executive. It resulted in a positive report and their contract with Bethany remained unchanged.

EDINBURGH

Here the work has continued to grow. By September 2007 the sixty-five Edinburgh flats had contracted 414 hours of support per week. This system of 'contracting' works by means of the Council stipulating a 'top limit' on the number of 'support' hours they are willing to finance and Bethany then invoicing them for the actual hours worked. 'Floating' support was being given to seventeen service users who had moved on from Bethany hostels or were otherwise in unsupported accommodation in the city. The staff were working with Edinburgh Council's Temporary Accommodation team and other agencies to develop a continuous supply of appropriate referrals, whilst improved joint working with Bethany residential services led to a further increase in referrals.

MANAGEMENT

While for most people, working with homeless and vulnerable people may well conjure up an image of front-line care staff working in a residential situation, this is only part of the story. The administration that underpins supported accommodation is a crucial aspect of the work of the Trust, and as the housing portfolio has increased, so has the workload, responsibility (and probably the headaches) of Adrian Currie, director of Property and

Housing Management, and his team. Adrian came to Bethany in April 1997 and brought with him a wide experience of housing management and architectural skills. Later that year he was joined by housing administrator, Hazel Boulton, who during her time with the Trust brightened up the lives of everyone with her cheery smile.

Adrian has worked closely with the Bethany Maintenance team, in addition to wearing various 'hats' which have included organizing the Bethany Christmas market and taking the production of Bethany newsletters into the 21ˢᵗ century.

One of the important issues when dealing with property is health and safety. These two words may evoke an adverse reaction because most people have 'suffered' under such regulations, but the following article in the spring 2002 newsletter shows just how vital it is to ensure everything is in working order. 'Early on Christmas morning one of the Bethany supported tenants was wakened by the piercing sound of his smoke alarm. He was able to get out of the flat through dense smoke and warn others. Later he was rehoused in another Bethany supported flat. The fire, which may have been started by a candle, caused extensive damage, but the fire brigade prevented it spreading to adjacent properties and the insurers paid for the restoration work. The "remains" of the smoke detector were a reminder of how important it is for all homes to be fitted with detector alarms, and also that they should be regularly tested'.

It may be thought that to be a maintenance worker does not require as much patience, 'people' skills or sense of humour as

Bill Johnston

those actively supporting people. However Bill Johnston's report in 2000 may well make one question that. At the time he was working as Bethany's maintenance officer and said 'there is no such thing as a typical day on Maintenance. You never can tell what may turn up. You can go from the mundane task of taking a mortice lock to bits, to the not very nice task of clearing a choked toilet. Incidentally, the pleasure it gives to locate the blockage, such as the holder of a rim block, must rank with an artist viewing the results of his efforts on a canvas! The job can be frustrating, as for example when in my efforts to gain access to the back court of a property in Leith Walk, I discovered I was actually trying to get into someone's basement flat. One of the most frustrating things is doing a job all over again because of wilful damage. But there are satisfactions like tracing the cause of flooding inside a certain building to a coffee mug left in a roof gutter outlet. At the end of the day, however, I feel that after forty-five years in the building trade, which I didn't particularly enjoy, I now have a purpose for my skills and they are being put to "good" use.'

And so in various ways all the different gifts of members of staff who seek to support people are brought together. People need houses in which to live, houses need to be sought, maintained and made financially viable, and people need to be helped to maintain their tenancy and turn the house into a home to be enjoyed.

Perhaps a poem written by a contributor to *The Bugle* should have the last word in this chapter.

A Poem for Support Workers

You're more than a support worker to me,
You're a friend – can't you see?
You make my calls,
You check my mail,
And listen to problems,
And take me out.
You make me laugh,
And make me feel worthwhile.
You don't have to do what you do,
But I thank God that you do.
You give me hope and are so kind,
Without you I'd go out of my mind.
You're always kind and cheer me up,
"Would you like a coffee?
I'll give you a cup!"
I'd like to do something worthwhile,
When I see you I want to smile!
I hate it when it's time to part –
When I leave here, my life will start.
I bet you're glad when you go away,
The jokes on you – Ha! Ha!
You've got to come back another day!

CHAPTER 5

'TURNING HOUSES INTO HOMES'
HOMEMAKER
(LEVEL 6)

Bethany Homemaker

In early 1991 Alan and son Stephen happened to meet a previous resident in West Granton. Alan asked where she was staying. 'Over there'. 'Can we come and see?' They followed her into a flat. It was dreadful. A mattress on the floor, nothing on which to cook, one blanket used as curtain, no kettle, no fridge, the only floor covering a two foot-square carpet, and certainly nothing to make the house look like a home.

It was another reminder of the gap in the provision of services within the caring process of which the Trust was becoming increasingly aware. All too often people were being allocated tenancies from the District Council only to find themselves inheriting a shell of a building which needed some renovating and decorating, quite apart from needing to be totally furnished to make it habitable. Often such people were dealing with other major difficulties in their lives. When the very limited help from DSS was added to this, the disincentive of structural damage, bare floorboards and empty rooms often seemed too much to handle, resulting in failure to establish themselves, with eventual loss of tenancy and return to a homeless and broken existence.

And so, as had been the case in the past, the need led to a widening of the vision. Later that year saw the Trust in the final stages of arranging a lease on a 5,000 sq. ft ex-Co-op supermarket. The building, to be used for an exciting opportunity to alleviate human suffering, was in Ferry Road Drive, West Pilton, and was to be called 'Homemaker'. Its aim was to help people who were living in extremely poor circumstances through lack of proper furniture and household effects. The idea was to take unwanted furniture and household goods such as crockery, kettles, irons, bedlinen etc and put a nominal price tag on them, thus retaining customers' dignity, while helping to pay the salaries of those who would head up the unit.

Whoever was appointed to mastermind the operation needed to have drive and vision, be unafraid of practical work and able to gather together a team of volunteers to share in the work of giving practical help and actually making things happen. Such assistance would range from the initial tasks of clearing out rubbish and painting and decorating, through to serving in the café and bookshop – both an integral part of the new unit, as was delivering furniture once things were up and running. Ewan Foreman was the man! He had worked for a short time as a project worker at the Centre and had all the qualities and enthusiasm for overseeing this new venture. He was to be ably supported by a local organizing committee comprising Rev. Andy Scarcliffe, Ronnie Mill and Jim Pennycook, from Granton Baptist Church, and Bill McGillivray, of Pilton Christian Centre.

Homemaker's aims were identified as follows:-

- To provide good-quality second-hand furniture and fittings at an affordable price to make kitchen, lounge and bedroom fully usable and as comfortable as possible.
- To provide help in the uplift, delivery and installation of all goods.
- To provide, where necessary, the skills of joiner, plumber and electrician.
- To provide a contact point where church and community met and where relationships could

develop through which individuals could become involved in church fellowships.

And there was a lot of furniture around!! Bethany had always received and supplied a certain amount but suddenly it was overflowing, as the Church of Scotland had closed their furniture unit. This coincided with Joe Kirkhouse's appointment as field worker, and he had to spend a considerable amount of time in a holding operation until the Granton project was up and running.

The first year's budget of £35,000 included funding for two full-time staff, one to head up the furniture initiative and have responsibility for the whole project, and one to manage the café and bookshop. The Scottish Office, through the Social Work Services Group, gave a grant of £10,000. Their recognition of the value of such a work was a great encouragement.

The furniture enterprise opened on Wednesday 11th March 1992, with an official launch on 2nd May, and the café was operational by the summer. The latter was small, but became a meeting point for the community with its significance far greater than its size. It also provided valuable work experience and placements for volunteers.

Initially furniture uplift and collection was in a Ford Transit Luton truck purchased from Tom McArthur, a plumber in Ayr who had done a lot of work for the Trust. By January 1993 extra transport was needed and a second van was on loan. When George Reiss joined the team as a support worker, he was able to do house visits for high-need cases, and this further assisted the assessment process.

Pilton was a culture shock for some of the full-time volunteer workers. Kelly, from Texas, had difficulty understanding the local 'dialect,' but rose to the challenge of working in a large housing scheme where the regular repainting of Homemaker's outside walls was necessary because some local residents saw them as a blank canvas which was ideal for their artistry! Shades of Banksy but without his price tag!

Another full-time volunteer was David Fisher. He was a quiet, unassuming young man with a very polite manner and a photographic memory! Two young people who had come to help set up the café during their holiday were heard to say 'he won't last in that environment'. But David lasted – more than lasted! He did a power of work, built up a real rapport with customers and designed the smiling house logo which illustrates Homemaker's desire 'to turn houses into homes'.

Although meeting real needs, the project was not without its challenges. In 1993 regulations were introduced which restricted the selling of any upholstered furniture which did not pass stringent fire retardant tests. This created quite a crisis as Bethany received very little soft furniture which had the necessary fire certificate. Added to this there was a shortage of transport, and demand for white goods outstripped supply.

Liz enjoyed her year on a training scheme working in the Homemaker café. After a break working in a hostel for homeless women she returned to the café as a volunteer, working with people to whom she felt she could relate. She shared her experience in the April 1996 newsletter saying 'the café is very important to me. I feel that the people in Pilton need a place like this as it is somewhere for them to meet and in a roundabout way see God working in Pilton. It is a place to witness to the public. Spreading the gospel is not just about telling people about Jesus, but about the way we live and how we put ourselves over to people. Let the people see us as ordinary people, on the same level as they are. We need to live as God would want us to and love the people that use the café as Jesus would. I love my new full-time job in the café as I have never loved a job before. Thank you Bethany for giving me a chance to prove that the café can work.'

Former Homemaker staff

But growing was not simply about size. As Ewan said, 'the Homemaker team learned (sometimes the hard way) that working in an area of high unemployment and low income demanded much more than good intentions. They found that combining Christian charity and commerce demanded skill and wisdom, and learned that helping people in need, whilst demanding and exhausting, had rewards that encouraged them to keep going'. But after six years in Pilton, Homemaker was on the move.

After an exhaustive search lasting over two years, and with more than the occasional disappointment, the Trust's commercial side, which by this time not only incorporated Homemaker but three charity shops,[1] found a new HQ and office base in an industrial unit in Jane Street, Leith.

Although the Hub was smaller than ideally required, this was offset by the advantages of being close to other sections of Bethany's work. Indeed, some said that it was rather like the prodigal son's homecoming to Leith. However all commerce staff strenuously resisted any such suggestions!

The Hub accommodated all commerce administration and incoming donated goods enroute to Homemaker and the Charity Shops.

The aim was to store items for no more than a few days which was quite a challenge. Homemaker in turn was to develop much more as a charity shop with a continued commitment to needy individuals and families in the Pilton area which it had just left and throughout the city. But where was it to be based?

In the summer of 1998 closer examination of a poster in the window of 32B Haddington Place, Leith Walk, revealed the wording 'Closing Down Sale'. There was, however, no sign of the usual 'To Let' board secured overhead. However, a brief discussion with the current occupiers revealed that they were indeed moving out and would be looking for someone to take over the lease. Within forty-eight hours an army of Trust staff had visited the premises (each with their own list of 'wants'). Without exception, all agreed

---

1. The story of the Charity Shops is told in chapter 6.

that the shop was not only ideal for Homemaker's planned use, but had a solid feeling of rightness about it. By the time the 'To Let' board did go up a few days later the premises were already under offer to the Trust.

The premises, which were spread over two floors, were large, in good condition and had off-street rear parking/loading. This could enable the ground floor to be operated as a regular charity shop, with the basement floor being used specifically for furniture for people who had been referred to Homemaker for help. Ewan was very much in charge of all the work but the move meant that two new teams emerged from what was previously one large staff team, with Emma Galloway heading up the team at the Hub, and Iris O'Neill heading up the shop at Homemaker. The new Hub central warehouse opened in March 1998 while the dedication for the new Homemaker took place on 9th May.

Skills Seeker Story

Over the years the Hub has given training opportunities for people seeking to realize their potential. One such was Paul, who as an eighteen-year-old spent a year there as a trainee under the government's Skills Seekers scheme. His duties included answering phone calls from people wishing to donate furniture and assisting with the van rotas. Speaking of his experience, he said, 'I feel the general office and computer skills I am gaining and dealing with the public are good experience in themselves, and will also benefit me in the career which I would eventually like to pursue in the police force.'

After six years at 22/24 Ferry Road Drive, West Pilton, the decision to relocate was never going to be an easy one. Strong links had been established with a number of regular customers, volunteers and trainees over the years, partly through the café, and many had come to be regarded as friends. Inevitably the move severed some of these links, although others said they would make the effort to help or visit the new Leith Walk shop. It was encouraging, however, that the Ferry Road Drive building was subsequently taken over by Fresh Start. They too were involved with homeless people, providing starter packs for new tenants and practical help such as decorating.

Since 1992 Bethany had been the recipient of a great number of good donations but in November 1998 through a new initiative and the generosity of the John Lewis department store, Homemaker began to receive white goods which were taken out of customers' homes when a new appliance was installed. Paul Mooney then had the job of testing and refurbishing any goods which were still of potential use.

Paul's own story is a testimony to the faithfulness of God. He says he was someone who was lost and has been found. After finishing school he worked in the hotel business where he discovered alcohol, which eventually made a complete mess of his life. He lost everything dear to him, including his wife and family, his home and job. He was in and out of rehabilitation and psychiatric hospitals and for a short period ended up homeless. During his darkest hour, while

Paul Mooney

staying in Dublin in a very unpleasant hostel, he met a Christian who told him about a Christian alcoholic support organization called Stauros. He ended up in rehab there and did so well that he eventually became a care worker in charge of work therapy for the residents who had alcohol and drug related problems. Unfortunately, he had a few lapses and it was suggested that he should get away from Ireland and the problems there which were contributing to his drinking. His boss contacted friends who worked at Bethany and they agreed to take him as a resident in Bethany Christian Centre. It was from that period on that his life took a change for the better. That was in 1991. He stayed at the Centre for six months, then moved into the 'halfway house' next door. His key worker discovered his ability with electrics and arranged for him to become involved with jobs that needed doing around the Bethany flats. He also worked on the refurbishment of Bethany House, and in 1992 Paul was put in charge of reconditioning white goods for resale in Homemaker.

When the first Bethany Shop opened in Stockbridge, Paul became manager of the electrical and French polishing workshops, which supplied electrical goods to all the Bethany charity shops and provided goods and a repair service to Bethany flats and properties.

In addition, re-gassing and servicing of refrigeration units was included in his remit. The workshop offered placements to train young people in electrical skills and help ex-offenders reintegrate into the community. Over the years Paul has had some good apprentices and two are now fully qualified domestic appliance engineers with a large company. There are many opportunities in the section and there is always a need for people to clean washing machines, cookers and fridges and carry out stock control.

Back in his native Ireland Paul used to be in trouble with the police. As he says 'back then I would have robbed the eyes out of your head and then when I knew you were blind, I would come back to rob your eyelashes too. But since I came to the Lord in 1987 I've really moved on and my sinful and devious ways are gone'.

Paul is the longest-serving employee of Bethany – now freed from his alcohol addiction. He is in contact with his family again and visits on a regular basis. They have regained their trust in him and are very proud of what he now is. Paul is grateful to Bethany for saving him from himself. He believes that everything that has happened to him was from the Lord. The Lord promised to take him to a quiet place and he believes that place was Bethany. He hopes maybe one day God will lead him back home to Ireland.

The 1998 change of premises also gave Homemaker the chance to re-organize the referrals for people in need of home furnishings.

 In the summer of 1999, Jonny Watson, Careforce worker, said Homemaker saw their role as crucial in the overall restoration process of people and their lives. At first glance a lack of furnishing appeared to be a very physical problem requiring a practical solution, but this limitation regularly triggered other deep emotional problems such as a feeling of self-worthlessness. These problems when coupled with difficulties such as isolation or family breakdown could create a situation which seemed beyond control.

Jonny told of a social worker who needed to obtain furniture for a client by the next day or they faced eviction. They were impressed when the necessary items were supplied in time.

Another client was a young girl who suffered from leukaemia. Homemaker was able to furnish her home and install essential electrical equipment, which gave her a degree of freedom and independence.

One young couple had a baby with severe breathing problems, and as the child slept on the floor he often needed resuscitation. Bethany Homemaker provided a cot, but were not optimistic about being able to supply a pushchair as it had to be a specific type so that the child could sit upright. There was one pushchair in the referrals section – and it was exactly right!

IDEALS

But as Ewan Foreman was at pains to explain, Bethany Homemaker wasn't just part of a charitable organization. It was also built on Christian principles and, whilst the Trust's trading and business activities continued to expand, there was the challenge to dare to be different. Ewan recognized this was both daunting and exciting because they were operating within the context of an increasingly free market which dominated every aspect of Western society. It pushed the boundaries of excess to the extent that it was willing to compromise the environment, the abject poverty of millions in the Third World and some extremely damaging effects on our own society in the longer term. He felt for most the issues were simply too complex and the implications of change too costly.

Ewan accepted that charities were, and are, not immune from the influence of modern consumerism. In order simply to survive they have to move with the times, employ professionals, measure efficiency, develop sophisticated fundraising campaigns, establish a trading income and, in some cases – if it did not present the moral problem which it would have done for Bethany, go cap in hand to the National Lottery because people would rather get rich quick than feed the poor. 'Homemaker's purpose', as Ewan says, 'was not merely to prosper, it was to make the best possible use of the donated goods they received; it was to give meaningful work experience to those that the majority of employers were unable to help; it was to provide a home-furnishing service for people in need that was second to none; and it was to generate income with true integrity. It was the same Jesus who overturned the tables of the money-changers, who also commended the shrewd manager. Achieving that balance was not easy; indeed it was a daily struggle. With Christ's help however, such things were more than possible.'

And so, as staff member Colin Foskett explained, Bethany Homemaker sought to create a normal retail experience, where, in our spoilt-for-choice, retail therapy, shop-until-you-drop age, they wanted their clients to feel like any other customer – in other words, to be given choice and not just to have to take what *others* thought they needed. The amazing city-wide support for the Homemaker concept ensured that a wide range of good-quality furniture, electrical goods and general household items made this possible.

Transport
Van drivers, the key transport men like Ian Taylor, were not just delivery men. Ian's experience of being out on the vans involved working as part of a small team, uplifting donated goods and delivering furniture to shops, Homemaker, the Hub and customers. Some members of the team might not have worked since leaving school and might well have preferred lying in bed to delivering a cooker or washing machine up a tenement stair.

Each team member needed to have confidence in other members and hope that they were not going to let go halfway up because the washing machine was getting rather heavy! Many of the deliveries were for Homemaker. Some clients struggled to cope with life generally and others with addiction. This could lead to a chaotic lifestyle and result in a house becoming totally 'cluttered'. It was sometimes difficult, therefore, for the van crew to find a clear space on the floor on which to deposit the goods being delivered. In an organization that is all about helping people, van drivers are no exception!

Development
In the summer of 2001 the shop unit next door to the charity shop in Haddington Place became vacant. It was an ideal opportunity to move the furniture referrals project there. Again cords were being lengthened to the right and left! It was in some need of renovation and stripping out before it could be ready for use as offices and inter-view rooms. The basements of the two premises were actually joined.

This enabled the staff to expand the referrals display area, and carry more stock, including fridges, fridge-freezers, new gas cookers and a range of new floor coverings, thereby giving a wider choice.

The move to the new dedicated premises took place in September of that year. The official launch, in the following February, was attended by the Lord Provost, the Rt. Hon. Eric Milligan.

HOMEMAKER CLIENTS' VIEWPOINTS

One client who benefited from the extended referrals was a girl who had experienced a turbulent home life which led to her staying in multiple foster homes and hostels. In her unstable teenage years she fell into drug misuse and was subjected to violent physical abuse and rape. She was on regular anti-depressants and was supported by a psychiatric nurse. She wanted to turn things around. She received her own council tenancy, gained a National Certificate in computing and applied for a further course. Homemaker was able to help her turn her house into a home by obtaining funding.

Alasdair had been in the Royal Signals Regiment for eleven years and had served as a mechanical engineer. After leaving the army he had worked in various jobs and when he was offered one in Edinburgh he left his temporary homeless accommodation and moved north. However, when he arrived, the job was no longer available. He was in Bethany House for a while but then found his own accommodation, and Homemaker was able to help him buy a bed and cooker.

And someone who not only needed furnishings but security was a lady who after almost forty years of serious sexual and mental abuse, left her husband. She had only a few bags of clothes, leaving behind sixty-eight years of possessions, photographs and home comforts in order to be safe. She had absolutely nothing and was very scared. One year later she was in her own sheltered one-bedroom council home, had received help with furnishings and carpets from Homemaker and was beginning to rebuild her confidence and her life.

FUNDING

Funding enabling a house or flat to be turned into a home has been a lifeline to Bethany. Agencies like The Prince's Trust, The Merchant Company and The Earl Haig Fund have over many years made an invaluable contribution to facilitating this help and making the work viable.

By 2002/3 Bethany was working increasingly in partnership with other charities such as the Shelter Families project and Fresh Start, providing starter packs and cookers for people who had previously been homeless and who were unable to obtain statutory help.

2003/4 saw Bethany also supplying furniture and starter packs in Fife in conjunction with Fife Council who had asked the Trust to help with furnishings for vulnerable people there. The Training and Supported Housing teams had been working in the region for a while and it was testimony to their good reputation that the Trust was called upon to give extra help in the area. For a period the Fife Homemaker work was coordinated at a warehouse in Glenrothes, but unfortunately the contract was later given to another organization whose tender was lower than that of Bethany's.

COLIN'S STORY

Colin Fosket, as social enterprises manager, coordinated the expansion of the Homemaker project throughout Edinburgh and for its duration in Fife.

But Colin wasn't always a member of staff. He was brought up in London and had always wanted to become a police officer. At eighteen that dream became reality and he joined the Metropolitan Police Service. His career progressed well and he loved the job. By the age of twenty-two he was a sergeant and things were looking great.

All that changed in the summer of 1992. He was involved in a shooting, was badly injured and his career in the police was at an end. His job had been his life and he felt lost. He drifted from job to job feeling lonely and angry. In 1997 he lost his job and his home and was running out of friends' houses where he could stay.

He came to Edinburgh and from the moment he entered the doors of Bethany House in September 1997, he was made to feel welcome, and was amazed at the love shown by the staff even in the most demanding situations.

He spent three months in Bethany House and was able to work on the issues that had led to him becoming homeless. He found that what was missing in his life was a relationship with God and in December 1997 he became a Christian. He found a church, some good friends and a fresh start in life. In late December he moved from the hostel into a Bethany flat and started helping out in the Bethany Shops. The Trust supported him through a training course in retail and he was employed full time in the shop in Leith. It was from there that he became involved in the Homemaker project and has recently been appointed general manager of RequipIT.

Today Colin's aim is to demonstrate the same compassion to those he helps as he received from the staff in Bethany House

STATISTICS TELL STORIES

The Commerce Section, which was brought into being to create jobs and generate income for the Trust, continually seeks to improve its services. In 2002 there was a drive to ensure that the logistical support systems at the Hub were working as competently as possible, resulting in various items of equipment being brought up to date. In that year alone 8000 phone calls were answered at the Hub, 3263 houses visited to collect furniture, 1194 deliveries made to Bethany shop customers and 649 Homemaker clients helped by delivering much-needed furniture and electrical items.

The 2007 statistics speak for themselves. The homes and lives of over 1,600 people were transformed through the provision of household furnishings, with a 91% success rate in meeting the demand. The number of households helped and income received increased as more staff time became available and better operating procedures were put into place. A system of monitoring the value of sales and the levels of waste collected from shops was working well, with the volume of waste below target. The number of appliances being collected from John Lewis under the new arrangement (between 50 and 80 per week) was having a significant positive impact on the throughput of the Hub and the electrical workshop, as well as Homemaker and the shops, while October 2007 saw the beginning of a new partnership in which the electrical workshop was to supply white goods to some other leading charities, thus generating extra income for Bethany's work.

FURTHER DEVELOPMENT

RequipIT came into being some years ago as a wholly owned subsidiary of Bethany Christian Trust. Its purpose was to upgrade and sell computer equipment. In April 2008 it changed its whole emphasis, and plans to refurbish and sell white goods and other domestic electrical appliances, thus supplying refurbished cookers, washing machines, fridges, freezers, TV and audio equipment to Bethany's own shops and to other charity shop chains across Scotland. The company will operate out of premises in Jane Street, Leith.

In 2007 Bethany's fundraising team had been working with Homemaker staff to develop specific proposals for block funding from potential funders, and were encouraged by the excellent news that for the first time in its history Homemaker was to receive funding from the local Council towards staffing costs.

The little house in the logo is still smiling as houses continue to be turned into homes and people genuinely helped.

CHAPTER 6

A LITTLE RETAIL THERAPY
THE CHARITY SHOPS
(LEVEL 6)

Shopping can be stressful! However, with helpful assistants, congenial surroundings and the time to browse, it can also be a pleasant and even a therapeutic experience. If the customer knows that their purchases are helping to support a charity working with homeless and vulnerable people, then that's an added bonus.

HAMILTON PLACE

In 1992, Homemaker's manager, Ewan Foreman, realized that some of the goods they received were suitable for selling through a charity shop and so began the story of Bethany's very own 'retail therapy'. A lease was signed on 60 Hamilton Place, Stockbridge, with the excellent premises allowing for a café and charity shop where a full range of overhauled 'white goods' could be sold. It was hoped 'The Bethany Shop' would be fully operational by the beginning of September 1993 and would help supplement the Trust income. Good clothes, bric-a-brac, household items and volunteers would be needed.

Ewan had the ability to know what would look good, but also the know-how to create the desired effect to attract custom. The large windows allowed plenty of scope for creative 'dressing,' whilst the high display shelves were a real eye-catcher, full of interesting objects which became quite a talking point. The only downside was that customers wanted to buy those as well. The shop carried a wide range of bric-a-brac, clothes, period furniture and guaranteed electrical goods in a most pleasant environment. Diane Stevens was appointed manager, with Paul Mooney on electrical goods, ably assisted by a superb band of part- and full-time volunteers.

The café area, which was situated in the window space, was ideal for sitting watching the world go by. Outside was a busy street with people coming and going to the library and the primary school. Many people just came in to relax for a while and enjoy a coffee before rushing off to collect children or finish shopping. The atmosphere was conducive to this and a rapport was built up with regular customers.

The tables in the café were a talking point too. They were treadle bases of Singer sewing machines and added interest to the shop. One of the real benefits of this particular shop was its size, allowing customers room to move around and browse. It all added to a pleasant shopping experience, as did the special events such as the Festival Open Evening and Silent Art Auction which featured paintings by Lady Lucinda McKay. Such evenings not only helped to widen the customer base but also established the shop as part of the Stockbridge community.

Jean and George Geddes worked as volunteers at Hamilton Place, before retiring for a second (or was it a third?!) time. They had heard Alan speak at their home church in St Andrews and felt they could get involved, and had time and talents to offer. George had retail experience and had also been a representative for the

Sue Ryder Foundation. They rented out their home to university staff and came to Edinburgh to manage the shop. They not only had a real rapport with customers but were a great support to other volunteers in the shop. Some of these were residents or ex-residents, who often needed a listening ear and a word of encouragement. Others were from overseas and suffered from homesickness, which after all is akin to homelessness in that it is a longing to be somewhere you can't be. George and Jean's befriending went a long way to making them feel valued and 'at home'. Reflecting on their time they wrote in the June 1997 newsletter, 'it is hard to realize that almost four years have passed since we came as volunteers to Bethany. They have been very happy and rewarding years and we give God thanks for the opportunity to play a small part in the ongoing work of the Trust.

We did not know where we would best fit in when we arrived but it soon became clear that we could be of most help in the first Bethany Shop. We must confess that we had misgivings about the suitability of 60 Hamilton Place for a shop but how wrong we were to doubt. We should have had more faith in what God can do. From day one, the shop has been a success and it has been great to watch it grow and develop.

We are convinced it is a very special place, evidenced in so many ways: the constant flow of donations which, like the widow's cruse of oil never dried up, the wonderful team of workers, the friendships formed with staff and customers, and the opportunities to share our faith. We are so grateful to have been part of it all and shall miss it very much – the Morning Prayer times together, the fun and camaraderie, the black bags, and not least the twenty stone stairs. No need for keep-fit classes! The

Lord has truly blessed this place and will continue to do so. We have gained so much from our time at Bethany and 60 Hamilton Place will always have a special place in our hearts'.

SUMMERHALL

Following on the success of the first venture, negotiations for the leasing of Bethany Shop 2 were soon in progress and in August 1995 Summerhall Place was operational, with Iris O'Neill as manager. She too had a flair for design and layout, making the shop inviting and welcoming. The premises were ideally situated for attracting student custom, people visiting the Sick Children's Hospital and those out for a walk on The Meadows. It also had a café facility in which Margaret Lochhead made the public feel very welcome, enticing them with good and varied things to eat.

The shop opened just in time to be caught up in the general 'buzz' which always accompanies the Edinburgh Festival Fringe. Taking full advantage of this, for seven nights the shop was host to live Christian music with artists performing between 8 and 10 p.m. creating a backdrop of relaxation and outreach for the many Festival visitors.

This initial venture was so successful that special events were organized during the Festival in the following summer. The Vreni Fry Quartette played a selection of classical melodies during lunchtime on one Saturday and Catrina Cunningham entertained customers with Scottish airs on the clarsach on another two Saturdays. Fireworks Night saw a visit of the Bethany Praise Band. Weekends, for Summerhall Place customers, and the public at large, were keenly anticipated.

RWANDA VISITS SUMMERHALL

But one of the evenings which Iris and Ewan organized stays in my memory for a different reason. It was the visit of Lesley Bilinda and a Rwandan couple. Lesley's husband, also Rwandan, had been murdered in the genocide. After we shared a meal and listened to music, both Rwandan in their flavour, Lesley shared her story which was one of triumph over tragedy and God's amazing healing of memories and reconciliation. The evening was a real challenge, and the donation ticket benefited Tear Fund as well as the Trust.

When Margaret moved on from the café, she was replaced by Iona Molleson who enjoyed her work in the shop and the opportunities which arose to share her faith. She felt there was something very special about being part of a team who were trying to do God's will. Iona was very talented artistically and did drawings of different aspects of the Trust's work. These were used to illustrate one of the annual reports, and later were printed on packs of notelets which were sold to raise funds for the Trust. When Alan retired from Bethany, the trustees commissioned a picture for his parting gift, and Iona was asked to paint it. She produced a wonderful collage which incorporated Bethany Christian Centre, Bethany Hall, South Leith Baptist Church and the first Bethany Shop in Hamilton Place. It has pride of place on our dining room wall.

Over the years since becoming manager of Summerhall in 1997, Lilias Currie has organized evenings of great fun when food and fashion have been the theme. Staff members have taken on a new role as models and as a result some of the attractive, young full-time volunteers might even have contemplated a career change!

It may come as a shock to Bethany supporters that Alan Berry was cautioned and charged with illegal disposal of certain items in regard to the Summerhall Shop! The items were two ladies' hats, complete with Bethany price tags, which had been disposed of in the wrong bin – the domestic, instead of the commercial. Needless to say, Alan, was not personally responsible for this, but as director the 'buck stopped' with him. The Council representatives who arrived with the caution were in deadly earnest. When Alan realized this, he asked if photographers might be summoned so that maximum publicity could be given to how the Council used taxpayers' money! It will not be a surprise to readers to learn that Alan still hasn't received a summons after all these years!

A SNAPSHOT FROM LILIAS CURRIE

The shops play a real part in expressing 'care' in everyday situations. Lilias gives a snapshot of one Saturday morning in the Summerhall café. 'A black coffee, a hot chocolate special and a scone' – the first order every day of the week from the recently retired couple who come in for a browse round the shop. Apparently the smell of freshly baked scones is too much to resist! Later more regulars come in for soup and meringue after their swim at the Commonwealth Pool. Many people use the café as a lunchtime retreat from work or as a venue to meet up with friends. There are also quite a few regulars who come in alone and obviously enjoy a chat with one of the staff if they are not too busy. This is so much more than just a charity shop.

GULLANE

In 1998 Bethany moved east. As Ewan Foreman reported, 'January 17th was an exciting date for the Trust as it saw the opening of its first charity shop outwith central Edinburgh. In the final days leading up to the opening, smiles on previously bemused local faces looking in the windows of the shop said it all. Dust and chaos had been replaced by soft new carpets, polished furniture and lovely donations which had been saved for weeks.

The peaceful village of Gullane proved the ideal site for the new shop with Sylvia Duff, manager, releasing its potential. The fabric of community was strong there and was immersed in its long and thriving history of golfing and tourism.

Having had experience of running her own guest house, Sylvia was used to working on her own and enjoyed the challenge of building up a project from scratch. Although the shop primarily existed to create revenue for the work of the Trust, it was hoped it would also play an important role in the development of community and the Trust's life and witness.

Ten days after opening, new volunteers were coming forward, income was over £2,000, an invitation had been received from a local church group to speak about Bethany, and annual reports speaking of changed lives were being picked up by customers. As Ewan said 'answers to prayer don't always come immediately, but it is good when they do!'

Sylvia said that as in most places the social strata were very extensive and ranged from single parents who didn't have much cash, to those who lived on the hill and whose houses were worth a fortune.

The Bethany Shop in Gullane represented neutral territory and was focused on enthusiastically building relationships with individuals irrespective of social class. Sylvia's genuine interest in people gripped the village and she quickly and successfully gained their trust. She practised Christian love in action, which indeed is the ethos of the Trust. As she stated 'People know that I've got a sympathetic ear and am willing to share their problems. The odd smile and a friendly face can make such a difference'.

Community ownership developed over the months as people loyally donated goods on a consistent basis. So 1998 not only saw the beginning of a new commercial venture for the Trust, but the informal partnership of Bethany with the community in Gullane.

GOING THE SECOND MILE, OR WAS IT TWENTY-TWO?

The following story is one example of partnership. In the autumn of 2001 an oak table had sat in the window at Gullane for weeks – it was destined for the Morningside shop (the fourth Bethany retail outlet), if it hadn't sold by the next Thursday when the Bethany van did its weekly visit. The van came, the table went. On the Saturday morning a couple arrived to buy 'the beautiful table'. Where was it? Good question. Sylvia checked. It hadn't arrived in Morningside so it was still at the Hub. She travelled eleven miles on her day off to Leith and eleven miles back. That's what you call the dedication of Bethany shop managers – and going the twenty-second mile! But it resulted in happy and impressed customers and £200 in the till.

FEEDBACK

In the world of business, service companies often go to great lengths to find out what their customers think about them. When

Bethany followed suit in 1999 and asked its customers their thoughts, it brought some interesting and encouraging results.

Colin Foskett, as part of his retail apprenticeship course, contacted 900 donors/receivers of furniture and shop customers, and asked them to complete a survey form. An amazing 330 responses came back. On the whole they were very favourable, with the information being used to help improve the service offered.

Of interest was that just over half said they visited the Bethany Shops because they were concerned about homelessness, with just under half saying that they were likely to spend more because of their concern for homelessness. Most were aware of Bethany through the presence of a shop in their area, through a friend or through their church.

As one reply said, 'Everyone seems to benefit, the homeless and the customer'.

MORNINGSIDE.

With the Shops proving themselves as real community resources, socially and economically, another shop was planned for the new millennium.

Iris O'Neill, Bethany's retail manager, said that having approached estate agents several months before to find another shop, they were surprised and excited when they located an almost new shop at 93 Morningside Road in a busy trading location in one of Edinburgh's prime retail areas. An inspection of the premises showed another answer to prayer. The shop had a large double-windowed frontage; was modern and spacious inside, and also had a large basement area. Best of all it was already painted 'Bethany blue', and required little internal work prior to opening.

With Liz McBean as manager and Shona MacDonald as assistant manager, within just a few weeks the set-up and refurbishment costs had been fully recovered. Despite some initial apprehension about the decision to move slightly upmarket in terms of location and therefore cost, it seemed to have paid off.

The following comments from the locals were favourable too. 'This disnae look like a second hand shop at all, it's awfae posh' (was that really a *Morningside* local!?)[1]... 'we are so pleased Bethany has come to Morningside' ... the shop is a credit to Christians' ...

---

1. 'Morningside' is definitely one of the more prestigious areas of the city!

and 'the ladies from Falcon House upstairs are delighted to have such lovely windows to look at as they walk round the block'.

And the windows are still worth looking in. In autumn 2007 a display of old clocks resulted in some being turned into sales and a train display encouraged good book sales.

HAMILTON PLACE AGAIN

The millennium year also saw Hamilton Place get 'a new look'. With some reluctance the café was closed and the renovations got under way. The shop was entirely transformed by Bethany's own tradesmen and the overall appearance was updated. The aim was to create shops within a shop and in so doing utilize the space in a fresh and appealing way so that the customers could enjoy the 'Bethany shopping experience' even more.

Jane Doyle, the new manager, brought her considerable retail skills to the job. She too was gifted in retail display techniques, so the windows there were also worth watching.

HADDINGTON PLACE

As mentioned in Chapter 5, when Homemaker moved to Haddington Place in 1998 part of the premises became a charity shop but when the referrals section took occupancy of the building next door in 2001, it allowed Haddington Place to operate fully as a designated Bethany Shop. This shop is in a prime location near the top of busy Leith Walk and has given training and placements to many from within Bethany itself as well as those on licence from prison through Training for Freedom. Speaking of those in prison, the shops have impinged on the lives of some in another positive way. An arrangement with IKEA whereby end-of-line and damaged items are collected and taken to Saughton Prison to be assembled by inmates and then sold in the Bethany Shops has worked well.

CHARLIE'S STORY

One former Bethany resident was Charlie, who during his time at Bethany Christian Centre was helped by his key worker who had gone through similar experiences and related well to his situation. Charlie initially volunteered in a Bethany Shop but is now the assistant manager in Haddington Place and a valued member of the team. He appreciated the friendship there and when he was married two years ago, his boss, Alastair, was his best man.

In the spring newsletter of 2001 Ewan Foreman reported that 'with many charities complaining that their shops were not doing as well as they would like, it was encouraging to be able to report that The Bethany Shops were having an exceptionally good year'. They were well ahead of budget, and contributed more to the running of the Trust that year than ever before.

Over the years much consideration has been given to the presentation and running of the shops. However, the real difference to their success was in the practical donations of clothes, books, bric-a-brac, furniture and electrical goods which were received from supporters daily. In terms of both quality and quantity, the support received was exceptional, and far from struggling to fill the shops, it was more a case of having enough shops to sell all the goods that they were given.

CORSTORPHINE

The opening of Shop No. 6 at 88 St John's Road, Corstorphine, was planned for 7th March 2001. With the acquisition of each new shop, more experience was gained and, given the number of charity shops already in the area, it was imperative that Bethany's new retail outlet would be an asset to Corstorphine High Street as well as to the Trust.

At the opening of the shop one of the dedicatory prayers was given by Rev. Mike Parker, who at that time was the rector of St. Thomas' Episcopal Church. Not only was he a 'local' but also a long-standing supporter of the Trust. I remember his visits to the Jane Street office each January with money that he and others had collected whilst carol singing outside Valvona and Crolla in

Leith Walk with the Rolling Barbers Choir. He said his wardrobe had already been very much supplemented from Bethany Shops, but with the new one on his doorstep it would make life even easier for him to remain well kitted-out!

The Corstorphine shop was one we visited regularly – but more often than not when it was closed! Being the nearest one to Bethany Home Farm, Alan and I could sometimes be seen late at night taking in trays of free-range eggs, and on occasions jam and marmalade for sale in the shop. I was always highly relieved when the security code we tapped in proved correct and the door opened. I had visions of creating chaos in Corstorphine High Street and being arrested for attempted breaking and entering. Although our nocturnal visits were well outwith trading hours, it didn't stop me noticing bargains, and I often had to write a note of explanation as to where such and such an item had gone and how much I owed.

Over the years John and Kate Veitch, Eileen Eschenbach and the volunteers have done a great job in what has not always been the easiest of situations, with trading targets getting ever more difficult to meet.

DALRY

In all the Bethany Shops it has been the aim to break away from the normal image that people have of a charity shop. This was particularly the case for Shop No. 7 in Dalry, adjoining Somerfield supermarket. Ewan said that experience had taught the section to become ever more 'fussy' when it came to new shops, and he came away from his first visit to Dalry Road with more questions than answers. However, initial concerns were overcome and by the time the shop opened in autumn 2001, the Commerce section were singing the praises of modern retail units. Not only was it located in a brand-new building, but the standard of the shop fit had been raised with much of this being paid for by the new landlord who was keen to have Bethany on his books.

An article in 2005 by manager Carolynda gave an idea of what it is like in a Bethany Shop as Christmas approaches. 'The end of November is always hectic. Christmas windows and displays have to go up, and it is the beginning of our sale offering bargains galore.

The team starts digging out decorations and pricing and organizing the stockpile of donations which they have gathered over the year especially for Christmas. It is amazing what is handed in: soaps, Christmas mugs and plates, stationery, beautiful handbags and scarves, all unused, still wrapped. One person's Christmas gift from last year becomes someone's stocking-filler this year.

Dalry's window that year featured a special red festive velvet dress. All the sparkly dresses and jewellery were looked out and the Christmas goods displayed on the bric-a-brac shelves ready for the sale.

Surprisingly best-sellers in December were dining room tables and chairs. They were bought for the family Christmas dinner and often donated back after the festive season. Extra dishes were also bought for the same purpose.

And while the staff could be seen in Santa hats they never lost sight of the true meaning of Christmas. Carolynda said 'the Santa hats made people smile but the central display with the large Bible open at the Christmas story, the manger with the Christ-child and behind it the Cross and the crown of thorns, prompted customers to reflect on the fact that the baby whose birth was being celebrated also came to die for us all.'

CHANGES

In 2002 Ewan Foreman moved on after ten years of committed and exciting service with Bethany. He had left an indelible mark on the Trust. He was replaced in October of that year by Christine Johnson as director of Commerce. She brought with her experience and expertise in the development and growth of new products and businesses which would add new revenue streams to the Bethany portfolio.

It was in that same year that the Bethany Shop at 60 Hamilton Place, Stockbridge, had to close. The landlords needed the shop to expand their own business and did not wish to renew the lease. As well as being the first and largest shop, Stockbridge was also the most profitable. Its loss meant a shortfall of income for Bethany for that financial year. Unfortunately relocation within the area was not possible as no other suitable shop was available. The shop basement had been used as a base for the overhaul of domestic and electrical appliances, and when the shop closed, this work moved to the Jane Street workshops.

LEITH

The Commerce section needed to offset some of the income lost from the Stockbridge shop for that year and to generate replacement income in future years. Having negotiated sufficient debt finance, Bethany, for the first time, bought shop premises – an exciting unit at 17 Duke Street in Leith. It was planned to refurbish it and have it open by December of that year. Jane Doyle, the Stockbridge manager, was to move to the Leith shop with her staff and, although she acknowledged the closure in Stockbridge was disappointing for many of their good customers, felt there was great future potential in the Duke Street shop.

It was opposite the Scotmid supermarket and had the advantage of several large display windows. On one visit to Leith, an item in the window caught my eye. I knew Bethany had a strict policy regarding 'display' items which were not for sale, but I thought I might try a little bargaining, as I knew Jane well, and the beautiful wooden plant pot stand would be just perfect for our lounge at home! I was successful and I've enjoyed looking at the stand ever since – I suppose it's quite safe to tell this story now, as Jane has retired from the Trust!

The Bethany Shops are not just about sales and purchases – they can each tell a 'people' story as the following illustrates.

Alastair, who was the manager in Duke Street asked one trainee about his experience of working in a Bethany Shop. He said Bethany had helped in many areas of his life including helping him to rediscover his faith and gain more confidence in himself. He never thought he could work in retail as his previous jobs had all been in security. When he first arrived he would try to do things without asking other people for help and sometimes this meant that his well-meaning efforts had to be redone, and this was pretty frustrating all round.

However, as time went on he began to change. He started to listen and accept suggestions. Then he began to actively seek out staff to help him. As a result of his increased confidence and the staff's encouragement, he developed his skills and began soaking up opportunities to learn. What he received from Bethany was confidence and trust. While working at the Bethany Shop he was able to find people who accepted him for himself. He became a trusted member of staff who reached out and trusted others.

HAMILTON PLACE ONCE MORE

In late November 2003 Bethany was back in Stockbridge among old friends and loyal customers with a new shop at 46 Hamilton Place, selling a wide selection of fashionable clothes, books, new and used electrical appliances, kitchen white goods, high-quality furniture and many other desirable items for the home.

KIRKCALDY

Usually when one of the shops is officially opened, Bethany's chief executive, local ministers and at least one trustee, are involved in saying a few words and in prayers of dedication. The new Homemaker premises had been honoured with the presence of the Lord Provost of Edinburgh in 2001, but on 1st June 2007, when Bethany's newest shop was open for business, they went one better – the Chancellor of the Exchequer, now the Prime Minister, was in attendance and did the honours.

Alan has had the privilege of shaking hands with ex-President Carter of the U.S.A. and with the Queen, and I was always the one who shook the hand of the person who had shaken the hand of famous people! But this time Gordon Brown shook hands with everyone present. As our son, Stephen, said, 'I hope he doesn't ask us who we voted for'. Being a 'local' boy and an MP for Fife, Gordon Brown had a personal interest in what was happening along the road from where he had been brought up in a Church of Scotland manse, and. was encouraging and enthusiastic about the new venture.

The shop is situated on the High Street and opposite the indoor market. Many people had worked hard to meet the opening deadline, and make the shop appealing and customer-friendly.

Over the years, there has been, and still is, much support for the Trust in Fife. With the Supporting People work in Dunfermline and Leven and the Drop-In centres, the awareness had increased and the prayer for the shop was that it would further highlight the problem of homelessness.

There is a good parking area to the rear of the shop, but being on the main street has not been as beneficial as anticipated, certainly in these early days. Just as Summerhall Place was once covered in scaffolding, and Haddington Place and Duke Street have suffered from disruption preparing for reintroduction of trams, so the Kirkcaldy shop has had to deal with major work right on its doorstep. For six months there was no pavement outside the shop. There were huge problems with lack of an entrance, loss of electricity, lots of noise, dust and dirt. The construction company and the Council both make the excuse that the replacement stone had to come from China, hence the 'delay'. Kirkcaldy shoppers and the staff at the Bethany Shop kept smiling but the disruption did affect business.

These problems highlight some of the difficulties the shops face. Business can fluctuate, meeting targets can seem daunting, and staff illness and changes can all add to the pressure. But by generating income, giving training opportunities, offering support, friendship and often fun to full-time volunteers who may be a long way from home, and finally giving a first-class service to customers, the shops remain a vital part of Bethany's operations.

SERVICE AND TRAINING
This chapter began by quoting Ewan as saying that some of the donations received in the early days were suitable for selling in a charity shop. One person who for many years made a valuable contribution towards this was Allan Turnbull, who was a qualified furniture restorer. In the furniture workshop he managed to provide a steady supply of quality items to the shops, despite a somewhat  erratic supply of 'nice old pieces needing a bit of work'.

He restored donated furniture to as near an original condition as possible. The aim of the workshop, however, was not just about raising money. Through Bethany's training scheme, it sought to give people from all walks of life who expressed an interest in furniture restoration the opportunity to do so in an actual working environment.

Some participants were involved with the Government's New Deal scheme. One such young woman in her early twenties showed great progress and interest, and was encouraged to pursue a full-time college course in the subject. Another trainee, a man in his fifties had not worked for the previous ten years through illness and lack of self-confidence. In both these cases, and others like them, Allan, Ray Bain joinery foreman, and contracts manager Ross Brown endeavoured to give them and joinery apprentices motivation.

This was certainly successful in the case of Mark, who when he started as a trainee in the workshop wasn't sure he had any aptitude for the work of furniture restoration. However, Ross Brown persuaded him to keep trying. He felt he had learned a lot and had had the opportunity to get involved in every stage of the restoration progress. He learned French polishing from Allan, who along with Ray patiently encouraged him.

Mark later enrolled for a full-time furniture restoration course at Lauder College in Dunfermline, hoping this would eventually lead to a full-time work in this area. As Allan Turnbull said 'in the workshop we like to think we help restore more than just furniture'.

There's been mention in this chapter of 'our own workforce' doing renovations, of trainees, of the Contracts section – examples of how the Levels of Care interface. The Commerce section provided realistic work-based training which often led to actual paid employment for people who had been involved with Bethany's other 'Levels of Care'. The whole culture and lifestyle created by long-term or second-generation unemployment is complex, but by working within clear parameters and expectations, trainees have been encouraged to adopt a responsible and motivated work ethic.

How did Bethany's involvement in training, job creation and education begin and grow? The exciting story is told in Chapter 9.

CHAPTER 7

BREAKING FREE
SPECIAL NEEDS
(LEVEL 3)

Bethany Hall

In his Gospel, Luke records that Jesus read from Isaiah 61 saying that He himself had come to fulfil the very prophecies written there. One of these was to set the captives free. Being captive to addiction is not easily overcome and this has been one of the main reasons for referral to Bethany Christian Centre. Over the years the staff there, including the specialist addiction workers, have sought to put in place structures and procedures that would help those bound by addiction and despair.

In June 1991 Gordon Weir reported that on the agenda was the creation of a group work programme for clients with addiction problems which would complement the Key Worker system with its one-to-one focus. Staff included Fiona Weir as deputy, Marion Gemmell, Ewan Foreman, Eddie Reevie and Barbara Neale as Care assistants with Andrew Gillies as full-time volunteer, and other voluntary help. Training remained a priority and the need for specialist skills meant inviting other professionals to share their expertise and experience on such issues as H.I.V./AIDS, time management, group work principles and stress-management for the staff.

Although the Centre catered for residents between the ages of eighteen and sixty-five, half of them were under twenty-six years of age. This brought its own stresses, but also gave the opportunity to help younger men break the cycle of an addictive lifestyle that could blight their whole life and possibly shorten it. The care package was modified on several occasions to offer help in new ways, and the newly introduced work programme involved care placements, a decorating team and candle making, with one previous resident employed to do house maintenance under Employment Action.

In 1992 there was a consolidation of the staff team, thus improving the stability and family quality of the home. Gill McKenzie served as Gordon' s deputy, with Barbara Neale, Stan Malloch, David Headley, Sandy Purdie and Andy Walker employed as Care assistants. When Gill left to have a baby, Stan became deputy. The group work monitored progress in five phases and proved effective. The spiritual aspect of the Alcoholics Anonymous philosophy was also being examined within a Christian context. House Bible studies, and group times which focused on addiction issues from a Christian perspective were entirely voluntary but proved popular with residents, some of whom found spiritual answers to their problems and that 'if the Son set them free, then they are free indeed'.

The Bethany staff believed that chemical substance dependency was in the main symptomatic of unresolved core problems within the individual. The aim of the Centre was to provide a residential community for men with such problems by providing a safe, supportive environment where a sense of security, self-worth and significance could be developed. It was hoped this would help residents to form relationships, lower their defences and deal with deeper core issues, thus paving the way to long-term change, recovery and hope. This was not easy for it required a high degree of honesty, acceptance and personal responsibility. The community was therefore geared towards abstinence, with the use of alcohol and other mood-altering chemicals being unacceptable. All residents were to be actively seeking a drug and alcohol-free lifestyle, with prospective residents normally seeking help with detox prior to admission.

Some of the project workers had had a wide experience before joining the Trust. Andy Walker had worked in the addiction field for ten years, initially in Hong Kong with Jackie Pullinger. Barbara had worked on the border of Cambodia and Thailand, and been involved in a rehabilitation programme helping refugees – many of whom had suffered the loss of limbs – to learn new skills and ways of coping. Sandy Purdie had had experience of working with H.I.V./ AIDS sufferers, and another staff member had known what it was to lose his freedom behind prison bars for a while. This meant that the staff understood many of the struggles and feelings of hopelessness which could so easily overwhelm the residents, but nevertheless could encourage them to hope for the future.

In 1993/4 the central government policy of Care in the Community became a reality, causing concerns but affording opportunities as it placed the Centre as a business competitor within the market place. The new arrangements meant that referrals were much slower even although the needs in society were increasing. Care in the Community brought significant changes in admission procedures and funding arrangements, making the administrative workload much heavier, and indeed making financial viability more difficult to achieve. Gordon and the staff tried to maximize resources by visiting agencies who worked in addiction and also considering referrals from any part of the country.

However, 1993 also brought some encouragements. The 'Dry House Band,' formed by residents with the encouragement and involvement of Gordon, was being increasingly used at ceilidhs, fellowship nights and sometimes as a praise band taking part in services. It produced a praise and testimony tape, and several staff and ex-residents ministered in meetings both in Edinburgh and around the country, thus encouraging both players and audiences alike.

One of the residents writing in the 1994/5 annual report told the story of his experience at the Centre. He said 'the circumstances of my life before I came to Bethany can only be described as utter turmoil in the true sense of the word. I had been divorced for approximately ten years and moved from one location to another hoping life would be different but it always ended the same way – discontented, frustrated and, on many occasions, to the point of suicide. Addiction to alcohol was giving me all kinds of problems, both financial and mental, and lack of purpose in life was causing me deep depression. An understanding social worker suggested that I make application to Bethany Christian Centre. Not knowing what was before me I accepted the opportunity that was offered as I thought it might be my last chance to put my life in order and get back to normality. After a very short time there I could feel a strong sense of belonging to what I can only describe as a family atmosphere. Every care was given to me – both medical by reference to doctors or dentists or whatever was necessary, and the advice on alcohol and social problems was given a very high priority. With the help of group discussions both with residents and staff I got a good insight into what was required to enable me to focus on the proper way of thinking and acting. Getting involved with voluntary work was another important factor which gave me a sense of purpose and fulfilment. The difference it has made to my life is far more than I expected and brought home to me the necessity to sustain my sobriety and hold on to all the things that had been shown and learned at Bethany. My present attitude to life is one of contentment and peace which has been lacking for so long and which I have been seeking desperately for a number of years.'

It was encouraging that in the above story the resident commented on the family atmosphere of the Centre and that the original vision of an extended Christian family was still functioning. Indeed when one resident returned to the Centre in drunken tears after a rampaging episode, he simply said, 'You are my family'.

The Halfway House
A further crucial development in the programme was that the Centre began using one of Bethany's three-bedroom flats as a 'halfway' house. It provided supported accommodation for men who had made significant progress in the rehabilitation unit, was vital to the ongoing work, and its success led to the development of a second similar unit in 1995. That year too, three of the volunteers, Vicki Grant, Denise Mair and Marion Young, commenced work as project workers.

Wedding Bells
Another item of staff news was very welcome. Quite a few staff members have met and married other members of staff, but Sandy Purdie went one better – he married a trustee – Gwen McDowall! He had to endure quite a bit of teasing about this as everyone said they needed to be careful how they behaved or what they said because 'Sandy's girlfriend is a trustee'. At the wedding, the couple had arranged for communion to be served to all present if they wished to share in this act of worship. Not only was there a real spirit of praise in the marriage ceremony, but this was further enhanced because those helping to serve the bread and wine were all residents or ex-residents who had come to know the Lord, and it all added to the joy of their occasion.

When Gordon became assistant director of Care in 1997, Stan Malloch served as interim project leader at the Centre. The admission criteria were widened and work was begun with addicted men who also had mild mental health problems and learning difficulties. That year too was significant in that Gavin Lawson, who was eventually to become manager of Bethany House, came into contact with the Centre as a resident.

Gavin's story
Eighteen years' fighting an alcohol addiction had left Gavin a beggar on the streets 'caring for nothing and nobody and having no desire to live.' Even when he managed to stay sober and hold down a job as a police officer, Gavin said he was hiding an unbearable weight of resentment, shame and guilt. He entered the rehab unit after a period in hospital, having previously spent some time in Bethany self-catering accommodation. In the Centre he found the help he needed, not just to stop drinking but to find

a way to recover from a destructive lifestyle and the darkness he felt. He said 'At the Centre I experienced love, combined with a depth of understanding I had never known before. I felt no condemnation or judgment, just acceptance. It enabled me to trust and share, and this was so relaxing.' Gavin gives credit to the dedicated staff and the help of other residents for making the difference, as well as what he learned about himself and addiction itself. Recovery was sometimes difficult and there were times when he felt like leaving the Centre, but he came to a full and transforming faith in Christ where he felt the hardness of his heart had been replaced with love.

He volunteered full-time at the Centre and felt privileged to be able to use his past experience in a positive way to encourage others.

THE ADDICTION UNIT

The years 1996/7 were difficult financially for the Centre. Given such continued problems and the ongoing developments of the work of the Trust, major changes were planned for the following year. For some time the Trust had wanted to widen the availability of drug and alcohol addiction advice to all areas of the Trust, including women. A free-standing Addiction team of Stan Malloch, Julie Lawson and Denise Mair was formed and began operating from the Bethany House basement in October 1998, while the flat at No. 48 Kirk Street offered supported housing specifically for women.

The aim of the new service was to reduce alcohol-and-drug-related harm and to improve the quality of life for residents. Working

Addiction work

closely with all sections of the Trust the team provided counselling, groupwork, a drop-in, advice and also a specialist service as part of the Government's New Deal programme.

Although there are similar issues for all who are homeless and have addictions, it had become increasingly evident that there was a need to develop more specific support for women and their particular needs. A women's group was therefore formed in 1998, initially running as a seven-week pilot programme open to all clients within the Trust. Patricia Tulley, from Supported Housing, and Julie Lawson and Denise Mair, of the Addiction team, addressed a variety of topics in a relaxed and non-threatening environment.

WELFARE TO WORK

Alongside this, the Centre was relaunched as a Welfare-to-Work hostel for men. Housing sixteen men, it developed a programme

Tom Farmer

of care and training to move people off benefits and into work, thus assisting them to break free from the cycle of unemployment and also helping to equip them for life back in the community.

On 1st February 1999, Sir Tom Farmer, of Kwik Fit, officially launched the project. Other invited guests represented organizations with whom Bethany interfaced, such as housing, social work, training providers and funders. The Centre is situated in the next street to Sir Tom's boyhood home and he spoke of his gratitude for the secure, encouraging environment of home and neighbourhood in which he grew up, and was glad that although 'Hope Street' as he had known it, had changed its name to Casselbank Street, hope and support could still be found there.

In the first year under its new remit, manager Alasdair Bennett, said the occupancy level had averaged 90 per cent. Sixty per cent had stayed at least three months, with 50 per cent of those who settled staying for more than five months. Of those who moved on during the year  and for whom there was information, 81 per cent were in their own tenancies or homes. Again from available information, 66 per cent were in some form of voluntary/paid work or training. A number of residents had made Christian commitments, and in February 2000 four residents of the Centre moved into the nearest halfway house and were doing well.

DAVID'S TESTIMONY

One of them was David, who in August 1999 had been referred to the Centre struggling in the throes of addiction and desperate for accommodation. He began a programme of groups, counselling and voluntary work and said 'I knew that God had brought me to Bethany for a reason. It is evident that God has given me this time for rebuilding and reshaping my life. It has been so important to be able to do this within a Christian environment, for which I am very grateful. I am enjoying all that I am learning and am trusting God for the future'. A future which has eventually led David into working as a staff member at the Centre.

Meanwhile the Addiction team worked with nearly fifty 'Bethany' individuals in the year 2000/01. In addition, as time permitted, they worked with those in the wider community who were struggling with various addiction problems. Stan said 'we believe it is vitally important that we help our clients grow in their faith, as for many this can be the single most significant factor in them maintaining long-term success in overcoming their addiction problems.'

The staff at the Centre were also continually seeking to improve the services they offered. Some aspects of the programme were obligatory, but there were also optional activities such as discipleship groups, accredited IT courses, other courses run by the Training section, music workshops, and arts and crafts work. All such helped to build confidence and create interest, while playing in a local football league and group holidays sought to create happy memories and contributed to the process of wholeness and healing.

There was also the opportunity to attend the weekly Stauros meeting. Graham, who at the time was a resident in Bethany House, and received support from the Addiction team said that when he attended the Stauros Foundation meeting he found there was the same basic message – 'to deal effectively with my drinking requires a change of lifestyle'. At the meeting there were people who had done just that, and Charlie Malone, full-time worker, who himself had fought against alcoholism for years, understood what he called 'white-knuckle sobriety', – 'sober and hating it!' Graham found it helpful to meet with others who had a real understanding of what addiction was like. The friendship and fellowship experienced all contributed to 'breaking free', as did the 15-week addiction recovery programme run by the Addiction team in conjunction with the Centre.

The men at the Centre were given support with budgeting, legal matters, health issues, family relationships, housing applications and benefit claims, and learned to work and serve each other as they participated in community meetings, cooking, cleaning and group activities.

DANNY'S STORY

Someone who benefited from the programmes was Danny, who told his story in the autumn 2003 newsletter. He said 'My life before coming to Bethany was, to say the least, unstable. Although I have always worked and had my own flat, the life I was living was very destructive; I was kept in bondage by circumstances that were out of my control. I tried to help others around me but I failed and until I helped myself it was impossible.

'Bethany gave me the opportunity to 'find myself', offering me the time, support, structure and most importantly the love to enable me to grow physically and spiritually stronger. The programme at Bethany works, but only if you are determined to work at it wholeheartedly. It's far from easy – painful and sometimes shameful. It looks at your past, allowing God to replace negative with positive things in your life.

'I'm not saying it works for everyone, but if you are 100% determined and open-hearted, you will succeed. Whether it's in the group work or the support work or the basic life skills taught, I believe every person's life could benefit from doing such a programme, even if you do not have an addiction. Bethany will offer you all they can and all you need to structure your life to enable a more fruitful one to blossom through Christ, but only if you really want it.'

CATH'S EXPERIENCE

In the same year members of the Addiction team were assigned to work in the different units. Cath Turrell, the Addiction support worker at the Centre gave an insight into her day. She wrote 'I come in every morning and check the logbook from the night before to see what's been happening. We have a handover meeting from 9-9.30 a.m. I may then have  an appointment with one of the residents, but if not I'll go to the prayer time. I do mainly one-to-one sessions which help people connect with the core issues of their addiction and the reason why they live as they do, whether it be through abuse, peer pressures, circumstances or emotions. I also work with the Phase 3 groups which offer a deeper understanding of addictions and the biological side-effects and traumas these can have.

'I think the Centre in particular gives an opportunity for people to step out of their lives for a period and to reflect on what they are doing. When they have time out to step back from their lifestyle they start to see longings within them they never knew they had. The Centre has a family feel with 24/7 support. The fact there is always someone for them to talk to provides the necessary support when the urge of addiction seems more than they can bear.

'I love people, and feel it is an honour and a privilege to be there when people tell you something about themselves that they've never shared before. I love to see their personalities and sense of fun start to shine through. As they spend time in the Centre, sober up and eat better, you can see them grow in themselves and start to enjoy life.

'But there are casualties of war. Relapse. That is unfortunately a realistic part of the job. Sometimes relapse can be part of recovery but it's frustrating when people go back to their addiction and have to leave the Centre because they miss out on the support offered here. It's devastating to go to the funeral of someone you've been working alongside'.

The reality of this was something Alasdair Bennett wrote about in the 2003/4 annual report. He said it was difficult to see men whom they had all grown to know well fall back into their old ways of life.

But the staff believe that there is a larger picture at work within the lives of those who come through the Centre and experience the love and warmth on offer. Change is not an easy process and the struggles involved with addiction can continue for many years, as was the case for John Paul.

JOHN PAUL'S STORY

Where John Paul had once found comfort from drugs, when he became a Christian he still wanted them but when he took them they didn't satisfy anymore, and he felt horrible inside. He would try to stay clean for a month or six weeks but kept relapsing. People, including a minister, did help but it just wasn't working. He battled for nine months to a year with addiction. In the end he found out about Bethany and being accepted into the Centre played a huge part in his recovery. He felt being away from his usual surroundings and the guilt that came with family pressures really helped. The onus is very much on the individual to face up to their problems, and Cath helped bring issues to the fore that he hadn't really dealt with and encouraged him work through them.

After moving out of the Centre he stayed in Bethany's discipleship flat next door and the ongoing support was important in him staying clean. Later he began working at Bethany House. He said he had previously worked with non-Christian homeless agencies but he found it frustrating because they helped people deal with the immediate problems, which didn't bring real freedom. He believed grace was a massive part of forgiveness because it helped a person deal with the guilt they experienced for all that they had done.

As Alasdair said, 'the Centre brings the real sense that a life free from addiction is no longer a distant hope but can in fact be a reality'.

And Cath, like the other addiction workers, the staff at the Centre and other Bethany units, is passionate about people's lives. She said she wants to see addicts unlabelled so people will accept them for who they are. She loves watching Jesus at work in people's lives and sees Bethany as the cross in the marketplace, but realizes how important it is that staff and residents are supported in prayer.

Gavin Lawson defined addiction as 'the out-of-control and aimless searching for wholeness, happiness and peace through a substance or event.' As life and society changes, people find themselves bound by new addictions, such as the young man of nineteen who was featured on the BBC News in October 2006. His was the first known case of 'text messaging and email addiction'. He was reported as saying, 'it is sort of comforting when you get one back. I like it'.

As I am writing this, Christmas is approaching, with all the added pressure it can bring to those who already feel life is a struggle. Following Christmas, people will start making New Year resolutions and probably break them soon afterwards. For those seeking to break free from addiction, each time they slip it takes immense courage and bravery to get up again, but with support from patient and loving staff, the prayers of supporters and above all God's strength, people's lives can be transformed. Cath says those seeking help need a strengthening of their wills so that their coping mechanisms in life are positive, and the staff need insight and revelation so that they realize how much the people they seek to encourage are loved by God.

At the Centre there is a room at the top of the stairs where people can meet Cath Turrell.

Here one resident who was tackling his addiction has written a poem to encourage others.

> The S.A.S. say 'who dares wins'.
> So put down the whiskys and the gins
> 'cos in here it is 'who wins dares'
> Tae gang tae the room at the tap o' the stairs.

> It is a chance for you tae clean,
> Yer past an 'a' the things you've been
> It could remove yer fears and cares
> The wee room at the tap o' the stairs.

> The start tae get ye feeling well
> Is tae tak a wee look at yoursel
> Pit down yer graces and yer airs
> Gae up tae the room at the tap o' the stairs
> Ye are nae gaing tae feel the wrath o' the Deil, the Pope or
> 'Auntie Cath'
> It's free, there are nae tolls or fares
> Tae the wee room at the tap o' the stairs.

CHAPTER 8

TIME FOR TEA
–*BETHANY HOUSE*–
(LEVEL 2)

When Bethany Christian Centre began operating as a rehabilitation unit in 1991 the question was asked what should be done about the missing second rung on the 'ladder of care' to provide a direct access hostel? Was the best answer to build a new emergency unit? There was a piece of land for sale in South Fort Street and although it was classified as an industrial/commercial site it was on the edge of the Leith residential area. It did have the disadvantage of being opposite Dofos dog food processing factory with its permanently strong smell. It was a good place for dog walking, and Perro and I often went right round the plot, with me praying and claiming it for the Trust if that was God's will. Alan had discussions with the selling agent and agreed a price. The trustees gave permission for a legal offer to be submitted, instructed the lawyer to put in the bid and asked God to stop them in their tracks if it was a wrong decision. They fully expected this offer to be accepted, but it was refused without any explanation.

Two to three months later, Alan received a phone call from Manus Gregor, a leading property owner in Leith who asked if it was correct that the Trust had submitted an offer for the land. When told this was the case, he was very annoyed, because although part-owner of the land he had not been notified of the Trust's offer. He asked if Bethany were still interested. Alan explained that the trustees had 'moved on' from the idea of fresh build but were still looking for property to serve as a direct-access hostel. He owned a building in Couper Street and asked if Alan would be interested in looking at it? Within an hour they were standing at the back of the building. Mr Gregor admitted that he did not have the keys with him but knew of a broken window at the back through which they could climb if Alan was agreeable. Once inside, Alan was immediately excited about its possibilities and felt convinced that this was the place.

Melrose Tea Factory

The building was a section of Melrose House in Couper Street, which had been used by Melrose's, the famous tea company. Was it 'time for tea?' It certainly seemed so for it had that all-important quality – potential. It also required, like most Bethany projects, an immense amount of work. The vandals had *been* in and the pigeons had *moved* in. Management committee and trustees went to view, and trustee Gwen Purdie and I looked out through one of the glassless windows and wondered! Even our daughter, Elizabeth, who has her father's ability to see what 'could be', was a little daunted.

It was like the *Mary-Celeste* – no-one in sight but signs of previous activity – tea bags everywhere, beams and chains for pulling up the great tea chests, maps on a wall showing trade routes, and abandoned cups in the deserted office.

In January 1993 the Trust placed an offer for £110,000, subject to planning permission. This was accepted, plans were submitted, a building warrant applied for and the result awaited. It certainly was the biggest project Bethany had ever contemplated and purchase and renovation were estimated at £258,000.

The vision was for a friendly, safe, comfortable, and well staffed immediate-access unit with the clear purpose of aiming to move people into suitable medium and long-term accommodation, via Levels 3 and 4. It would take organization, hard work, networking, and result in an expansion of all other levels of activity.

The trustees agreed in principle to appoint a master of works who would coordinate the whole project and where possible involve volunteers from the Centre and churches. But how would such a person be found?

Alan was friendly with the minister of Inverkeithing Baptist Church, Rev. Ian Paterson, who was a qualified electrician. He read of the project in the Bethany newsletter and phoned Alan to ask if he could help with the electrics. He came across and inspected the 'antediluvian' equipment in the basement and decided the only thing to be done was 'gut it'. After further discussion and prayer, Ian stated his willingness not only to be responsible

Ian Paterson

for the electrics but to act as hands-on master of works for the whole project if his church were willing to grant him leave of absence. It was an immense task. The work started on 17th May 1993 and Ian gathered together a skilled team of workers, including joiners Ray Bain, Ronnie Mill, Bill McMillan, and Graeme Corbett, as well as sub-contracting out to specialists for the brickwork and steel stairway. It was also an opportunity for 'Training for Work' personnel to become involved. Paul Mooney painted, David Brown 'plumbed,' Jim Tully helped with electrics, and many volunteers offered their own valuable contribution.

After clearing out all the rubbish, the first priority was to make two offices ready for use. This was important because since we as a family had moved to our own home, all central admin had been carried on there, including interviews and staff supervision. As the work grew, this became increasingly difficult, especially when a newsletter was being prepared and collated, and hundreds of sheets of paper were laid out on the lounge floor. It was difficult enough to negotiate round the room if one had two feet, but with Perro's four, she was firmly banned on such occasions. However, the administrative side of the work was greatly helped when through the good offices of supporter John Rennie, the Trust acquired a Canon Starwriter to replace the typewriter. In these days of computerization it would probably be regarded as a museum piece, but back then it was 'progress'!

At some point most of us have probably commented on an untidy room, saying 'it's like living in a building site'. This comment became reality. Fiona Weir, Alan and I picked up safety helmets at the door, climbed the old wooden stair and went into the sanctuary of the offices while the workmen hammered all around.

Ian had names for some of the sub-contractors. One of these was known as 'Duck & Dive', who on one occasion bit off more than they could chew. The task was the 'slapping' of a door at the foot of the new steel emergency stair. They gave a price thinking that they had to go through two, or possibly three layers of brick. To their horror, each time they took out another layer of bricks there was more to follow. They actually found that the basement level of the building had no fewer than six layers of bricks! At times their language would not have been found in the 'Sankey' hymn book.

Bethany House comprised five floors including a basement. The steel stair had to be prefabricated in the north of England and delivered and fitted on site by the construction firm. After the contractors had left, Ian was doing some final measurements of the bedrooms and found to his dismay that the contractors had put the stair in the wrong place. It was only about a foot out, but there was no possibility of moving it and so the rooms on either side of the stairwell had to be changed accordingly. (Not Ian's best day!).

There were bars on the windows of Melrose House to keep people out, but when it became Bethany House these were removed in case the wrong impression was given and it was thought we were going to try to keep people in!

The workmen went home, but sometimes Alan stayed on or returned in the evening. Doing so could bring its own complications. Bethany House was situated at the beginning of Leith's red- light district and not everyone on the street assumed that the person coming into view was just wanting to return to the office! Later, when working at the House, John Rodgers was approached by a young lady on several nights as he arrived at work in his car. It was his first car and therefore very special. He had explained each night that he was 'just going to work', but on the final night was in such a hurry to get past the girl that he jumped out of the car and rushed into Bethany House. Several minutes later he realized that in his haste he hadn't put on the hand brake. The precious car had rolled down the road and compressed itself against a lamp-post. Sometimes doing the right thing can be costly in ways never imagined!

One evening, however, 'overtime' for Alan brought its own rewards. It was the night of the firework display which is the spectacular finale to the Edinburgh Festival when the orchestra plays in Princes Street Gardens, synchronizing the music with the fireworks. The centre of the city is absolutely mobbed but Alan and I had our own special viewing. I met him at Bethany House, we climbed up and through the trapdoor on to the roof, put on a radio, took out a flask and had a marvellous view of the fireworks. If anyone from Bethany House is reading this, don't as they say 'try this at home'!

The goal for completion of the renovation work was 'heads on beds for Christmas'. Could it be done? It was pretty nearly achieved. Added to the tremendous work done by Ian and his team was the generous volunteer labour of staff from the Royal Mail, Standard Life, Scottish Widows and The Prince's Trust, who worked in their own free time to share in the decorating.

Unlike other projects, the official opening for Bethany House took place before residents moved in. New project workers were appointed under the leadership of Simon Laidlaw. They were Gael

Andrews (later Belton) as depute, Ian Bruce, Ian Robertson, Gillian Porter, James Belton, John Rodgers and Andy Wright. Along with Graham Findlay (Training) and Andy Davis (Careforce), their first jobs were not actually with residents but preparing the building and facilities ready to receive them. The Friday night before opening was a frenzied hive of activity. Everyone was involved. My mum and her friend who had travelled from Nottingham for the opening were pressed into service with Hoovers and by the time of the dedication service in Leith Baptist Church on Saturday 5th February, staff must have wondered what they had let themselves in for. Paul Oliver and James MacInnes, both of whom were volunteers at Bethany Christian Centre, were taken on at the last minute as night-shift workers. They missed the hoovering but made it for the dedication.

Workers at Bethany House renovations

One thing that could not have failed to impress the new staff team, however, was the support for the project. It was overwhelming. There had been a tremendous financial response from individuals, trusts and churches, but even more importantly, there were approximately six hundred people in Leith Baptist Church to commit the project and the staff to the Lord. After the service Bethany House was open for viewing. I am not sure if the Fire Officer was one of the people who actually looked round the building on the Saturday afternoon but I think if he had been, we might have heard officially from him. One person who did visit that afternoon was Gordon Atherton, representing the trust's then insurance company, General Accident. In the spirit of the occasion, Gordon turned a 'Nelsonian' eye to the crowd on somewhat narrow staircases which at other times would surely have elicited comment for remedial steps to be taken. It was like the January sales, though everyone was well-behaved and orderly. The premises were also open on the Sunday afternoon, and between the two occasions approximately eight hundred people visited. It had certainly caught the imagination of Bethany supporters.

On the Monday following, the opening ceremony was performed by the chairman of Lothian Region Social Work Committee, Councillor Brian Cavanagh, accompanied by Mr. John Chant CBE, director of Social Work.

The House comprised six centrally-heated flats of varying sizes. Each flat had its own lounge, kitchen and bathroom/shower. On the ground floor there was a large kitchen and dining area for central catering, a laundry and offices.

Rental income came from two sources – Housing Benefit and Care Allowance and in March 1994 the unit was registered with the Social Work Department so that up to ten of the spaces were available for more vulnerable single homeless people.

Residents, both men and women, between sixteen and fifty-nine years were eligible to apply. This meant that people with learning difficulties, mental health problems, addiction issues, ex-offenders and people at risk from financial/sexual exploitation could all be helped. Even in situations where people had to be turned away, help and advice was given and alternative accommodation organized if at all possible.

One of the new staff had had experience of working with Bethany before and it had had life changing consequences. In 1992 Gillian Porter was in her second year of social work training and did a six-week placement at Bethany Christian Centre. There she was touched by God's love and shown the power He had to change people's lives. She accepted Jesus into her life and His love began to heal her inner pain.

It was also very encouraging that two of the new staff members, Graham Findlay and John Rodgers, had trusted the Lord when they themselves were Bethany residents. Graham had arrived at Bethany Christian Centre a broken man who felt he didn't have much longer to live, because he had used drugs daily for about four years. Coming to Bethany was a turning point. For the first time he said he felt accepted for who and what he was. But the craving for drugs was still there. He told a staff member that he needed them, and they replied that God could help him overcome the addiction. He experienced the truth of this and began to rebuild his life. In joining the staff team he wanted to give to people what God had given him.

John had drunk himself into becoming homeless but in Bethany he found a refuge. Not long after being there he asked God into his life, and his future took a whole new direction. He married Susie, had his own home and after holding down a responsible accounting job and another as a Care assistant with the Salvation Army, he came to work at Bethany House, believing God had brought him there to pass on to others the love and hope that had been given to him.

This feeling of security was the experience of one of the early residents. He said that 'since arriving in Bethany House feeling lost and fearful for the future, he had found a haven in which he could form a new, more positive infrastructure and develop a faith which he hoped would be honest and true.'

Yet another resident, who had become a Christian while in prison, greatly appreciated the welcome he received after his release. The staff helped meet so many of his needs and encouraged him. He later moved to a supported flat, worked as a full-time volunteer at the House, then became a paid member of staff there and in Supported Housing. Now, many years later, he is serving the Lord as a Baptist minister and sharing the good news of the gospel with others.

And someone else who came into contact with Bethany after release from prison was Dougie McVey. His pre-Christmas shopping(lifting!) trip to Edinburgh was brought to an abrupt end with a stay in Saughton Prison. From there he went to Bethany Christian Centre where his life took a new direction, eventually leading him to become the mainstay of the Bethany House nightshift.

In February 1995 the Bethany House basement was opened up, giving excellent recreational space, a quiet room, storage and therapeutic workshops. After the dedication service for this further facility, the Scottish Baptist Singers gave an excellent benefit concert in Madeira Street Baptist Church. By March a craft workshop was firmly established, providing therapy for residents from the Centre and the House. They created a large selection of candles, and with the help of an increasing band of 'outworkers,' were able to produce cards, jewellery, tapestries, cross-stitch, quilted items, fridge magnets and badges. The workshop received many invitations to provide craft stalls at various events, and there was also a public sales counter in the basement itself. Project worker Andy Walker was also very 'crafty', and his 'Ewe' cards and pictures were in demand. Derek, who was helped by Bethany Christian Centre, managed the workshop and was a skilled picture framer, and this too brought in the customers. When our daughter was married we were indebted to the workshop for their expertise in producing small candles which were used as 'wedding favours,' and for the excellent framing of pictures which were given as gifts.

Tom was only one of the residents who felt he benefited from working in the Craft Workshop. Before coming to Bethany he had spent his life alone and afraid. Unable to face each day without drugs or drink, he had lost two families and had nothing to live for. After drying out in hospital he had nowhere to turn. He was homeless and so turned to Bethany. He found compassion and a kindness he had never known before. The Lord Jesus came to him and with the help and love of the staff at Bethany House he responded to Him. For the first time in his life he had hope and wasn't afraid. He was training to be a candle supervisor in the workshop and using his artistic skills in a way which would never have been possible in his previous life.

By the time the unit had been opened for eighteen months, Simon Laidlaw reported that 'two hundred and forty-two people had benefited in varying degrees from the care it provided. Half of those successfully moved on to longer-term accommodation of their choice in the community. Unfortunately the rest either returned to no fixed abode or simply parted from Bethany House to places unknown.' The staff constantly strove for more successes but it was hard and further complicated by the fact that almost half the number of referrals were under the age of twenty-five.

Later in 1995 three new bedspaces were created because the Trust offices, including the director and administrator, Douglas McCormick, moved to the newly acquired Bethany Hall in Jane Street, Leith, where I faced my newest challenge – a computer!

The speed with which these new offices were finished and the extra accommodation created at Bethany House was due in no small measure to visitors who had come all the way from Bolivia, and had a great effect on the life of the Trust in a very short time.

They paid their own travel costs and were given hospitality by Bethany in exchange for a month's work. They were reciprocating the generous labour of British students who had gone to Bolivia through the Latin Link Steps Programme and who accompanied them to Edinburgh. They camped out in Bethany Hall but also found a 'second home' at Ray and Jacqui Bain's.

Besides the renovation work at Bethany House and office removal, they were involved in preparing a new Bethany Shop and furniture removing They worked hard, played hard (especially football), smiled a lot, laughed a lot and shared their faith through music and testimony in quite a few churches whilst they were in Edinburgh.

To mark their time, a farewell ceilidh, Bolivian-style, was organized in South Leith Baptist, and an opportunity was given to contribute towards the boys' travel costs and buy some of their handmade waistcoats and musical instruments. Alan was presented with a beautiful waistcoat and there is a set of pan pipes mounted on a piece of Bolivian cloth on our hall wall, which keeps alive in our memory their irrepressible zest for life.

Simon Laidlaw said the additional three rooms meant that staff could give support to twenty-eight people at any one time. In the year 1995/6 fifty per cent of referrals were again under twenty-five years and most had challenging behaviour, calling for real commitment from staff.

The basement facility was so well used each evening that it was decided to open it during the day as a drop-in centre for residents and ex-residents. This enabled valuable ongoing contact and support.

Alongside addressing vital life issues, there was also an increased opportunity for recreation in weekly arts, crafts and guitar activity groups as well as the House's very own football team, kitted out in strips kindly donated by Tranent Christian Centre.

Simon Laidlaw had done a power of work from day one and had put in place procedures and policies that had set the course of the House over its first formative years. He had run 'a tight ship' where everyone knew what was to be done and was expected to do it, but in 1997 he took up a new post as the Trust's assistant director for Development and Finance and John Rodgers became project leader at the House, with James MacInnes as deputy.

In the following description James paints a graphic picture of a 'typical' day in the House. 'One resident was dispatched to court, while a second was referred to the Training section. Another had to collect a payment from DSS, while a fourth was referred to the Supported Accommodation team. Number five attended an interview with the Housing Department, while the next was accompanied to his GP appointment. One poor chap was informed that he must leave Bethany House in fourteen days' time. Number eight was running out of clothes and arrangements were made to get him some. There was a key worker session with the next to address his housing need, while another tripped, fell and was taken to hospital to have her leg plastered.

A social worker attended a meeting with their client and Bethany House staff, at the same time as someone else had a lawyer's appointment. Another had left the day before, so a bedroom was cleaned and prepared for the person who was interviewed and immediately moved in. Devotions were held in the afternoon, and five clients decided to attend. The flat meeting in the evening was for four folks and about thirty had lunch and dinner.

'Four people paid rent money and an unknown number played pool in the afternoon and evening. Danny the chef found time to go shopping and made chocolate crispies for supper. Coffee was drunk in the lounges, enquiries were dealt with, TV was watched and referrals taken. Flat 3 did the washing-up after dinner and the repair man fixed the washing machine. The manager sought refuge with staff and residents between meetings, the night shift came in, files were written and reports made.' (Exhausting to just read it never mind live it!)

It is not surprising then that in 1999/2000 John Rodgers said that 'in all my nineteen years of employment I have never worked with such a group of people who are so totally committed to what they feel called to do. The effort, time, patience, kindness and love that is invested in clients has made real inroads into building meaningful relationships. When residents say that they feel accepted just the way they are in Bethany House, the staff are encouraged in that whilst they seek to promote independence as a resettlement unit, the residents feel that during their stay they are very much part of a family community. Unfortunately there are still some people who continue to reject the help that is on offer and more often than not, they find themselves back on our doorstep a few months later. What makes it all worthwhile is when men and women have caught just a glimpse of the hope that is offered, then make that 'glimpse' a reality.'

By 2001, 1826 men and 312 women had lived in the House. The high turnover had taken a huge toll on the physical environment, and the decoration and furnishings had generally become shabby and worn out. It was important that each person who presented themselves at Bethany House should be given the best service that was available, and the physical surroundings were important as they communicated to the individual that they were important, that they had worth and were valued. A major refurbishment was undertaken which raised the standard of the service offered while responses to an evaluation exercise carried out afterwards showed residents were 'impressed' or at least 'satisfied' with their bedrooms.

When John Rodgers became director of Residential Care, Gavin Lawson replaced him as manager of Bethany House. Like John,

Gavin had had his own issues to deal with in the past, but he too had experienced the transforming power of God in his life. Both of them, therefore, had a real understanding of the struggles that residents could face and an ability to empathize. When residents said 'you don't know what it's like', they could honestly answer that they did. Because of their own experiences they were also good at recognizing the devices that residents used to try to 'pull the wool over the eyes' of staff – and they weren't easily fooled!

| Simon Laidlaw | John Rodgers | Gavin Lawson |

Over the last few years Bethany House has faced the challenge of an increasing number of asylum seekers from countries including Iraq, China, and Algeria. The different mix of nationalities and potential language barriers have placed new demands on the team, but also given further opportunities to bring renewed hope to vulnerable people.

In February 2007 a new initiative was taken for 'a test drive' by residents in Bethany House. The programme is called Supporting Homeless Individuals for Future Tenancies, or SHIFT for short. Statistics and experience showed that many people could not cope with being in their own tenancies and so it was hoped that this new programme would help address this problem.
The programme had four parts:-

1) Turning a house into a home

2) Getting occupied (by volunteering or working)

3) Managing money

4) Building social networks

Over a five-day period a variety of topics were covered such as DIY, debt management, learning about potential housing areas and writing a CV. The course drew on expertise from Bethany staff and external services to provide sessions which would be relevant and interesting to all service users. Ex-Bethany residents were also involved in the programme by sharing their experiences and knowledge.

Jess Philbrick of the Community Education team was pleased with the outcome of the first course in April 2007 and another seven were planned. By choosing which sessions to attend, service users were able to benefit from the areas most relevant to their needs and given a better chance of achieving long-term change in their lives.

What James MacInnes wrote in the 2000/1 annual report is still the case. 'No-one's time at Bethany House is easy. Becoming homeless and living in a hostel does not mark a particular high point in many careers. No-one sets out to become homeless and often it is the culmination of a long road of frustration and disappointments. It would be misleading to suggest that Bethany House can explain to individuals why everything that has happened to them has happened. It would also be misleading to suggest that Bethany House is able to make everything right. What it can offer is the sure and certain truth 'We care. We want to listen, we want to take time, and you're no longer alone.'

CHAPTER 9

EDUCATION, EDUCATION, EDUCATION
EMPLOYMENT TRAINING AND EDUCATION
(LEVEL 7)

Bethany Hall

Since its inception, part of the Trust's vision has been not only to help people with accommodation but also with employment. The two so often impinge on each other. If people do not have an address they find it difficult to get a job, and because they have no job, they find it extremely difficult to get or hold down an address.

As far back as 1990 the important step was taken of appointing the Trust's first Employment Training trainee. 'Scotty' had been helping in the kitchen at the Centre for a considerable period but the arrangement was formalized and included college work, and he was answerable to Marion Gemmell.

By 1992 although Bethany's Employment Training and Work Creation section, the new Level 7, was still in its infancy, there were eleven people on the Government's Training for Work initiative and two had moved on to full-time employment with the Trust under the TEGS[1] Scheme. This involved the Government paying 60% of salary costs for the first six months plus training allowances. Two of those on Training for Work and one volunteer

---

1. Training and Employment Grant

had driving lessons. One of these, on passing his test, became a full-time paid driver at Homemaker. Those involved in heading up this latest 'rung' on the Bethany ladder were constantly looking for new and imaginative ways of finding people meaningful full-time employment.

IAN PATERSON

By March 1994 Ian Paterson had completed his task as master of works for Bethany House and was appointed as project leader for Level 7. It was an exciting development. Ian had a real vision for the work and a heart for those whom he was seeking to encourage. Alan wrote in the March 1994 newsletter that part of the dream was 'to give really good training for work, particularly to people being helped through the other six levels of the Trust's work'. The aim was to give job satisfaction, a sense of worth, real prospects and hope for the future to long-term unemployed and homeless people through a recognized programme of work experience and employment training. This would include some teaching on social and job-finding skills. Following an initial assessment, Training for Work would offer a 6-12 month work experience placement through recognized training providers in building trades as well as catering, computing, decorating, retailing, social care and general warehouse work.

Bethany Hall

The renovation of Bethany House and a building owned by Castle Rock Housing Association, and the upgrading of Edinburgh District Council flats, were all projects which had afforded first-class experience for trainees and several of those involved in skills training completed a major job on the windows of a church manse and renovation of a private domestic bathroom.

Every area of the Trust was active in promoting purposeful employment and in the year 1994-5 the Commerce section was able to offer several SCOTVEC[2] and SVQ[3] courses to their trainees, many of whom had been out of work for some considerable time, or had never worked. The Bethany Shops offered retail training; Homemaker, experience in furniture sales and removals; and the Centre and Emergency Units, training in the caring field. These were ideal in-house opportunities within the Trust, complemented by college placements organized for trainees.

Important as these were, they were not the areas of advance that really encouraged Ian. Rather, in consultation with the Leith Job Centre, the new Level 7 had become increasingly aware of a need for a Drop-In centre and telephone helpline for unemployed homeless people. The purchase of Bethany Hall in Jane Street in 1995 provided the ideal location and opportunity to develop this.

BETAN

Most of the people for whom Bethany sought to provide accommodation had also been unemployed for a long time. In many ways it is easier to settle into a new home than to get and settle into a new job. Ian recognized how difficult it would be to find jobs for many of the people the new section were trying to help. Some of them had never worked before; many of their parents had never worked; some had alcohol, drug abuse or mental health problems; and they were seeking to address these problems in a climate where many in mainstream society were also out of work.

The more the new team tried, the more difficult they found the task, but then they believed they had found an answer. It was summed up in the slogan 'You Can With BETAN'. The idea was to provide a pre-work training course, the first of which was

2. Scottish Vocational Education Council
3. Scottish Vocational Qualification

scheduled to start early in February 1995, and the Department of Employment gave a verbal firm commitment to give an annual grant to help finance it.

It was based on what Ian had learned from the Peckham Evangelical Churches Action Network group, 'PECAN', a very successful project organized by the churches in Peckham, London. They had been running courses for five years and had the distinction of being one of the first Christian groups to get European Social Funding to help develop the programme.

BETAN stood for Bethany Employment Training Action Network and was the Trust's own modified course designed to suit the needs of their clients, to raise the individual's self-esteem, help them identify their skills and show them how they might promote themselves on the job market or increase their employment prospects through further education and training.

Of the eighteen students who completed the first two courses, four found full-time employment, seven went on training for work, four on community action, two were engaged in adult basic education, and one applied to college and was awaiting a placement. The group involved did have a wide mix of experience and ability, with some having been recently employed. The results were extremely encouraging, so much so that the course was partially funded by the Scottish Office with a grant of £22,500 per year for the following three years. The Department of Employment and The Prince's Trust said they would also consider funding, and there was the possibility of European Social Funding in the year 1996-7. Ian was greatly encouraged and believed the potential was tremendous.

Alongside the training programme there was the Drop-In Café, initially called the Pastor's Pantry! Ian likes his food and there were always goodies on offer, though not necessarily of the kind that were beneficial for the waistline. Although not widely advertised at first because of proposed redevelopment of Bethany Hall, the Drop-In Centre provided a point of contact and resources for the unemployed homeless.

Although Building and Maintenance interfaced with Levels 4-7, this area of the Trust's work was flourishing and rapidly becoming a department in its own right. As well as completing a refurbishment at Bethany Christian Centre and the Supported

Housing offices, the remaining accommodation at 5 Casselbank St had been turned into two self-contained, three-bedroom flats.

The basement at Bethany House was fitted out as a recreational facility and the property above South Leith Baptist Church, which had been purchased in the previous year, was completely renovated and turned into two single-and one two-bedroom flats.

Ongoing maintenance work to other Trust properties and several outside contracts were also completed. In addition to facilitating the other levels of Bethany's work and providing some extra revenue, these works enabled the Trust to offer three apprenticeships and four Training for Work placements in the building trades, mainly to ex-Bethany residents as part of a new Contracts section. The team was pleased to quote for joinery work but also offered plumbing and decorating. A further three Training for Work placements in administration and training were provided at Bethany Hall.

By the year 1995/6, the training team comprised Ian, full-time volunteer Susan Baxter (doing a marvellous job making sure Ian was in the right place at the right time), Anne Jackson coming on board as trainer, and George Scott working in the Drop-in Café. Ian Paterson had cooked some wonderful Christmas dinners for the tradesmen, but George's chocolate cake was definitely top of the list in its category – I remember it well!

The BETAN courses became well established, giving assistance in finding work or accessing vocational and further education courses. Anne and Susan made direct contact with the Job Centre to encourage support for the course, completion of which could achieve a SVQ Level 1 in job-seeking skills. The scheme got a good write-up from students. As one young lady said 'I thought I knew everything about applying for jobs – after all, I'd had enough practice'. She had spent a year without permanent work before attending a BETAN course. There she realized that in learning about her skills and who she was, she was able to offer a lot more information to a prospective employer to enable him to have confidence in her. Another said he found it 'very helpful, a good laugh as well – a good opportunity to find out skills that you never thought you had, to improve on them and use them to do work you enjoyed rather than taking any job that came along.' Others spoke of the course as 'great for boosting your confidence, helping you to get to know yourself, seeing the good points that you have ... and getting you up in the morning'; and the all-important factor 'providing back-up help after the course is over.'

It didn't take one student long to identify his skills and discover that he had a knack for selling. He came to Bethany from prison seeking help with his heroin addiction, and while in the Centre started doing voluntary work at the Bethany Shop to keep his afternoons occupied. He had some experience from helping out at the family market stall in 'the Barrows', Glasgow, and BETAN helped him turn something he was doing in his spare time into a career.

Doing a six-month Training for Work scheme gave him more structured work experience along with an SVQ Level 2 qualification in retail. He became a full-time paid employee at the shop and worked on a modern apprenticeship in retail management. He was a natural with the customers and enjoyed what he did. 'I get a buzz out of it sometimes', he said ... 'we can turn a couple of chairs into 160 quid and put it on the street to help people who are homeless – people who've been involved in crime and addiction'. He said 'it felt good because you know that money's going to help people in the situation I was in and it's putting my bit back into Bethany'. There was one famous incident involving this obliging salesman when a customer admired the carpet on the floor in the shop. Everything resting on it was moved, the carpet rolled up and sold to one pleased and rather amazed customer! I'm not sure what Ewan Foreman, Commerce manager, felt about it!

Because of their previous problems, a large percentage of clients hadn't sought employment as they didn't believe anyone would employ them and were unwilling to face the possibility of further rejection. As a consequence some had little motivation and usually no conception of the value of employment in terms of self-worth and were not ready to consider a career. An accredited modular core skills training programme was therefore introduced.[4] This not only offered down-to-earth training but could

---

4. This programme was developed for and with the aid of the homeless unemployed by Baker Brown Associates of Bristol, along with The London Connection.

also form the basis for future training, because all GSVQs[5] and modern apprenticeships included mandatory core skills training.

'Core Skills' offered training under a number of headings, including Education and Employment, Housing and Self-Reliance. There were individual modules on such subjects as Personal Goals and Action; Establishing New Patterns; Understanding Homelessness; Living in a Hostel; Finding Accommodation; Moving into Accommodation, and Money Management.

Gaining such awards was hugely important to those who received them. Perhaps for some it was the first time they had completed a course and it helped them to see themselves as people of value. As one person said 'I didn't realize I had so many skills. I thought I hadn't done anything worthwhile. I was hopeless at school, in fact I didn't go much after primary school'. As Anne Jackson said 'God had a plan for these people's lives. He wanted to give them a hope and a future and the courses were there to give them a vision of that future and the confidence to reach out and take it. A job was only part of that hope, because the independence it gave could be instrumental in establishing them in a stable lifestyle'. By this time I was working in reception at Bethany Hall, and it was a delight to see the pride and pleasure on the faces of those passing through to be presented with their awards.

Partnerships were formed with local colleges. Iain MacIntosh, head of community development of Edinburgh's Telford College said, 'Partnerships are vital so that organizations can make a meaningful contribution to the economic regeneration of areas of deprivation in the city. In the past two years collaboration between Bethany Christian Trust and Telford has developed in a positive direction. Our particular partnership offers individual adults an enhanced level of support to rediscover a role for themselves in our society through training towards integration into the community of work. I believe that the creativity, professionalism and commitment shown by the Trust, along with the pragmatic and practical approach taken, provides a level of support for many of those in need within our community which should be commended.'

---

5. General Scottish Vocational Qualification

The contact with the college enabled the Trust to deliver accredited training courses which helped in boosting clients' confidence and were a crucial building block towards college and further qualifications, with a new information technology course among the range of options.

In April 1997 the Bethany Training team was one of four projects hosting the first Christian training and employment conference in London where one hundred delegates from more than fifty organizations met. Ian Paterson set the agenda for the conference, highlighting the need for professionalism combined with the ability to identify with people's problems. Topics covered included 'How to apply for funding', 'How to get a project off the ground' and 'Government initiatives on training'. The conference raised many important issues and was declared a resounding success.

RAY BAIN

Another innovation was the delivering of training within Bethany itself. The apprentice joiners spent Friday afternoons with Ray Bain learning the theory of their trade, which complemented the practical work experience. It was a task that kept Ray on his toes for it meant brushing up on the theory he had learned when an apprentice himself, but he felt it all worthwhile when the lads passed a module.

Ray Bain

A tradesmen with his own business for thirteen years, Ray had experience of working on Bethany property before joining the Trust full-time. When asked to be clerk of works to renovate Bethany House, he turned it down, getting cold feet because he felt he would let his customers down. The next Sunday in his sermon, Ray's minister said that if we don't do what the Lord requires of us, He'll get someone else to do it. Ray thought, 'that's me'. He phoned to offer his services but the job had already been filled. Shortly after, however, Ray did join the team renovating Melrose House. This marked a new chapter in Ray's history and when the renovation of Bethany House was completed, he became a full-time staff member with the Trust.

The lesson is nevertheless typical of many that Ray learned in his time. Although a master at his trade, he found no room for complacency at work and many aspects represented a challenge to him. He enthused about opportunities to chat with residents while doing jobs at Bethany House, the Centre or Supported Flats. The real needs around him there and those that arose naturally through day-to-day job training helped him recognize the need to pray continually and rely on God. And although his faith was stretched, it also grew. He attributed much of that to being with so many different types of Christians, working, praying and learning together. His own faith was stimulated as he led a Discipleship group with interested residents at Bethany House. As one of the apprentices, who did not deem himself to be a Christian, said, 'Ray is everything a Christian should be'.

Later the apprentices had the opportunity to gain modules at Telford College, and when Rev. Ross Brown joined the Trust for two years as contracts manager, he brought with him his own particular expertise as a highly skilled joiner and also his pastoral gifts of caring and encouragement.

STAFF TRAINING

But it wasn't just residents and tenants who were learning new skills and coming to understand that learning was a life-long experience. In the spring of 1998, staff at Bethany House had the opportunity to learn more about mental health, schizophrenia and depression, issues with which they as staff found themselves coming up against more and more. New volunteers were able to take advantage of a comprehensive induction time, which sought to familiarize them with the background and aims of the Trust, and prepare them for their new role which would inevitably have its ups and downs. Those in residential units completed the mandatory food hygiene course and undertook basic first aid training. And completing Scottish Vocational Qualifications, diplomas and sometimes even postgraduate studies in various relevant fields has all been part of staff seeking to do their job competently and with professionalism. Some have gained certificates in counselling skills while members of the Addiction team and Care section received training from Jane Wilson, of the Scottish Drugs Training Project, and a grant from Edinburgh Youth Social Inclusion Project enabled an action research project on anger management to be undertaken.

In 1998 Marks & Spencer made its own contribution to Bethany training by helping to put together a training manual. That same year there was a lot of media coverage about the Government's New Deal Programme. Amidst all the hype and political talk it eventually became clear that the programme demanded that all young people (18-25) who had been unemployed for more than six months had to meet a personal adviser. Under the Welfare to Work programme each had up to four months' 'Gateway' time to prepare them for the employment options that followed. It was at this stage that the training team's expertise was called upon. They were already helping those sent from the Job Centre with advice on job search, confidence building and making up personal profiles. Memorably, one satisfied customer, whose family owned an Indian restaurant, took round some sample dishes one lunchtime for the staff who had helped him put together his CV!

On the practical side, the Trust's involvement brought in vital funds from the Government for these services, and even in its initial stages one trainee continued with the Trust after the Gateway period. It was not all plain sailing though – along with the increased number of people coming to the team through New Deal came a mountain of paperwork.

In seeking to provide new skills for those coming to the courses and Drop-In, the 'Journeys' programme was developed. It encompassed the 'Moving On' basic lifeskills course and the 'Moving Up' course (previously BETAN). When Bill McNicoll and Liz McHugh joined the team, things really began to expand and basic information technology and first aid courses were introduced. Bill had previously been to the Leith Job Centre regarding employment for himself when he had been made redundant, and they suggested he sign up for the BETAN course. On completing it he was offered a job as the Drop-In co-ordinator! Both he and Liz had patience in abundance and an ability to get alongside those they were seeking to help. Successful European

Social Funding and Scottish Office money for one year and three years respectively enabled the team to look further afield in Scotland and make some of their expertise available to other groups interested in what the 'Journeys' programme offered.

Trainer Alex McGowan adapted the 'Moving On' Programme for residents in Bethany House. He felt those who had experienced addiction and homelessness were able to trust him because he had faced similar problems. In sharing how finding faith had turned his life around, he encouraged others to believe that they also could 'move on'. For all who completed the programme there was a sense of achievement but also the completers' outing to enjoy archery, go-karting or a similar activity, and the possibility of progressing to the 'Moving Up' programme.

However as the following extract from Anne Jackson's 1998/9 report makes clear, patience and perseverance were needed by staff and clients alike. She asked 'what can we offer in terms of a safe place? The barriers are huge: Will clients turn up? The first time round, probably not! Bethany is the place of the second chance. However, that does not mean you let them come at their own time – you set up another appointment for them – at the same time next week. There have to be boundaries or the placement will be so flexible it will collapse in on itself. However, if there are too many rules, then it will not start. Some trainees find the discipline of getting up in the morning very difficult. They hear the alarm but put it off without waking up! Maybe that is because they don't want to get up or maybe it is because they turn night into day and find it difficult to get up in the morning. Whatever the reason, they need to know that being late is not acceptable, but that there is a second chance'.

CREATIVE WRITING GROUP

But Level 7 did not only provide opportunities to prepare clients for re-entering the world of work, it also encouraged the use of the expressive arts as a way of helping them to appreciate and understand gifts that they had – gifts which might never have been used to benefit themselves and others. This was the rationale behind the Creative Writing Group which was led by volunteer Patrick Duncan, who encouraged the residents 'to have a go'. As he said 'we're made in the image of God, to reflect the Creator – to be ourselves creative. Being creative is fun, full of life; as essential a part of us as the correct intake of food or Vitamin C. Without some outlet for our creative part, we shrivel up.'

None in the group had any real experience of creative writing but from the very first session two things were obvious. The first was that each of them had a vital something to contribute; often that was simply to affirm what someone else had written. And everybody shared, nobody was silent, and each felt they mattered. The second was how important it was for them to get out of their head into their feelings. Experiments with music, candlelight, clay and pictures helped them to do this and thus enlarge their senses. Besides giving members of the group the opportunity to express themselves and tell their story, better literacy and social skills were developed, and they felt empowered by having a voice.

The hope was to submit entries for a book on aspects of life in Edinburgh due to be published in the summer of 2000. If work was not included there, then somewhere else would be tried. It was hoped using words and pictures to be creative in a supportive environment would add another dimension to the lives of some of the residents and encourage them to achieve potential they maybe never realized they had.

Success did follow. Participants like Joe found great satisfaction and release in their writing. He had been through the Bethany system and was always to be found when there was something arty or creative on the go. He was a published poet. and although he had experienced many problems, was full of enthusiasm for the project. Out of the group's work two poems were selected from thousands of submissions and were published in 'An Intimate City,' an illustrated Anthology of Contemporary Edinburgh Poetry. Other members had work published in *The Big Issue*. The group received funding from the Campaign for Learning's co-ordinated BT Reading Challenge. They joined one hundred innovative community reading projects in the UK, selected from over 700 applicants. At an award ceremony at the Royal Society of Arts in London they were congratulated by Mersey Sound poet Roger McGough, as the Scottish regional winners.

Their next big challenge was to prepare for their first exhibition entitled 'Letters Home' the following year. And this was a success too. Their work was beautifully mounted and displayed in the prestigious surroundings of the Writers' Museum in the Lawnmarket in old Edinburgh where visitors could gain an insight into literary giants of the past such as Robert Louis Stevenson and Sir Walter Scott. It is not big as museums go but has an atmosphere of calm as it perches at the top of the Mound, with views over the old Nor' Loch to Fife in the distance. When the loch was drained to create the beautiful gardens that lie beneath the castle, it made Princes Street one of the most picturesque shopping streets in the world. Sometimes it is easy to think of 'homeless people' as an amorphous mass whom we don't really understand and who lack the normal feelings, as well as a stable home. This exhibition would certainly have changed that view. Along with other visitors, it helped me to get to grips with the fact that the writers had the same hopes and aspirations as anyone else but maybe had experienced more disappointments than most. After all we all have our own personal hang-ups, insecurities and vulnerabilities, a need to be liked, a need to be tolerated and forgiven. I found the work profoundly moving.

Indeed, the write-up said 'the mark of good writing is that you can reach out and touch the characters, smell the air, feel the mood, get inside the mind. There was never any lack of talent among these sensitive artists; just the natural reserve of those who had fallen on hard times. Drawing on diverse influences, such as the work of other writers, news articles, holiday brochures, or focusing on a photograph or piece of music, group members explored in poetry and prose their inner feelings and experiences'. After the exhibition, the work was taken on tour to The Festival of Learning and several libraries.

JUNE

For some the Adult Basic Education work in numeracy and literacy helped to bridge the gap in their education, giving the opportunity to improve maths and English skills. Anne Jackson told of one such student, June, who spent Monday afternoons catching up on things she had missed out on at school. When she was there, somehow or other reading just seemed too hard to conquer and she was labelled a non-reader. As a result she became adept at avoiding situations where her inability to read would be exposed and often said 'I've not got my glasses'.

But June felt she was missing out. She had always had a fascination for Helen of Troy, and felt that if only she could read she would be able to find out more about Helen's exciting and romantic life. So June overcame her apprehension and applied herself to painstakingly learning to recognize words and see patterns and shapes in words and spelling through the ABE[6] group at Bethany. With lots of support and encouragement when the hard work and frustration made the going difficult, the day dawned when she could get to the library. There she met with a sympathetic librarian who understood that she still found reading a bit of a problem but wanted to find out about Helen of Troy. Imagine the thrill of getting your first library book in your thirties, of discovering the joy of books and the world it opens for you.

June's achievements were featured in the 2000/1 annual report when the accompanying photograph showed her proudly receiving an adult learner's award from Scottish Television.

And June used her new -found skills in remembering others also. When the Queen Mother died, she wrote a letter of condolence to the Queen, and was delighted to receive a reply from the Palace sent by one of the Queen's ladies-in-waiting. She read the letter to the group, emphasizing the best bits, such as 'Her Majesty,' in a loud voice and feeling ten feet tall!

It was especially gratifying to the Training section in particular, and the Trust in general, that courses were being recognized by outside agencies. November 15th 2001 was a special evening when the annual dinner of the National Training Awards was held at the Glasgow Hilton, and the winner was to be announced, chosen from six finalists, of which Bethany was one. This was a UK-wide competition promoted by the Scottish Executive, Scottish Enterprise and Highlands & Islands Enterprise, celebrating the best in training and development across the country. They were

6. Adult Basic Education

recognized as the most prestigious awards for training and skills development in the UK and aimed to identify examples of exceptionally effective learning that had had a significant impact on business or individual success.

Unfortunately, trainer Bill McNicoll was ill and unable to accompany Anne Jackson and Liz McHugh, who were dressed for the occasion in their 'little black numbers'. Being one of the finalists was impressive enough, but when Bethany was chosen as the winner for their category it was rewarding that the growing reputation for excellence, dedication and relevance of the courses offered had been recognized at such a high level. It was especially good to be able to tell those participating in the courses that they were attending 'the best'.

WISE WOMEN

And recognition didn't stop there. The Wise Women Group also received sponsorship. This large group of women came together in 2002 initially as a survival group who had experienced the pain of homelessness. All had found themselves in a place where they had forgotten that they could still make choices to change the direction of their lives. The group offered a safe place to discuss such issues, to explore possibilities and, with the support of others, to investigate options that up to that point had always been regarded as for other people.

Liz McHugh and Anne Jackson

The idea for the course resonated with the plans of Telford College and City Literacies and Numeracies, (CLAN), Edinburgh. Sponsoring the group, they gave a recognized personal development award accredited by Telford College to all who completed the course. Topics included healthy eating, looking after your body, exercising your mind and what it means to respect yourself and others.

From that initial group, five members decided to take up the challenge of lifelong learning and enrolled for college courses. They all discovered the joy of friendship and trust within a group, as well as the satisfaction of encouraging others and developing a sense of belonging, and appreciated the crèche that was provided.

The group went from strength to strength and in 2003 gained a Millennium award from the Scottish Community Foundation to set up a self-defence class in Leith. The popularity of the Wise Women's Group and the desire for women to meet together to learn resulted in a joint project with the Acorn Centre where a weekly women's Drop-In was provided. Once a week all the children went to a crèche and the women at the Drop-In were free from distractions to participate in discussion groups, workshops and have the opportunity just to chat 'child-free' for an hour. In the sessions, issues were touched on such as how to relax after a terrible day, how to manage aggression and talks on further education.

When the doors for the Women's Group first opened just one person turned up. The following week two women arrived. After a short time there were on average fourteen women going along every Tuesday. The group grew by word of mouth and was important to those who attended. One described it as a 'lifeline'.

ART

In May 2001 the first of the Art Group sessions took place. These too proved to be very successful and rewarding for all who participated. Not only was work exhibited in Leith Library but in 2003 a joint arts project with Telford College culminated in a remarkable exhibition called 'Face to Face' at the Ocean Terminal Shopping Mall. This prestigious retail outlet is part of Leith's dockland regeneration project, with its penthouse suites and Royal Yacht Britannia visitor attraction. Diane was just one member of the group who contributed to the exhibition. She said she loved going to the group because all her friends were there. When Bethany won a Scottish Arts Council Award for this project – which was collected at a ceremony in Dundee – she rated going on stage and winning the award as one of her greatest moments.

The Ocean Terminal was also the venue for the Bethany Photography Exhibition – 'Images and Words – Through our Eyes'. This was an exhibition of work resulting from a course operated jointly by CLAN and Bethany Training section which explored literacy and communication through technology. Using digital cameras the group learned various techniques as they captured a range of powerful images in and around Leith.

All the clients derived great fun from the course, as well as a real boost in confidence and skills. Some surprised local residents on Leith Links found themselves (and their dogs) co-operating obediently and enthusiastically in the project.

The results were interesting and sometimes poignant, showing that beauty can be found in unusual places. The group learned that it was good to stop and stare and to appreciate the wealth of experience to be had by just looking around. Added to this was the satisfaction that Community Education, Edinburgh, would use a copy of the exhibition as a teaching resource for students.

COMMUNITY EDUCATION

By 2004 Bethany's Training section had also found a new name – Community Education – because more and more the team and clients were interacting with the local community in encouraging lifelong learning and bringing colour into people's lives. The Big Draw certainly did that. During a week in October 2004 the Ocean Terminal Shopping Centre was bursting with creativity as Bethany Community Education staff and clients took over the Forum space to put Leith 'in the picture'.

The Big Draw was a national initiative to encourage people to engage with the arts, and Bethany's project provided clients and the general public with the opportunity to represent the Leith area through artistic media.

Bethany's Big Draw was an interactive art exhibition in which any member of the public was welcome to drop by and join in. Images of Leith were projected on the wall and then traced on to brown paper running the length of the walls in a mural. The outlines were then filled in in the most colourful and expressive ways, using crayons, paints, pencils and collage materials. There were no restrictions on style or colour – everyone had a great time experimenting in their own way with the art materials supplied. The finished mural was stunning and was displayed around the walls of the Ocean Terminal before being taken for more permanent housing at Telford College. Bethany was very grateful to the students and staff from the college who helped to run the project. Visitors from all spheres of life enjoyed the Big Draw, discovering their own hidden talents and boosting their creative confidence. Leith had never looked so colourful!

That year too saw Bethany becoming a European Computer Driving Licence test centre.

PUBLICATIONS

One very special project of which everyone involved was hugely proud, was *Sharing Lives*, Bethany's first clients' book of short stories and poems. The book helped writers develop their spelling, punctuation and grammar, as well as giving them the motivation to do well knowing that someone would actually read what they had written.

This was followed by the first edition of *The Bugle* newspaper which rolled off the press in December 2005, and was available at hostels and drop-ins across Edinburgh, libraries, churches, and doctors' and dentists' waiting rooms in the Leith area. Written solely by those overcoming problems of homelessness, the idea came as a direct result of positive feedback from service users after *Sharing Lives*.

The Bugle is a bi-monthly magazine written and produced by the Bethany Press team, a group of people who have been or who are currently homeless. It provides an opportunity for Bethany Service Users to share their experiences of homelessness, develop literacy and self-confidence, provides skills in working to deadlines and project completion, and builds a sense of community among the team. They meet weekly at Bethany Learning Centre and receive support from the staff there, decide the contents, interview contributors, write articles and take photographs.

The latest innovation in which Community Education and Supported Housing are involved is the men's Drop-In which started in September 2007. (After the success of the women's group, the men were feeling hard done by). The aim is to be a real draw for men who feel isolated, for example those living in hostel accommodation and who don't have good support around them. Sixteen men went along to the first session, and it is hoped the momentum builds and more men are encouraged to attend.

The Bethany Community Education team is the only homelessness charity team in Scotland accredited by Learn Direct. It is now able to provide accredited accessible training in Edinburgh, West Lothian and Fife, supporting homeless and vulnerable people to reintegrate into their communities and prepare for employment.

The following story not only illustrates how the Levels of Care impact upon each other, but how an individual life may be enriched by the courses, activities and events organized by the Community Education section and through which friendships have been made.

Jimmy McCurdie

We are all good at something – the problem is often finding out what. For Jimmy McCurdie, who was one of Bethany's long-term residents, this journey of self discovery has been a long and winding road. Jimmy's first involvement with Bethany was twenty-four years ago after some years of mental illness, including a spell in the Royal Edinburgh Hospital.

He eventually moved to his own tenancy and has been involved in a voluntary capacity in several sections of Bethany and many other charities within Edinburgh, always looking to be helpful and to find his particular place in life.

Jimmy has clear artistic gifts, and enjoys drawing and painting. For some years he dabbled with creative writing, producing some short stories and cartoons, but it is in the realm of poetry that Jimmy has found an avenue for expressing his feelings and views on life. His talents in this area have  been recognized, both by Bethany, who produced a volume of Jimmy's poems for sale, and by outside publishers, two of whom accepted poems for published anthologies. Jimmy is thrilled by his success, but remains typically modest, and continues to work away quietly within Bethany.

Chapter 10

Stops as Well as Starts

Have all the things that the Trust hoped to achieve actually come about? Definitely not, but the Scriptures do say that our stops as well as starts are ordered by the Lord. Sometimes looking back it can be seen that God had something better, or it was not the right time, or, as in some cases, we still don't know why the answer was 'No'.

Rosyth

One such 'stop' was Watson House in Rosyth, a town set in the shadow of the Forth Rail and Road Bridges and home to the famous dockyard. The Bethany story here begins in 1996. At that time it was apparent to Christians in several church fellowships in the area that there were a number of people who were much loved in God's eyes, but who had 'fallen off the bottom rung of the ladder'. They asked 'What can we do?' They had already answered the question in some measure by taking gifts of food to families on a council estate and by collecting, storing and distributing furniture to people in need.

In January 1996 Alan went to Dunfermline, just a few miles from Rosyth, to speak to an inter-church group in Viewfield Baptist Church about the Trust's work in Edinburgh. That was the catalyst needed. Several of the people at the meeting agreed something could and should be done to help the needy and homeless folk in West Fife. Twenty-four local churches were contacted and eventually representatives from seven of them met to discuss the issue. An action group was formed which became known as Christian Concern (West Fife). From the beginning the value of the expertise of Bethany Christian Trust was recognized and a close partnership began.

In 1997 the Trust was invited by Christian Concern (West Fife) to outline what could be done for the five hundred people thought to be homeless in the area. Ian Paterson, who was then Bethany's Training manager, and Alan had discussions with Gordon Brown, the Kirkcaldy MP, and found him very sympathetic to the vision and eager to offer support.

A meeting was arranged at the Pitbauchlie Hotel in Dunfermline at which there were representatives from nineteen churches, Christian organizations and local authorities, all of whom were seeking to ascertain the way forward. Fife Council's Alan Davidson reported that in the previous year in terms of statutory homelessness there had been 2600 referrals to the Council's housing service. They could not address the problem without the help of organizations and groups such as those who had come along to the meeting. He commended them for seeking to make the important connection between concern and care through to provision.

There was the possibility of transforming one of two buildings opposite the entrance to the new 'Rosyth 2000' development in what was the naval base. One was the former Rosyth Families' Centre and the other, Watson House, had housed police at the dockyard gates. The latter was the preferred option. Because of Rosyth 2000 there would be opportunities for training, and an approach to the neighbouring dockyard owners, Babcock Thorn, resulted in the firm agreeing to give training places to ten people.

Rosyth also seemed an appropriate site as it was not unusual to encounter people who had been in the Services and upon discharge struggled to live independently.

It was estimated that the project could be put together for around £350,000 compared to the £2 million approximately which it would cost to create a new building.

In July 1998 there was confirmation that the project would definitely go ahead. In August a planning application was lodged for a twenty-four bedroom residential training centre and twelve supported flats at Watson House which had been bought by Fife Council on the 3rd of that month.

On 16th November Christian Concern (West Fife) launched the Bethany Centre (Fife) project with about sixty people representing many churches meeting in Rosyth Baptist Church. The churches aimed to raise £80,000 to help provide twelve supported flats and two staff flats to complement the Council's proposed residential training centre, all of which would be managed by Bethany Christian Trust. The 'There is Hope' Youth Committee in Dunfermline began fund-raising to support the venture, and organized a craft fair and fashion show.

It was a real blow when tenders for the work came in far above what was expected, resulting in the Trust no longer being able to be involved in the £500, 000 provision of supported flats. Bethany was, however, still committed to training in West Fife and developing the partnership with Christian Concern (West Fife). Chapter 12 shows how very important this partnership was to become. However, at this stage it was a question of 'watch this space.'

GLASGOW
Over the period 1996/7 there were also discussions about possible work in the Drumchapel area of Glasgow, and in Alloa. The hope was that the work would expand to different locations by invitation when there was clear local support for such initiatives. However, by spring 1998 due to circumstances beyond the Trust's control, such discussions were not furthered.

BETH-HAVEN
About the same time as the disappointment regarding Watson House, another project got under way. The beginnings of this

go back to 1997/8. The annual report for that year told that the City of Edinburgh Council had asked Bethany to be responsible for a twenty-bed reception centre and an eight-bed Challenging Behaviour unit. They were to be part of the Rough Sleepers Initiative which was designed to provide a nationwide network of resources for homeless people so that no-one needed to sleep rough in the UK. Various premises were considered, including a site in Candlemaker Row but this was deemed unsuitable because of strong local opposition.

 However, on 15th February 1999 a temporary reception centre for male rough sleepers was opened, with Gavin Lawson as manager. It was called Beth-Haven and operated in the former Leith House, which had been a 'model' lodging house, run by the Council. It was to offer basic accommodation for up to twenty-eight men for an initial two-week period, after which it was hoped that residents would find more permanent housing in a hostel or tenancy. It was a far from ideal environment, with some rooms only large enough for a small single mattress on a raised built-in platform which was against three of the outside walls – certainly one would have had more space in prison. Rooms like this were left unused and the better ones utilized. At one time almost a hundred men had lived in this 'model' lodging house. Reducing the number to twenty made the environment tolerable.

'Model' was not quite the word Bethany staff would have used on taking occupancy. There was soiling on some of the walls, they found metal legs of an ironing board taped together to create a shotgun, and there was a spring-loaded reception hatch left by the old regime which was activated by quickly pulling out the brush handle that had kept the window open a little! Beth-Haven by contrast was to be a place where workers *engaged* with clients.

On day one there were fourteen admissions and by the end of the first week the hostel was completely full, and this pattern continued. Many of the early residents came from the Night Care Shelter which had just closed until the next winter. It was very hard work, emotionally as well as physically for the twenty or so staff and volunteers. I think the words 'commitment' and 'stress' took on new meanings for the staff. It was difficult for them not to feel overwhelmed by such a large number of people, all with significant needs. There was a continuous changing of staff and this made it difficult for a full staff team to develop. Added to this, the reliability of the heating system left much to be desired.

The unit was operated on a self-catering basis; but with a large number of residents coming straight from the street and having nothing, on admission they were given a 'starter pack'. Contributions to these and donations for the clothing cupboard were much appreciated, as was the kindness of a team from Greenbank Parish Church who volunteered to serve a shared meal each Friday and thereby help create a sense of community.

A 'haven' is an inlet of the sea that affords good anchorage or shelter. The idea of refuge and security did seem to have been a reality in the experience of some of the residents at Beth-Haven. Brian took time to write 'thanks for helping me and pointing me in the right direction', while Mike, from Poland, said 'Bethany Christian Trust were working to try and help me and my family. But that is not all, I received understanding about life; all people need each other'.

And residents weren't the only ones to benefit. Carole, who was a domestic assistant within the 'Haven,' felt she had found a whole new family there. Previously a medical receptionist, she said 'I came to hear about Bethany from my own church and, feeling God was leading me in a new direction, I applied for a job within Bethany. I didn't know what to

Beth-Haven staff

expect. The first thing that struck me was the acceptance, openness and love. There was a strong sense of family feel within the team. God has developed me and given me a new level of trust in Him.'

From the day of Beth-Haven's opening, the project had been plagued by uncertainty. Up until the end of October there had been 385 admissions, with fifty-five being in occupancy more than once. Most of these people had been refused access to other hostels – even with this, the staff succeeded in having an eighteen-day average turnaround and saw more than half the residents going on to longer-term accommodation in another hostel, council or other let, back to family or previous tenancy.

However, on 4th November a crisis point was reached where two more staff gave notice of leaving, two were off sick and there was still nothing in writing to say the tenure was to be extended to 31st March 2000, as had been hoped. The Trust did not feel able to advertise without having written confirmation when all that could be offered was a four-month post which certainly wasn't long enough to expect people to make a career move.

The decision to close on the 6th December 1999 was accompanied by a great feeling of sadness. As Leith House, the hostel had been open to receive hurting, homeless and vulnerable people for 105 years. The only thing that took the edge of this a little was that the Care Shelter was due to open the next night and so there would be that facility open to any of the men who had nowhere else to go.

Although the project came to a 'stop,' there had been positive 'starts'. Residents had enjoyed outings, some had even appeared on TV as 'extras' in an episode of 'Rebus', a Scottish detective series, some had made constructive changes to their lifestyle, and others had also come to faith. Some of the staff, though having had 'a baptism of fire', went on to serve in other areas within the Trust.

The Farm

But what about other dreams? Very early in the life of the Trust there had been a vision to find a country location where agricultural/ horticultural work could form part of a 'rehabilitation/training package'. By 1994 it was felt that the work in the 6 Casselbank Street building was very constricted and also near many of the temptations which residents at the Centre were seeking to overcome. Strong links with the city were absolutely necessary but it was thought a healthy country location would be helpful and therapeutic.

The Monastery of the Poor Clares at Liberton was going to be sold. Was this the place? The trustees had a long discussion sitting on a seat in the peaceful graveyard there, and although Bethany submitted a bid in September 1994 there was no response and we had to presume the answer was 'No'.

Cheylesmore Lodge in North Berwick and Murieston House in West Lothian were considered. The latter mentioned had definitely been designed for gracious living, and the property included two cottages, outbuildings, an old stable and an orchard. Just a shame about the price!

But then supporters were asked to pray about whether we should put in an offer for Middleton House, situated south of Edinburgh on the A7. It had 113 acres of mixed woodland and arable grounds. The wooden dormitory buildings were badly in need of repair. They had housed evacuees during the war, Hungarian refugees, and had been used for school camps. The main house, built in 1710, could have housed a rehabilitation unit, and conference and retreat facilities. There was plenty of scope for agricultural/horticultural development.

I remember this particular property well because a decision had to be made whether or not to put in a bid, and the final date was to be while we were on holiday in a remote part of Orkney mainland. The holiday cottage had no phone and the nearest one was a mile away. At least once a day Alan could be seen going into the phone box to make contact with the trustees. I wondered what the locals made of this behaviour. Did they have a spy in their midst, was he enquiring after a sick relative, or did he just have a fascination with old phone boxes? There weren't many houses around, but after all, it was island life, and I am sure they would have been aware of his obsession with telephoning. However, the outcome of these many calls was that it was decided not to offer for the property.

Later the land known as Hayscraig farm, at the top of Greendykes Road in Broxburn, was for sale. Was the property bought, did the Centre relocate, did it work out as planned? The answer to these questions will be told in the next chapter, because although this venture has been the most disappointing, frustrating and puzzling of all those in which Bethany has been involved, for some, including me, it has had its positives and has been a special place.

CHAPTER 11

THE WEST LOTHIAN QUESTION!
(LEVELS 3, 6, 7)

Last year Alan and I visited the House of the Binns, in West
Lothian. It is the ancestral seat of the 11th Baronet, otherwise
known as Tam Dalyell, the longest-serving MP in the Commons.
He will always be remembered as the one who persistently
raised the 'West Lothian Question' (named after his original
constituency) about why, post-devolution, Scottish MPs should
continue to vote in the Commons on English legislation. The
Trust has had its own West Lothian Question, which has also
been persistently asked!

THE FARM
When the Trust bought Hay-
scraig farm at the top of Green-
dykes Road on the outskirts of
Broxburn, West Lothian, it was
not the kind of picture post-
card location one would normally consider for a holiday.
But the crucial question was,
could and would people want
to live and work on its sixteen-acre site? The land had suffered
from various changes of use – it had been a pig farm, a landfill site
and a depot for heavy earth-moving vehicles, boasted a large derelict building, was situated on the top of a very windy hill, one
side swept down steeply to the Niddry Burn and it was altogether
in great need of trees to form windbreaks. It was not, therefore, as

157

Elizabeth Bennet exclaimed on first seeing Pemberley in *Pride and Prejudice*, 'most happily situated' – but it did have potential, and unimpeded views over the south-west towards Livingston. One cold day, therefore, various trustees and members of staff stood on the little knoll overlooking the site and commended it to God.

By December 1996 plans were beginning to shape up for the renamed Bethany Home Farm. The project was based on the 'foyer' concept and was Bethany's most ambitious response to the increasing demand for such care.

A residential training unit was planned as an extension of the work of Levels 3 and 7, with a farmhouse housing up to twenty-four men or women. The accommodation would consist of three shared flats and six single houses. It was envisaged people would stay for one or two years living in shared accommodation before progressing to a single house within the complex. Staff would assist them in the development of basic life skills.

The on-site training factory would provide daytime training to residents and local people in building trades, market gardening, vehicle maintenance and decorating. The remaining land would be developed for horticulture and forestry. Courses would be run in conjunction with further education colleges and the accredited SVQs offered by each training unit would aim to finance themselves by offering products and services to the local community. The home-styled care and real work training on the farm would aim to restore self-worth and give hope and opportunity for a better future to vulnerable and homeless people.

It was an exciting vision, but a mammoth task, and the total budget was estimated in the region of £800,000, with the project being built in four manageable and sustainable phases.

In January 1997 David Headley moved from Bethany Christian Centre to head up the work at Broxburn. It was 'a time to uproot and a time to plant' involving much hard practical clearing of the land, but, with the tremendous help given by Raymond, Alex and other volunteers and residents from Bethany's Edinburgh units, 3,500 trees were planted. There were strict guidelines regarding which species of trees had to be planted and the Trust owed much to the generosity of Dr John Blyth, both in the initial stages and on an ongoing basis. He not only gave advice, bought and supplied many of the trees, but paid for others to help with the planting and undertook some of this work himself. Such support was invaluable.

The derelict building was demolished, and some of the tradesmen from the Contracts section put plumbing in the garage and worked on its roof. The latter was a cold job and some of them felt they had been banished to Siberia for a spell. However working at the farm gave the opportunity to make contact with local people. One such lady from the nearby village of Faucheldean asked Bethany to quote for a job – and Alex, Bethany tenant, and Stephen, joinery apprentice, ended up on another roof. There was the compensation that the lady was a remarkably good baker and very keen they sample the cakes!

Development in the countryside is quite often frowned upon, but Bethany asked West Lothian Council to treat them as a special case. The Council replied that the project seemed to be well thought out and they would consider whether it fitted in with their policy.

By June 1997 planning permission had been granted, and a project launch evening was organized. A marquee was erected, and David Headley and Adrian Currie were in charge of proceedings, which included a time of praise, an outline of plans and hopes, prayers of thanksgiving and dedication. Home baking was provided by local churches, and photographs and models were displayed in the shed. The visiting dogs behaved, the resident goats behaved, the sun  came out and about 170 interested people attended. The following day specially invited guests and councillors had the opportunity to look round the site.

Goats! – they were an absolute menace. Goats have an amazing ability to act as 'Hoovers', devouring everything in sight. This is beneficial if there is just a small area which is needing cleared of rubbish, but the small flock at the farm felt a particular affinity with cars and realized a better view could be had from the roof of such vehicles. They were spoilt for choice at the first staff fellowship/barbecue event at the farm when the cars started rolling in. Their time in Broxburn was short-lived and they found a new home at Edinburgh Zoo. Unfortunately for them, visitors never got to see them, but some of the other animals were delighted with their arrival. In other words we didn't know *exactly* what happened to them, and it was better not to ask!!

It was hoped to get funding from local, national and European Government sources, training providers, local businesses and charitable trusts. Application was made to Government through the Council for £200,000 under the Rough Sleepers Initiative, but by November 1997 funds from the latter and Resettlement had proved unsuccessful.

There was, however, some good news. A portion of land which bordered the farm was purchased, and the access road up to the farm was bought for the amazing cost of five pounds. It was encouraging too that bulldozers cleared the steepest part of the land. Thousands more trees were planted over the winter, with some supporters contributing £1 towards each new sapling, each with its own protective shield to keep out the local 'munchers',

Even with these positives, 1997 was a difficult year. David Headley left the Trust in December and there were more disappointing delays and refusals for funding. One of the weaknesses of seeking Government funding was that the package had many parts. For the whole project to go ahead each of these needed to be guaranteed, otherwise it could not proceed. On several occasions the whole package fell because one 'funder' was not able to deliver at that time. Plan B, or 'the Bethany way' was set in motion in the hope of speeding up the process by making fresh applications for Phase 1 only and the building of two staff houses. Drainage of the land was a particular priority and volunteers were sought to clean lime plaster from bricks which could be re-used for this or building.

The Houses

Planning permission was granted to import 7,500 cubic metres of soil to cover the former opencast works, and the Trust was indebted to Mr Kennie and his father, who owned a local heavy transport firm, for donating, delivering and using his bulldozers to landscape the site. Peter Gordon Construction dug the founda-tions for the two houses, Thomas Mitchell Homes delivered and erected the 'kits', and the houses were fitted out, all of which was celebrated with a barbeque and bonfire.

Just as a 'city set on a hill cannot be hid', so the erection of two houses (at one stage sporting bright yellow cladding) and perched on the top of Greendykes Road, was very difficult to disguise. They became a talking point and everyone in the area was aware that 'something was going on.' Alan and I were to live in one of the houses to be a 'presence' on site and to be as involved as our working life in the Trust offices in Leith allowed. When we went to register at the doctor's surgery, we were greeted with 'oh it's you who are living up there,' with the doctor being far more interested in this news than he was in the state of our health! As is always the case with such projects, stories around them grow arms and legs, and there was some hesitation in the area about potential residents, though it was hoped that locals would be persuaded that the farm could be a benefit to the community.

NEIL

With the arrival of Neil Fisher as farm manager things began to move – literally! Neil joined the Trust with many years' diverse agricultural experience from crop trials to cabbage growing. The time spent doing this in Kenya and Nigeria was followed by thirteen years of specialist advisory work with the Scottish Agricultural College. He had written a thesis on Brussels sprouts, and as one of our family, who has no love for this particular vegetable, commented 'how can anyone find enough to write a paper about them – you either love them or hate them, end of story'. He heard Alan speak at his church and felt he could and should get involved. Needless to say he didn't come to Bethany because the salary offered was an improvement on his existing one – rather he felt he could use his considerable experience and expertise for the Lord. A timely, generous grant from The Jerusalem Trust guaranteed his funding for three years. On taking up post, if Neil had been asked what working in Africa and West Lothian had in common, he might well have said 'a rainy season' and 'a challenge'. The month before he arrived was about the wettest October on record. Alan and I were to occupy No. 2

Bethany Home Farm, and the land to the front of this house was by that time boasting its own unscheduled lake. Family members suggested we might keep it as such, creating a stop-over for birds using the regular flight path from the Broxburn Canal to Linlithgow Loch!

A continued wet winter, transport problems restricting potential help from Bethany's Leith Projects, and unforeseen problems with the land itself meant there was no such thing as a 'normal day' in Neil's first six months. But there was potential! Three or four residents benefited from travelling out to work on a daily basis, though the work at that stage was mainly heavy and uninspiring. As Neil said 'when you have dug a hole for one tree, the next three hundred are pretty much the same!' However, the men from Leith enjoyed the odd chance to drive the tractor and the opportunity to be out for the day. Neil felt that in no sense was the project at that stage providing vocational training other than one or two forestry skills, but rather skills related to the discipline of life, being capable of doing a decent day's work, starting at a reasonable time and working steadily during the day. As with every job there was a degree of boredom and repetition, and he felt clients would benefit from knowing that, even if they didn't realize it at the time. So holes were dug for another block of about a thousand mixed broad-leafed trees, and grass sown in preparation for spring and the coming of livestock.

Neil led by example. He arrived early, stayed late and found practical solutions to most problems. He had an amazing mixture of intellectual ability, common sense and down-to-earth (literally) know-how, and just got on with it.

IN RESIDENCE

Alan and I moved from Leith to Bethany Home Farm in November 1998 and our own house in North Fort Street became another volunteers' flat. We were greatly indebted to Margaret Rees for showing such practical friendship when she came to help me clean the flat, and to former residents who assisted with the flitting. It was amazing how much stuff we had gathered over the years. It reminded us of a fellow minister who had occupied a very large manse, and was moving to the north of Scotland. The removal firm kept adding on another vehicle when they saw the amount to be transported. Alan has used this as an illustration of how people coming to Bethany may appear at the door with all their worldly goods in one poly bag, but carrying a whole load of other unseen baggage which is weighing them down. Some people felt sorry for us going, as they thought, to the 'wilds of West Lothian', but it was our choice and we were excited about the move. We had greatly enjoyed living in North Fort Street but when we arrived at the farm felt very happy to be there. Unfortunately the houses had been left surrounded by builders' rubble, just about enough to build another one; and what was to become our back garden was quite dangerous, even more so when the following month keen frosts and ice transformed it into a landscape of deep, slippery crevices.

The second house was still empty at this stage, and so on a winter's night if one approached the property on foot it was very, very dark. I quite often came home from the office on the bus with Perro, walked three-quarters of a mile up Greendykes Road and then the quarter of a mile up the farm road. I was never afraid, but I did often wish that Perro was a white dog with a fluorescent collar, rather than a predominantly black one who metamorphosed into a completely irrational creature whenever she saw the beam of a torch!

It took Perro a little while to settle. She was an obedient dog and had been used to walking to heel in the city. Now when the front door was opened and she was allowed the freedom of a large open space, she had to be coaxed to go out by herself. Eventually she made friends with Brodie, the exuberant, irrepressible golden retriever (who couldn't retrieve himself) belonging to our near-neighbours, the Kirkwoods.

It was quite something to be living in a 'brand new house', with en suite facilities, and an amazingly large lounge that had windows looking in three directions. The one to the front gave a good view of the red shale 'bing' which was Broxburn's answer to Uluru (Ayers Rock), very colourful when the sun shone, and from the top of which one could see for miles in all directions.

RESIDENTS

Shortly after our arrival the first residents moved into No.1 Bethany Home Farm. Neil often stayed overnight in the house and there was cover at weekends from other staff members, and it was hoped that Christians from local churches would also get involved in providing this.

Funding and expertise was sought to develop more labour-intensive horticultural enterprises including polytunnels and other propagation facilities. More trees were planted, including fifteen rooted trees from Leith greengrocer Farmer Jack's, where they had been bought and returned after Christmas so they could be planted out and hopefully mature. Fences were erected and a generous donation of £24,380 received from The Auldcathie Trust. This trust, which was funded by landfill tax paid by companies dumping waste at the site in nearby Winchburgh, gave the money for environmental improvements. This allowed the access road to be upgraded to meet the standard required for use by the emergency services, and this made life much easier for everyone.

Drier weather in the spring enabled vegetable sowing. In April a new staff member, Robert Cochrane, who had experience in landscape gardening, joined the team and encouraged residents from the hostels in Leith to work on the farm on a daily basis.

In the meantime I was having what an old friend would have called a 'serendipity' experience. I was finding 'one surprise after another'. The first was bunches of snowdrops down at the side of the Niddry Burn; and later, down the valley, which I named 'the forgotten valley', there was wild garlic, and primroses growing among and even on the trees. This was a special place for me – a great place to go and be quiet, read and pray with just the babbling of the Niddry Burn for company. The land across the stream belonged to the Hopetoun Estate and occasionally deer could be glimpsed through the trees. The whole place had a 'Narnian'[1] feel about it. I never actually saw Aslan softly padding through the undergrowth, but it was a place where I felt the presence of God. I was excited and wanted to share these lovely surprises with the guys next door – for ever practical they said 'is that what you're making all the fuss about' when I showed them the primroses! The next surprise was a 'host of golden daffodils'

---

1. The land of Narnia where Aslan the great lion is King, described in C.S.Lewis' *The Lion, the Witch and the Wardrobe* and other books in the Narnia series.

in among the tree belt to the left of the access road. I never even mentioned these to our neighbours!

In the early spring there was a clear view down the valley to the burn, but later the butterburr grew to such a height that Perro could disappear altogether, and the path became impenetrable. It was like a parable. We were needing a clear vision of what the farm was to be about but there seemed plenty of things to obstruct it.

The verges and the area immediately in front of the houses were grassed, and a rabbit fence erected at the back of the gardens. After much hard work, our own garden took shape, with vegetables and flowers planted, and a big rockery which covered all manner of stones too big for us to move. Neil planted potatoes and brassica in one field, and the first flock of hens began to lay.

Gordon and Jim, from Bethany Christian Centre, came to help erect a 50 x 26 polytunnel, and Neil, Robert and the residents of No. 1 Bethany Home Farm set about fitting it out and planting peppers, courgettes, cucumbers, tomatoes and ornamental plants.

Neil hoped that feeding the hens and collecting eggs would give some pattern to the day and would add interest for the residents and visiting workers. He rightly surmised that it was a certain type of person who would enjoy being a resident on the farm. The initial ones settled well and the daily work experience given to clients from Leith had the added bonus that they could let potential residents know what they would be in for.

HARVEST

Harvest time came with potatoes, green beans, cucumbers and tomatoes all ready for gathering in, and some flowering plants and bushes ready to enhance the landscape. Surely, everything in the garden was lovely? Not really, because the residential side was not working as expected. Part of the problem was that

the residents provided neither a viable community nor a large enough group to justify full-time staff cover. Neil did go far beyond the call of duty in this, although he admitted that he did not see himself primarily as a 'Care' worker, but rather a motivator and facilitator of meaningful employment, through which he could

165

seek to get alongside the men. There was also the problem that some offering themselves as residents were not physically fit enough or well motivated to develop their skills in agricultural and horticultural practice. Added to this, residents had to be willing to at least try to live together, even at times when habits, interests and differing ages made this challenging. All this was difficult to resolve with the ideal of developing both further accommodation and alternative training opportunities more or less simultaneously.

Instead of just providing the usual British topic of conversation, the unpredictability of the weather often determined the day's programme at the farm. Winds could feel particularly strong on the top of the hill, and in December 1999 with the newly planted tree belts still in their infancy, there was little to break the ferocious gale that swept over the exposed site just before Christmas. The residents were sharing in my birthday meal when we heard a tremendous crash – the polytunnel had been uprooted. We chased outside, grabbing twisted metal, trying to salvage anything we could, but it became too dangerous and we had to abandon the operation. It was particularly sad because we had been assured by the seller that this would not happen, but there was no redress. Not only was there the loss of outlay for the polytunnel itself, but also the loss of a facility which had enabled work to be done inside even through the winter months when everything slowed down outside.

During one very cold spell the residents of No. 1 built an amazing snowman, complete with hat, scarf and boots. It lasted for a quite a few days and greatly puzzled Perro: was it animal, vegetable or mineral? On another occasion the children from the 'Story-Keepers' group at South Leith Baptist Church came to visit. The were going to look at different types of soil as they had been studying the Parable of the Sower, but on the morning of the planned visit, there was an unexpected and very heavy snowfall. The access road 'disappeared', and Alan had to mark it out for them. They did all arrive and had a great time in a white wonderland instead. On only one occasion was it nearly impossible to get out of the farm. Having heeded the weather forecast the night before, we took the precaution of leaving the car at the end of the drive. It was just as well – by morning the snow was several feet deep. We had to carry Perro, wade our way through the snow, and enlist the help of the tractor, but we did eventually arrive at the Leith office.

Although the project wasn't functioning as hoped, it wasn't all unrelieved gloom. Mark stayed at the farm quite a while; his practical abilities and experience as a blacksmith were appreciated and he experimented for a while trying to get his own business off the ground. John fully entered into the outdoor life until he left the farm to return to his job at sea, Larry enjoyed using the strimmer to keep the undergrowth in order, Kevin was enrolled in the New Deal scheme and worked hard outdoors. Alan Berry, who had been away from agriculture for many years, realized how much he enjoyed working out in the fresh air after a day in the office or on a Saturday. I did what I could, especially in regard to the hens and attacking the weeds.

However, from very early on Neil felt it would be difficult to make the project work if funding was not forthcoming, but he and Alan planned and worked and the farm gradually took shape and became an attractive place to live.

New Plans

Various staff members from different 'Levels' of the Trust contributed their own ideas and feasibility studies, but there was no real consensus, and no clear way forward without funding. By 2000 there were still hopes and plans for a training factory at one end of the site and a residential unit at the other, but by then 'Animal farm' could increasingly be applied to Bethany at Broxburn. Fencing, bought by another generous gift from The Auldcathie Trust, made it possible to increase the variety and number of livestock, whilst the balance of their donation supplied a second tractor, extra machinery and materials to create pathways through the tree belts. These latter, plus a flight of steps, were achieved after much back-breaking work, but made it possible to walk right round the edge of the farm. Indeed, when the trustees of The Auldcathie Trust came to see how the money had been used, they could hardly believe that the site was the same place they had seen previously.

More hen runs were added. Some of this work was done by Colin, who was a resident at the Centre and helped out twice a week at the farm. With the acquisition of another flock of very attractive hens, there was a total of 150 birds. Some of these were housed in old caravans and some in wooden hen houses, but they were all free range. Successful registration of the flocks and egg packing arrangements for free-range production meant that the eggs were able to be sold in various outlets such as the Bethany Shops, the staff room at the school where our daughter was teaching and to a regular clientele from South Leith Baptist. The sale of the eggs had the spin-off effect of raising local awareness of the farm, and our nearest neighbours, the Kirkwoods, and other locals put in regular orders. Besides this, the first batch of seven home-grown chicks were hatched from the little flock that was gifted from Rutherford Farm in the Borders.

Collecting, checking, weighing, sorting and labelling the eggs was time-consuming. Unlike most of us, hens do not take holidays, and so even on Christmas Day the routine had to be followed. One resident who was more than willing to be involved in this was Jim MacNab. Jim was neither young enough nor physically fit enough to do any heavy manual work around the farm, although there was one occasion when he managed to dig up some daffodil bulbs that I had just planted, smiling afterwards and saying that he thought 'that bit of earth was easier to dig than I expected!' However, he was a good cook and the boys next door appreciated the fact that their catering was taken to another level. He spent many hours in the 'egg packaging' room at the back of the garage and he also renewed his friendship with his faithful friend, Perro.

Perro had a long coat and shaggy tail which got very untidy and dirty, and was often matted with sticks, undergrowth and mud. We used to snip the ends but on a certain occasion when we were away on a holiday minus Perro, she was left in the care of Jim, who took her for a No. 1 haircut at a local grooming parlour. When we returned I wasn't sure whether to laugh or cry. Poodles may get clipped in a certain way, as do terriers, but not collies! She looked like a pathetic, skinned rabbit. To add insult to injury Jim said 'you owe me £13.50!' Poor Perro, she knew she looked ridiculous and crept around keeping out of sight, but she, along with us, was signed up for a sponsored walk. The only picture we have of Perro Mk.2 is in Maggie Currie's wonderful photograph of the North Berwick sponsored walk which appeared as centre spread of a Bethany newsletter. Fortunately, the long coat did grow again and she was restored to her shaggy self and self-respect.

ANIMAL FARM

Certain people in *The Archers* (and I must confess to being an avid listener to life in Ambridge), have a affinity with pigs, and also ferrets – and for a while both of these creatures lived at the farm, with twenty female pigs settling in well to the newly built pig-sty. When they were all stretched out sleeping, their snoring had to be heard to be believed. On one occasion when I was feeding the hens I heard what could only be described as terrified squealing. The herd had ganged up on one particular pig and were bullying her. Larry, Alan and myself did eventually manage to extricate her from the sty, doused her with water and checked for injuries. She recovered, but had to be kept apart from the rest, which meant in the end she got thoroughly spoiled. She was called Penelope, even though we had been warned that giving names to animals made it much harder when they did finally go for slaughter. She grew so fat that we were sure that she would fetch a better price than all the others, but alas 'fat' outside meant 'fat' inside, and as opposed to lean meat, it doesn't bring a good price. I was sad though when the herd went off to the factory in Broxburn and felt I couldn't possibly buy a packet of Hall's sausages from the local supermarket for a good few weeks, just in case Penelope might be in there somewhere.

And the ferrets were another first for me. One of the residents arrived complete with ferrets and built a little hutch outside the back door of No.1. He was determined that I was going to admire them and eventually did persuade me to stroke them. They were beautiful in their own way and under their owner's supervision did manage to make a little impact on the rabbit population. Rabbits were a constant menace and delighted in the munching they thought had been 'provided' for them in the gardens.

Eight Shetland ewes and a ram were over-wintered in the newly fenced fields and fifteen lambs arrived the following spring, the first one at Easter. Shetland sheep are small but hardy and the Bethany flock all lambed without difficulty, even when twins were born. Having the sheep brought us into contact with a local farmer, David Foster, who over the years as the flock increased was a considerable help and a source of all manner of useful information regarding the Shetland breed – as well as being the 'lender of rams' and sometimes vehicles in which to transport them.

When the ewes and newborn lambs were back in the field, one of my delights was to watch their antics. The lambs were full of the joy of life, leaping and frolicking over the new spring grass. They would take off, almost vertically, at a great speed, ponderously followed by their mothers. When the ewes eventually caught up with them, the lambs would race off again and the games continue until it was 'milk time'. One was reminded of the song 'All in the April Evening' with its words 'I saw the sheep with their lambs and thought of the Lamb of God'.

With the arrival of the sheep there were new jobs to do and new lessons to be learned. They needed tagged and recorded, their toenails clipped, feet cleaned, treatments given orally and applied externally, supplementary feed given through the winter and they had to be sheared. Neil was learning some of this 'on the job' but he was competent and a good teacher.

CHANGES

But there were disappointments concerning No. 1 Bethany Home Farm. Some of the folks who had come out to stay in the house with a view to being responsible for the others had their own problems and didn't stay long, or it just didn't work out for various reasons. Things came to a head when during our holiday some of the boys and their visiting friends behaved completely irresponsibly, and used vehicles in such a way that they not only damaged them, but endangered themselves and also the animals. Their behaviour was totally unacceptable.

This meant that although by April 2001 the first loop of the outer circle footpath through the southern and western tree belts was complete, a new tree belt had been planted along the west side, and a small polytunnel gifted, there was sadly only one resident remaining in the house, and far-reaching decisions had to be made regarding the future of No. 1. It was decided that until 24/7 cover could be put in place it was no longer viable to use it as a house for residents.

Added to this, funding for Neil's three-year contract was to end in the late autumn and, although he was willing to help out on an occasional basis for as long as he remained in the area, the uncertainty of the way forward and again lack of funding meant only 'a holding' operation seemed possible. It was a tremendous disappointment, and Neil had worked so hard.

However, No. 1 Bethany Home Farm was available and staff member Alex McGowan and his family moved there in August 2001. Alex continued with his work with the Trust in Leith while wife Marie helped to keep the farm running on a day-to-day basis, assisting with the livestock.

One of my earliest recollections of the McGowan family is of us all out in the newly mown field raking up the grass and enjoying the lovely sunshine. Shortly after they moved in it was all hands on deck preparing for an open day at the farm, when Robert Doig, B.B. Captain of the 18th Leith Company, kindly allowed us the use of their marquee. Home-grown produce, jam and marmalade and the ever-present free-range eggs were all on sale, as were teas, coffees and home baking. There were flower arranging demonstrations, guided tours of the site and children's games. It was a great day and rekindled the hope that just maybe the farm could still fulfil its potential and the vision be realized.

MORE ANIMALS

Neil sometimes despaired at my sentimentality when it came time for hens to be culled or rams, large and small, to leave the farm. I was amazed on one occasion, when surely only out of a sense of duty and showing support, Gordon Weir *volunteered* to come and help with the hen culling! Alan never slept either the night before or after such events! But the sentimentality was worse with the arrival of the McGowan family who all threatened to wear S.O.S. tee shirts (Save Our Sheep) at the time, when having done their duty, rams Magnus and Rambo left the farm. Some of the little lambs were also given names, and those that had to be bottle-fed or kept warm for a spell in Marie's kitchen answered their names for a while. Again the words of Jesus about calling His sheep by name and them hearing and knowing His voice came to mind.

And then there were the verses about 'sheep going astray'. Our flock very rarely did this, but the fence of our neighbour's field left much to be desired and we quite often had visits from his sheep who could be loath to go home. Our flock increased each year, but its undoubted character was Brownie, who, although small, always produced twins – one large ram and a much smaller female. If one wished to move the sheep the job was greatly facilitated if Brownie was feeling co-operative. If she decided to comply, the whole flock would follow her and the process would be completed in no time – if not, one could be chasing sheep for a very long time. Perro might have looked like a sheepdog, and indeed became quite good friends with them, but they were definitely in charge and were far more likely to have rounded her up than the other way round.

And Perro wasn't much good with another species of resident either – the rats. She had no more love of them than I had. We tried traps, Marie kept outdoor cats for a while, Environmental Health were on the case, but because of the burn and the easy access to the hen food they were just part of life. They would gnaw at the hen houses and the food store and when I was on 'hen duty' I would pray hard, and bang saucepan lids together until I was sure that anything lurking had fled – at least in the short term.

There were other unwelcome visitors too – the foxes. Perro and I came face to face with one in the bushes behind the houses one day. I was amazed at the brightness of its red coat – it was beautiful. However, that was hardly how we felt about them when they attacked and killed some of the hens, and left their bodies lying. The result was time and further expense involved in electrifying the fence.

By Christmas 2001 a large caravan was housing the latest 140 hens, and twenty birds were donated by a supporter who worked at the Agricultural College in Ayr. Then came a gift of excellent nesting boxes from a chicken farm in Fife. Our very popular egg production was in full swing.

Being on top of a hill with no factories or built-up area around to obscure or pollute it, the sky above the farm seemed a vast expanse. Marie and I would often step outside to enjoy the starry heavens or marvel at a complete rainbow arching over the site. Recently I was reminded of this when I read a portion in 'Our Daily Bread' Bible Reading Notes which read 'The earth's population is now over 6.6 billion. And depending on where we live, finding moments of solitude where we can gaze at the silent night sky is increasingly difficult. Yet, according to the writer of Psalm 19, if we were able to steal away to a spot where the only sound was our heartbeat and the only sight the canopy of the stars, we could hear a message from those heavens.

'In such a moment, we could hear with the ears of our innermost being the noiseless testimony of God's breathtaking creation. We could hear from the heavens as "they declare the glory of God". And we could watch in amazement as the sky "shows His handiwork". We could listen as day unto day utters speech that fills our minds with the unmistakable awareness of God's splendid creation. We could marvel through the night as the firmament shows in unmistakable splendour the knowledge of God's handiwork. Our Creator tells us "to be still and know that I am God". A great way to do this is to spend time in His creation admiring His handiwork. Then we will certainly know that He is God.'

Memories such as these went with us as, being well and truly retired by January 2003, we left the farm and moved to Dunfermline. For a while Simon Takarinda was employed there and other Bethany staff members such as Liz McHugh and Marie, focused on tidying the farm in preparation for people on placements from the Social Work Department who came and worked with them two days a week. Clients like Craig enjoyed spending time with the staff, sheep and chickens, as well as working on the land. There was still the vision for the farm to develop a full-scale therapeutic learning centre with a building equipped to assist people with all abilities to learn new skills. The environment was conducive to relaxation and learning, and West Lothian Council had given their full support, but again, where was the funding?

MATTHEW HOUSE

Later that year, however, No. 2 Bethany Home Farm was again occupied, this time operating as Matthew House, developed by the Trust, in partnership with West Lothian Council, in a way that would best meet the needs of vulnerable young men between the ages of sixteen and twenty-one who had a history of homelessness. It was envisaged that probable potential residents might already be working with staff from the local Council Housing office and perhaps Social Work as well.

Matthew House was a safe and secure place where for a short time young men could take time out of the spiral of homelessness with all its anxieties and uncertainties to ask 'Why am I here? Where am I going? How will I get there?'

The 24/7 support provided by the staff team, originally David Craig, Andrew Jones and Callum Henderson, gave ample opportunity to nurture confidence and provide assistance with the various indepen-  dent living skills – skills that were so necessary to prevent the spiral from continuing and to try to find appropriate longer-term accommodation. Another staff member, David Jamieson, had himself been helped while staying for a short period in Bethany House and wanted to be able to provide similar support for other men in this new project.

MARTHA HOUSE

About the same time as Matthew House was opened, a similar project for young women, Martha House, also came into being in West Lothian, not at the farm, but in West Calder. As part of the growing picture of broken families and homelessness, many women in their late teens and early twenties were desperately looking for a place of safety and security. Martha House was a response to this need.

Working with such an age group was never going to be easy and many challenges faced staff in both Houses as they sought to develop innovative ways of working with residents and encouraging them towards a future full of hope. Many of them had hardly known a loving stable home and brought a fair degree of challenging behaviour to the two units. One girl, who arrived at Martha House with a host of crisis issues, said she had had a chaotic and troublesome past, due to homelessness, abuse of all kinds and drugs misuse, but began to see a way forward when she arrived at Martha House. She started a part-time college course which she hoped would help get her life back on track and was glad to be settled into a friendly atmosphere with positive influences.

Early in 2004 the twin projects were officially launched with a celebration service in Dedridge, Livingston at which Callum Henderson, manager of the Houses spoke movingly about how Christian love in action was making a difference in the lives of the young people in the units.

Statistics in Bethany's 2003/4 annual report showed just how vital were these services. Over 25% of homeless people in Scotland were eighteen to twenty-five-year-olds. Many of the residents going to these units were even younger, sixteen or seventeen, and found themselves homeless at an extremely vulnerable time in their lives. The Houses sought to provide an atmosphere of Christian love and support where staff worked tirelessly to deal with the very real challenges facing such young people. Many of the residents had a history of care, with multiple previous places of stay and with nowhere to really call home. Some thought of the trauma of homelessness as a further confirmation that society was against them and had already given up hope of a decent future. A fulfilled and stable life seemed an impossible dream. The caring support of the staff helped to rekindle that hope in some, though sadly not all.

The units provided a variety of activities helping young people towards their own tenancies, including budgeting, cooking, DIY, life skills, anger management, sport and recreation, and the Addiction workers organized group work programmes at both Houses.

One of the residents at Martha House said how easy it was to judge people by a label, adding that not all homeless teenagers were alcohol and drug-addicts that hung around street corners causing trouble. She arrived at Martha House just a few weeks before she was due to take her Standard Grade exams. After a series of traumatic family events, she had no option but to present herself as homeless to the Young Adults team. Thankfully she was able to secure a place at Martha House, meet new people and get support on the issues affecting her.

During the year 2004/5, thirty-six young people, all from different backgrounds and with different needs, found accommodation and advice at Martha and Matthew Houses. The one factor they had in common was that they had their whole lives before them but the challenges of youth homelessness placed many obstacles in their way. What was particularly encouraging was the strong rapport that often developed between staff and residents and enabled them to work together for the best outcome.

Later, mothers with infants were also able to be supported at Martha House. One such was Jill who said she was a happy, bubbly, caring person but had never had the chance to 'take lessons'. When she moved to Martha House she wanted to learn to look after herself so that one day she could be more independent and have a house of her own.

She had been in foster care since she was eight years old, was then seventeen and had a little girl of her own. She need-ed to find somewhere safe, and when she heard about Martha House was really excited. She appreciated the routine in the house, the support she received in looking after her daughter, learning housekeeping skills and the activities which the local church organized. She had been learning how to sew but so far had only managed to stitch her fingers! Her dreams for the future included 'a house and a nice guy to spend the rest of her life with, someone to be a great daddy for the wee girl'.

Being in the two units also meant that young people could access support from the community through opportunities to build relationships with other agencies and West Lothian churches. Both houses operate a resettlement programme and work with Edinburgh Cyrenian's Youth Inclusion Project. Cyrenians have a lot of services available and provide transport to their programmes, and this networking complements what is offered within the Houses.

But staff do face the inevitable discouragements. In October 2007 two residents in Martha House were arrested for wilful fire-raising, which damaged one of the bedrooms in the house. It was a close thing, but the fire brigade managed to stop the fire from spreading, and the officer at the scene commended the staff for their swift and effective reactions. Matthew House had its ups and down that month too, with one resident leaving and another being placed on a notice to quit. It was a difficult time for staff and residents but, as is so often the case at such times, God sent some encouragement, and the arrival of a generous donation from HSBC Bank was, in one staff member's words, 'definitely a hallelujah moment!' Another encouragement in regard to finance is that when Martha House was purchased with joint funding from West Lothian Council and Bethany, the understanding was that the Council's indebtedness would reduce year on year. This has indeed taken place, and by May 2008 the whole property should be owned solely by the Trust.

Because the outworking of the original vision for accommodation and training at the farm had not come into being, the livestock was sold and hen runs dismantled, and there were negotiations to try to sell the site. One or two organizations, some doing similar work, showed a degree of interest, but nothing materialized. Application was made to West Lothian Council for permission to divide the land and sell the two houses as separate entities, each with their own plot of land. As the book is being written, this has been granted and No.1 Bethany Home Farm has been sold.

All of which raises mixed emotions. Neil says 'guidance is not an exact science'. The farm project illustrates this well. Recently, Neil, Alan and I walked round the farm for 'old time's sake' – it was windy!! The snowdrops were blooming and the trees, including two of the three chestnuts that were planted, were growing. Further tree belts had been planted in accordance with regulations from West Lothian Council. We still don't know why the outcome was different from what was hoped for and expected, but we take comfort from the fact that as this piece of ground was transformed and rejuvenated into a farm many people were helped along the way, and it has formed a bridge into West Lothian. It is planned that in 2008 the work now being done in Matthew House will relocate to a more central location in the region. The premises that are being considered will allow a much larger and more cost-effective service to operate, thus making the service more accessible to others. The property at Bethany Home Farm will be sold to finance the move. We will watch this space with prayer and interest.

Chapter 12

The Toast of the Town
–*The Toastie Club*–

The Watson House Project in Rosyth may not have come to pass, but in 1999 Bethany finally made it over the Firth of Forth to the Kingdom of Fife (so called because Dunfermline had been the ancient capital of Scotland). The Trust's training vision for the area was still alive and well, and the partnership formed earlier with Christian Concern (West Fife) was about to be actively worked out. The plan was to offer a pre-vocational 'Moving Up' programme to homeless/unemployed people in the Dunfermline area, using excellent office facilities provided by Christian Concern West Fife in the Viewfield Centre. It was to be headed up by Bethany's newest trainer, Lisa McBean. Contact was made with two other homeless agencies in the locality and they were receptive to the plans.

Bill McNicoll

By the summer of 2000, the project was really getting off the ground, and trainer Bill McNicoll was in Fife each Thursday to offer support to Lisa and a regular clientele of homeless and unemployed people who met at the 'Drop-In' every week. It had taken time to become established, but it was never anticipated that it would happen overnight. Help and support were offered, and the breakfast and games of snooker were proving popular.

What was encouraging were the positive comments from the clients and knowing that the word was 'on the street'. The 'Toastie Club' was gaining credibility. The name Toastie Club was discovered when a social worker phoned Bill McNicoll to discuss a mutual client and asked 'are you Bill from the Toastie Club?'. Bill almost said 'no, I am from the Bethany Drop-In', when he realized that *he was* Bill from the Toastie Club, and since then the name has stuck.

Choice is important and it is possible to have a cheese and ham toastie, a ham and cheese toastie, a cheese toastie with ham, a ham toastie with cheese, etc., etc ., and it works. Two things contributed to the early success of the Drop-In. Firstly it had its own dedicated space behind the Viewfield Centre (with its own front lawn for smokers to huddle on in winter and sunbathe on in summer), and secondly a toastie machine was introduced. The demand placed upon it was such that this standard domestic model could not cope, and a large industrial-scale machine had to be sourced. Toasties are after all the heart of the business; it is easier for someone to say 'I am going for a toastie and a cup of tea, than it is to say 'I am in a mess and feel a little vulnerable and insecure and would like to get some advice and support from Bethany'.[1]

By the time the project had been running for a year it had begun to make a real impact on the homeless scene in Dunfermline. The barriers to the clients' ambitions to have a home and a job were addressed through group discussions dealing with such issues as self-awareness and rights and responsibilities, while basic courses dealt with literacy/numeracy and anger management.

Bill McNicoll visited Dunfermline every Monday and Thursday, and a dedicated group of volunteers from Christian Concern made the Toastie Club a welcome place to be. Men and women, aged sixteen to seventy attended, and in the six months from January

1.   see chapter 10

to the summer of 2002, the team worked with 122 individuals of whom 94 per cent were male and over 80 per cent were offenders and/or substance abusers, and some had mental health problems. All appreciated the warm food, provided in partnership with Fare Share, and this was important for some may not have eaten for forty-eight hours. There was also the opportunity to use a phone, look at the daily papers and magazines, and receive any necessary help with reading official letters or addiction advice.

In the September 2004 newsletter Bill said the best part of the day for him was mid-morning when people had settled down, were playing pool or sitting around chatting. He loved the feeling of peace in the room. But he could also face difficult parts of the day such as seeing someone in distress and under the influence and needing help, and he himself struggling to know what to say or do – though he found that God provided the words. There were bad days too, when he had to acknowledge that some people just couldn't be reached. From time to time there were incidents where workers had to intervene, and very occasionally sadly it was necessary to ask someone to leave.

Bill was clearing up the Drop-In after one such occasion when there was a knock at the door. It had been a difficult morning; one young man had arrived simmering with barely controlled anger. Almost immediately there was great tension within the whole group. This escalated further and he nearly came to blows with another young man. Although Bill had been successful in defusing this and preventing anyone from actually being hurt, the young man turned his frustration upon him. He did leave but with much shouting and threatening at Bill. It was with some relief when Bill answered the knock at the door that he found it was someone else who had been in the Drop-In earlier. He explained that he wanted to apologize to Bill on behalf of everyone who had been in the Toastie Club for what had happened earlier. He said, it was not right that Bill, who did so much for other people, should have to put up with such abuse. It was only with some effort that Bill convinced his visitor that while he greatly appreciated the visit and the kind sentiments expressed, he did not want– as was suggested – anyone to 'sort out' this fellow for him!

The Drop-In was well supported by local commerce, churches, and the police. Indeed, as reported in an article which first appeared in the *Dunfermline Press* and then *The Courier and*

The Sun, the police gave credit to Cheese Toasties for slashing Dunfermline's crime rate! They said that the hot snacks given at the Drop-In meant that desperate folk no longer needed to steal food, and they recorded a significant drop in theft and shoplifting in the area whenever the Toastie Club was open.

By December 2004, the Toastie Club had expanded to three sessions every week and had its own football club. Keeping fit was good for mental as well as physical health, and the team enjoyed training sessions which included short talks on health topics, healthy eating, alcohol and fitness. During the summer they took part in several tournaments and played a friendly match against a local amateur league team, enabling the men to improve their physical fitness as well as build confidence and self-esteem.

At a celebration evening supporters and clients enjoyed a presentation about the progress of the Toastie Club and medals were awarded to all members of the TC football team in recognition of their hard work and achievement. Local pharmacist, J.B.B. Dick, was presented with a medal too, for all the support he had given the team, including providing football strips.

Recognition was also given to the Toastie Club volunteers: people like Derek French, Lady Martha Bruce, Anne Clayton and Marie-Clare, who for four years had shown real commitment and care for homeless and vulnerable people in Dunfermline and without whose efforts the Drop-In could not have operated. As volunteer Ruth said it gave them an opportunity to put into practice Jesus' love and a chance to actually feed the hungry. Christian Concern were pleased to report that they had seen some people move from positions of vulnerability and homelessness to a more stable lifestyle in their own accommodation.

By October 2005 the Bethany newsletter was reporting that the Toastie Club had received an astounding 3,747 visits over the year. It was definitely the place to be, with the comforting smell of cheese wafting from Viewfield Centre.

LEVEN

The newsletter went on to explain that, building on experience gained through the Dunfermline service, in July of that year Bethany launched a six-week pilot Drop-In further up the Fife coast in Leven. It received forty-five visits from homeless people in the first five weeks and, on that evidence, Bethany, together with churches in the local area, committed themselves to long-term involvement.

Ian Gunn, who had lived in the area for over fifty years said, 'Leven has had a lot of problems with drugs and the needs are great, so we hope that the Drop-In will make a big difference'. This second Drop-In also provided a vitally open door for individuals and a starting point from which to move in a positive direction. One man commented 'when you're on your own all the time, wandering round the streets, it gives you somewhere to go and someone to talk to'.

ANDREW'S VIEW

Andrew, a volunteer in Leven, said he had heard about Bethany from someone at Leven Baptist church who had been involved in training service users in painting and decorating, and gained a fuller understanding of the work after a presentation at his church. It was obvious that, despite there being many drug problems in Leven, he felt people were just sitting in their pews every Sunday, so far removed from these people's lives and doing nothing to reach out and help them.

Andrew started volunteering at the Drop-In. The team had put up posters in local shops and they spoke to people they saw on the streets. Andrew felt this was God's work in action and it was something in which anybody could become involved.

He explained that along with offering food, hot drinks and toiletries, there was the opportunity to share problems and access other agencies. A Fife Council housing officer visited the project every Friday seeking to help people to obtain more permanent accommodation. Andrew remembers one man in this situation. He was about sixty-five years of age and had become homeless when he divorced from his wife. He said 'we reached an agreement over the house – she got the inside, I got the outside!' He had been staying in B&B accommodation and was miserable because his belongings kept getting stolen. Through the housing officer the team were able to secure accommodation for him.

Andrew explained that those who attended knew each other but there never seemed to be any aggro. They all knew the rules; no drinking, drugs or swearing on the premises, and people abided by that. As Andrew said, going to the Drop-In was voluntary, not something imposed, so that was perhaps why they were respectful, and they seemed willing to trust and confide in those there to help them. Some people were curious as to why volunteers should offer their services without expecting anything in return.

It was encouraging that the numbers of those finding suitable accommodation was increasing, with some being moved on into Bethany's Housing Support service

Visitors to the Leven Drop-In enjoyed reading previous editions of *The Bugle*, the bi-monthly magazine which the Bethany Press Team put together, so the team paid them a visit, and the October 2006 edition featured jokes and poems from Leven. Also in that edition, Andy Wilson interviewed members of the Toastie Club football team at their training site and spoke to Michael, Jimmy, Daniel, Steve and Mick. The team had spent the last three months training and competing in a local tournament, and finished a very respectable third.

When asked what the training had meant to them, the lads said 'It's got us a lot fitter. It gives us something to do on a Monday and Wednesday, instead of just kicking about drinking and taking drugs. It's bringing the guys together as a group and means we are working on team skills'. And it was obviously very important for one person who phoned Bill to say he had been released from jail and was now available for selection! I wonder if he had been in Perth prison because apparently the word about the Drop-In wasn't only 'out on the street'. A new referral to Housing Support was asked if he had ever heard of Bethany before being referred. 'Yes' he said, 'the boys in Perth jail talk about the Toastie Club all the time, they say it's great!'

More Toasties

By 2007 the Dunfermline Toastie Club was meeting four times a week, with Monday afternoon being given over to activities and a women's group meeting on Thursday afternoons. Writing in *The Bugle*, Janet, who attends the group, said 'we have a cuppa and a roll, and sit down and have a chat. We also read magazines and talk about articles in them, about what is happening on the TV and in the news. We just chill out with our feet up. It's really good.' Julie also attends the Drop-In and says it serves up the best toasties in Dunfermline. She likes just getting out of her house and enjoying the company the club provides.

The Toastie Club has so developed that it now offers addiction counselling, advocacy, a liaison service with local doctors, health services, job centres and local housing providers. Addiction worker Cath Turrell said she loved meeting up with the folks there. If they need to talk in a more personal way there is a room set aside. Her addiction support work is tailor-made to each individual. She helps people work through the consequences of their addictions and put in place mechanisms for relapse prevention. Help is also offered in filling in forms, as well as life skills courses and boundary awareness. The environment is safe from the perils of the street, but the demand is growing and the vision is to be open full-time. In order to achieve this, a sum of between £30,000 and £40,000 will need to be raised each year, and different fund-raising events have already taken place toward making the vision a reality.

As the October 2007 newsletter said in its article 'Reaching Out', 'Bethany understands the need for personal contact and interaction between service users and service providers; the need to remind them not only of the services available to them, but also that someone cares. Bethany's street work provides a point of contact for some of society's most vulnerable and inaccessible people; those whom other services providers do not reach.'

BILL'S INPUT

One such person told of Bill McNicoll's work in this respect. He said 'the doctor wanted to stop my methadone script three years ago but Bill came with me and talked to him. Without my methadone I probably would have gone back to heroin. Since then I've managed to put on a stone in weight and have got a two-bedroom flat with my cousin, thanks to Bill's support.'

The Bethany newsletter acknowledged that 'Bill is a trusted and friendly face to many who use Bethany's services in Fife, and his approach is simple: to make himself visible and available on the streets around Dunfermline and Leven on a daily basis; talking to between five and twenty people every day, constantly reminding them of the dates and times of both Drop-Ins and encouraging them to attend. From the first contact with a person needing help, he seeks to gain their trust by showing he cares through remembering their name, always being available for a chat and offering practical advice on homeless issues. Bethany's street work bridges the gap between "service users" and Bethany's other services, and encourages a trusting and lasting relationship of care between the two parties'. But this work is not without its dangers. Those supplying drugs are unhappy at losing clients. On at least one occasion a dealer has tried to run Bill off the road.

Some developments have brought much encouragement to the staff and volunteers. For just over a year the 'Toastie Church' has been operating. It was something that clients asked for themselves, and between ten and twenty attend and discuss various issues in the light of Scripture. As Derrick and Janet wrote in *The Bugle*, 'Every second Sunday afternoon anybody is welcome to come, we have a chat and a roll, and then we talk about Jesus and what He does for people. We then finish with prayers.'

Recently there have been further developments. Christian Concern and Bethany Christian Trust staff decorated the premises, modified the serving area and put down a new carpet. This greatly improved the facilities and was much appreciated by those using the Toastie Club. As the book goes to print, one of the Dunfermline Toastie sessions has moved to the Abbeyview housing area and is beginning to become part of the local scene.

Perhaps the ethos of the whole project is summed up by Bill's comments when he said he did his job because he knew God loved him and he wanted other people to experience that love. Through the Drop-Ins, the street work and the Toastie Church, that love is being shown and the prayer is that God's Kingdom may be extended in the Kingdom of Fife.

CHAPTER 13

MONEY MATTERS

The title of this chapter is deliberately ambiguous. It deals with *matters* that require finance, but it also emphasizes that *money* matters – that it is indeed essential for the fulfilling of the Trust's vision. It also highlights that *how* it is given and used should always be seen within the context of it being God's work and therefore handled with transparency and integrity.

RECEIVING MONEY

From the inception of the Trust, God has been faithful in supplying the finance to do the task. Much of the gift income initially came from friends, family and fellowships connected to staff members and often arrived with notes of encouragement and assurance of prayers. In the early days a substantial gift was received from a young man who had been left a legacy, but did not at that time feel in need of it. At the other end of the spectrum, though nonetheless sacrificially given, have been the regular gifts – often one pound sent in each month by senior citizens from those who had committed themselves to giving through Bethany's Partnership Scheme. Correspondence with partners was built up over the years. Many of them were spread throughout the country or even abroad. Although never met personally, they came to be regarded as friends through their letters.

The Trust has reason to be very, very grateful for the amount of money which has come through central and local Government. (Recognition that Bethany was doing work that would help to achieve what they wanted done). Initially this help came through rent money, and more recently through 'Supporting People'. Currently approximately half of all income comes from this source and has enabled the Trust to increase its staffing which, in turn, has meant an increase in the number of people helped.

Sometimes in spite of disappointments at how circumstances turned out, new friends have been made. One such instance was in regard to our desire to purchase the Monastery at Liberton. This did not materialize, but the Sisters of the Poor Clares, whose home it had been, became regular prayer supporters and periodically sent financial gifts and words of encouragement.

There were even occasions when saving or receiving money was not the right thing for Bethany to do, even though it was offered with the best of intentions. One of these involved a famous Edinburgh hotel which offered to host a sponsored event, the main feature of which was to auction off drink supplied by the breweries. The gentleman who approached us found it hard to understand why we couldn't accept. We did try to refuse graciously and not give offence, and no doubt another charity benefited from their generosity.

Breweries also featured when Ewan Foreman was offered a large consignment of umbrellas to sell in the Bethany Shops. Unfortunately they had the name of a famous brewery boldly emblazoned across them. On another occasion, a joinery firm who had supplied materials for a major roofing job and wished to be supportive of Bethany's work, offered to make out their invoice and exclude VAT. This would have been perfectly in order if *they* had actually done the job themselves, as in such cases the government allowed contractors to zero-rate planning consent work done on listed buildings. The snag was *Bethany* was doing the actual work. Again, the kind offer was refused. God honoured this witness and the next week a gift was received which matched exactly the sum which would have saved if the VAT offer had been accepted. God was thanked for His faithfulness, and the good news shared with the joinery firm!

E.E.R.A. Appeal

In 1992 there was one project, headed up by Ewan Foreman, where neither the Trust, nor people using their services were to receive any financial benefit at all. It was a one-off and heralded a great success. The Scriptures highlight a spiritual principle about giving. However much there is a personal need, if the needs of others are also remembered, God prospers the givers. In this case it was concern about the plight of refugees in the former Yugoslavia. It was estimated that between 100,000 and 400,000 people could die during the winter. There were between two and two and a half million people displaced, with about half of all refugees being children and nearly three-quarters female. We wanted to do something. After an intensive period of fact-finding in order to provide necessary reassurances, the 'Edinburgh European Refugee Appeal' was formed.

Over a two-week period in November, over £19,000 was raised. Some of this was turned into food, some used for transportation as each black bag of goods cost £1 to send. Over and above this, two 40ft-trailers were filled with over 1,500 boxes of medical supplies, toiletries, bedding, children's equipment and clothing, and the greatest specified need – underwear.

The support received from individuals, churches, schools, companies and other organizations was overwhelming. Teams of volunteers undertook the painstaking job of sorting, packing, and labelling goods in a disused warehouse in Couper Street. In January 1993, the massive trucks left Edinburgh and the drivers were committed to God's safe keeping for the long, hazardous journey.

For a while there was no word of the trucks and then a message to say they still had not arrived. There was a very emotional response and cheers and hallelujahs when eventually a fax came through to the office from the Resource Centre in Croatia telling us 'We see the trucks coming now!'

The centre was run by Dr. Branko Lovrec, who had given up his medical practice to concentrate on Christian communication both in print and practical relief work. It was a well established relief agency and Christian publishing house supported by TEAR Fund, Samaritan International, the Slavic Gospel Mission, and accredited by the Government of Croatia. They were to distribute the aid on our behalf, and, in thanking us, they wrote 'we will be using the money for buying food as we are distributing parcels daily to new refugees from Bosnia.... We gave gifts with books to a children's hospital, to Institute for Handicapped Children, to Institute for Retarded Children, who have appreciated much our gifts. We thank God and you for your gifts of help.'

SAVING MONEY

But saving money as well as giving it, was important. Maybe because we knew of the circumstances of many supporters – and because in a very real sense they had seen their giving as 'to the Lord,' – not wasting money and looking for ways of saving it was always on the agenda. We tried to impart this attitude to residents, sharing with them the kindness of others in their giving and how it hurt when, at best through carelessness or at worst through wanton destruction, property and equipment were damaged. Staff were encouraged to switch off unnecessary lights, make do and mend if possible and never, never, ever use a new envelope to send a note to the director through internal mail when a second-hand one would do! Amazing to think that the prayerful deliberations of Alan and Gordon about the way forward for the Trust (mentioned in chapter 2) were worked out initially on the back of an envelope and that, of course, a second-hand one!

Over the years many companies have made Bethany the focus of a special appeal or committed themselves to ongoing help. For years Marks & Spencer donated food that was coming to the end of its shelf life; Fareshare consistently delivered food; Standard Life sponsored the publishing of an annual report; and our lawyers, Balfour & Manson, paid for stationery costs over several years. Such generous sponsorship is still continuing. In the current year, 2007, the annual report has been designed, produced and sponsored by Teviot, with photographs by David Mcintyre. All such generous support has saved the Trust much money.

One initiative in the late 80s which did this, but which stretched the ingenuity of the staff, was the Government's desire to decrease the EEC food mountains. Bethany, along with other charitable organizations, became the recipient of an amazing amount of long-life milk, cheese and butter. That was the good news – the slightly more complicated news was that the Salvation Army also received several hundredweight of meat which was frozen solid and needed to be cooked professionally, otherwise the outside would have rotted by the time the inside had defrosted! One of the Edinburgh colleges took this on as a project and made it into steak pies – hundreds and hundreds of them! Alan collected Bethany's share, being all but buried by them, and when our own freezers were filled, filled those of everyone else who was willing to store them for us! All this was accompanied by an endless supply of tins of minced beef and stew. There are only so many things one can do with mince and stew but staff were to be congratulated that, even if they didn't manage one hundred and one different ways, they deserved full marks for trying.

RAISING MONEY

When it comes to raising money, rather than just saving it, it seems that staff and supporters have indeed devised one hundred and one ways.

Some have been straightforward financial giving, often on a regular basis from individuals or sometimes the result of a church offering on a special occasion, such as the £800 received from one church at harvest-time. Many have used the cardboard flatpack 'bed' which makes up into an attractive collecting box. Such gifts enable Bethany to pay the many expenses that are incurred in the day-to-day running of the Trust. Very few services have their costs covered completely and some services like the Winter Care Shelter, Bethany Homemaker, drop-ins and Passing the Baton, receive no statutory funding at all. Bethany struggles to fund many of its services, and gifts from individuals, in the form of one-off gifts, standing orders and legacies continue to play a huge role in Bethany's ability to provide life-changing services.

Some ways of fundraising have been just hard plodding. Anne Berry, Fiona Weir, Andy Davis and, later, members of the dedicated Fundraising department, have spent hours searching through the Charities Book, identifying which category of trust might be willing to benefit Bethany and then applying for a grant. The fundraising team usually focus on specific campaigns such as seeking support for Homemaker or the Care Shelter Project. One obvious aim is to ask for financial assistance, but they also seek and receive support from many people through volunteering, prayer and furniture donations. Although the team does not work directly with those who use the Trust's services, they are constantly amazed and heartened at the stories of how so many people have made the journey from a chaotic and hopeless existence to a far more structured life with hope for the future. As Chris McNeil, fundraiser, says, 'Now that I work here, I understand much better how vital and urgent the need for the work undertaken by Bethany is, and I realize how important it is for this to continue and expand. Seeking funds can be challenging, but particularly satisfying when the results are positive.'

Several trusts have been consistently generous, giving a grant year on year and even at times adding to this. This was the case in 2007 when £100,000 was urgently needed. The matter became an earnest prayer request and God's faithfulness was seen in a trust which had already generously supported the work giving an 'unexpected' extra gift of £100,000.

In the early 1990s the representative of one such trust was to be in Edinburgh on business. He wished to visit the Centre prior to his organization making a decision regarding funding for Bethany. The date was duly recorded in Alan's diary, but unfortunately he double-booked and went off to a meeting in Glasgow, blissfully unaware of the situation! The representative arrived in the late afternoon, and the director's nineteen-year-old daughter, Elizabeth, took charge. She explained, without telling any falsehoods, that her father had had to go to Glasgow but she would show him round and hopefully be able to answer any questions he might have. He was given a grand tour and didn't even blink an eye when a very enthusiastic resident, who had just become a Christian was introduced to him in the corridor and immediately asked him if he 'was born again'. Elizabeth felt that the visit had gone well and jokingly said he would probably be well impressed with her fund of knowledge and charming manner. There were smiles all round when a letter came authorizing the grant and using Elizabeth's very words to congratulate our charming and knowledgeable daughter!

Some ways of raising money really caught the imagination. Such was the 'Coppers Count Appeal'. It started in 1994 with supporter Jack Sutherland saving one and two-pence pieces in a jar. Jack, like many later collectors, was also known to put in the odd silver! What a simple but effective way of fund-raising. Soon labels were available to stick on jam jars, and groups and many individuals started collecting. Davidson's Mains Sunday School was one of the first to participate. They had a large jar for donations beside the coffee table in church each Sunday. One primary school drew a line along a corridor to show their 'copper' progress and eventually support became so widespread that the Six o'clock News might well have had a special investigator on the case of the nationwide disappearance of copper coins!

Donald Macmillan in the finance department spent many hours counting it all. In the midst of a busy day taken up with his bookkeeping duties, he was particularly grateful when people sent in a cheque for the value of the money rather than the copper itself! This was never more so than when on his visit to the Centre in 1999, Sir Tom Farmer gave a generous donation of £10,000 to the copper appeal. But copper was not only 'counted', coppers 'counted' in themselves. Every metre of mixed coppers when laid in a line was worth approximately 62p; and every mile worth £1,000. It was possible in the early 1990s to buy a flat in Leith for around £25,000. The rent raised from a supported flat was not sufficient to pay the mortgage on this figure, but if £10,000 was put towards it then it lowered the amount which had to be borrowed and made it self-supporting. By the summer of 1999 the first 'copper flat,' which was located in Leith, had been fully renovated and was occupied.

Other fund-raisers used their talents and time. Carol-singing was a favourite means of raising money. One children's group had a garage sale, whilst another sold their baking at school break-times and staff compiled a cookery book. In his fourth year at secondary school, our son, Stephen, along with other pupils and staff, organized a snooker tournament. Rugby, football and athletics personalities joined with representatives from local companies and Bethany Christian Centre in a successful fund-raising event.

Others such as the Baroque Brass Quintet from St Petersburg, Rod & Marco, Ian White, the artist MOIR, Terry Clark, Bob McQueen and a wonderful group of singers and musicians, and Philip Hacking gave the proceeds of their concerts, exhibitions or recitals. 'Crafty' supporters made greeting cards and knitted toys which, along with homebaking and jam, were always in demand at the Christmas markets. (Incidentally, Audrey Macmillan's apple pies took some beating and Andy Davis's grandmother, Mrs Biddlecombe, has continued to send a box of her beautiful knitted toys year after year, even though Andy left the Trust some time ago.)

Some fundraising events required a great deal of stamina and not a little courage. One supporter, who had previously lived in Leith, left after an Open Day to walk all the way to Leicester, his new home, in support of the newly acquired Bethany House. Some risked the safety of life and limb by running marathons, and a group of staff and residents parachuted out of planes. Residents who had stayed at Bethany Home Farm paddled canoes for eight to ten miles down the Union Canal from Broxburn to Linlithgow.

WALKS

Groups of walkers trekked along the Southern Upland Way. A trio of two sisters and a brother walked seventy miles along the Dorset coast strapped together at the ankles. It was a case of when one fell, they all fell. At one point they inadvertently strayed on to Army land and were taken by Army Landrover down to the bottom of the hill they had just climbed!

In 1991 Alan and Stephen Berry, plus Perro, Gordon Weir and Joe Kirkhouse (an experienced Munro Bagger), attempted a sponsored climb of the 3619ft Beinn Ghlas and 3983ft Ben Lawers, but the venture had to be abandoned because of gales and torrential rain. However, their second attempt was successful and completed in record time.

And reaching for the heights is still continuing. In July 2007 the 'ageing and increasingly decrepit Supported Housing manager' (the team's words not mine!) and three valiant compatriots crawled up Ben Nevis and raised over £400 for the Trust.

Sponsored sleep-outs have been a valuable way of raising money. Although not giving a real idea of what it is like to be homeless, because after a cold and uncomfortable night most participants can go home for a hot shower, they do raise awareness of the problem and make participants grateful for the safety and security of home. Venues have varied from outside St Mary's Cathedral, York Place, St Margaret's Church, Dunfermline, and latterly Edinburgh City Chambers.

Sponsored walks have had the added benefit of giving the opportunity to see beautiful scenery, get healthy exercise, renew old friendships and make new ones. Locations have included Glen Tilt in Perthshire, the Loch Ard Forest, near Aberfoyle, the Water of Leith walkway, the Pentland Hills, Ben Lomond, Cramond, the coastal path from Yellowcraigs to North Berwick, and Loch Katrine. This latter walk had the added attraction of a 'shoogly' ride from Stronachlacher back to Aberfoyle on the 'Trossachs Trundler' bus. Perhaps the most spectacular walk was the twenty miles from Pitlochry round Loch Faskally, via Killiecrankie. Both on this walk and the Loch Katrine one, it was possible to do a circular route, on which one could greet people coming in the opposite direction, encourage them about the easy bits ahead and console them over those that were just a hard slog. Loch Faskally was a favourite, and some of the folks from Cupar Baptist with caravans in Pitlochry joined the walkers. They loved this part of the country so much that when other venues were announced, they just did their own 'Loch Faskally walk' and sent in the money. September 2007 saw a large number of supporters, who among them raised over £17,000 by walking the coastal path from Elie through St Monans to Pittenweem, the glorious weather enhancing the beauty of Fife's East Neuk.

CEILIDHS

Some fundraising events were great fun – though a lot of hard work behind the scenes. Catering preparation for the first ceilidh took a group of us many hours in the kitchen of Bristo Baptist Church, but the end result was worth it. Those held in the splendid surroundings of the Ballroom in the Assembly Rooms in George Street, Edinburgh (with its magnificent chandeliers), were thronged with people.

It was wonderful to see so many supporters, staff and residents coming together to enjoy themselves. Some of the overseas volunteers had never previously seen, or at least never attempted the dances, but their energy and enthusiasm made up for the fact that most of the time they had no idea what they were doing! On several occasions Iris O'Neil organized the bountiful supper, with her whole family being 'volunteered' to help.

The proceeds of one Christmas ceilidh were destined for the new Bethany House project. Joyce Watson and Gordon Weir were vocalists, there was a piper, and Gillian Porter performed Highland dancing. Later when Andrew Purves joined the staff we had the benefit of another medal-winning Highland dancer. We were blessed with staff and residents who were incredibly talented musically. The Dry House Band were amazing and tireless in their energy. Ceildihs were also held in Linlithgow Academy and, courtesy of Andrew Purves being an 'old boy,' also in George Heriot's School.

CYPRUS

In the millennium year great preparations began for Bethany's biggest fundraising challenge – a trek through parts of the Holy Land to the town of Bethany itself. Planning meetings were under way with Classic Tours who, in conjunction with Bethany's Adrian Currie, were organizing the trip.

Unfortunately, because of the increasingly volatile situation in the region, Classic Tours did not feel that the trek should take place in the original location. Somewhere with a biblical connection was still preferred, and so Adrian undertook to head up an expedition to Cyprus, with the base being in Paphos, where tradition has it Paul was tied up and beaten for his faith.

Whilst wondering if we were going to be fit enough to complete the trek, Alan and I had other preoccupations. Our first grandchild was due to be born on 23rd October, but by the beginning of November still had not arrived – and we were leaving on the 10th. However, on 6th November, Oliver Gillies finally made his appearance and, at the risk of boring all the rest of the party and never enquiring whether they really wanted to see it, his photograph was duly carried around Cyprus and shown at every possible opportunity!

There were eleven in the group and most lived within easy distance of each other, and therefore had the opportunity of meeting beforehand. Lin Ball, however, from Milton Keynes, had seen the advert for the trek and wanted to be involved. Lin was to celebrate her fiftieth birthday and felt that, while undoubtedly receiving from others on that occasion, she herself would like to contribute to a worthwhile cause and chose to support the Trust.

It was quite a thought for her to meet ten unknown people at Glasgow Airport. She recalls her first impressions. 'I mentally used the phrase 'motley crew' as I looked around the sleepy group meeting up at the check-in-desk. Little did I guess that this group of highly assorted individuals would become so precious to me in the coming week – like a very special sort of family. We were six women and five men, ranging from the 30s to 60-plus, and we soon found we had all sorts of interesting connections as well as fascinating differences.'

Adrian had done an amazing amount of work in planning the daily itinerary. The weather was much hotter than expected and, quoting Lin again, 'the terrain for trekking was more varied and perhaps more difficult than expected, though it's amazing what you can do with the encouragement of good companions. Routes included the coastal area of the south and west of the island but also we were trekking steep slopes, narrow gorges, sandy clifftops and muddy tracks. The day we had been expecting to be the most physically demanding in the Troodos mountains turned out to be perhaps the easiest, as the tracks were well marked and softened by layers of pine needles.

On the Sunday we visited Nicosia, where as guests of Iain and Karen Gordon, who were working with Sat7 in Cyprus, we worshipped with the New Life International Church, ate a wonderful lunch and saw for ourselves the Green Line which splits this last divided European capital between Greek and Turkish. Adrian confided in Alan that he thought Iain would make an ideal director of the Trust when Alan retired. Little did he know that Iain was already seriously considering such a possibility and they were to meet again soon afterwards, this time when Iain was appointed chief executive of Bethany!

Lin continues 'On the day before we left Cyprus we spent several hours walking to and around two World Heritage Sites in Paphos, marvelling at the amazing mosaics there and also visiting the Pillars of Paul.

Five or six years before, the youngest member of the group, Ali had been involved in an horrific accident on a RAF mountain rescue course. He needed brain surgery, was in a coma for five days and his damaged left leg had to be amputated at the knee. Ali and his girlfriend Tricia became Christians at an Alpha course in 2000 and were married later that year. By the end of day three of the trek, Ali's stump in his artificial limb was suffering heat rash and the skin began to break up, making every step painful. But he completed the whole course with tremendous courage. He never complained once, but talked most of his newfound faith in Jesus. Lin ended her report, 'As you might imagine, no-one complained about their blisters. Others too shared their faith. I'm so glad I celebrated my special year getting to know Bethany. The trek is likely to remain a highlight of my entire life.'

Since then there have been another two treks, one in 2002 to Greece and another ambitious and physically challenging one undertaken jointly with Edinburgh Medical Missionary Society to the Sinai Desert, when a visit to Sat7's Cairo studio was included in the itinerary.

CARING CHRISTMAS TREES

In February 2006 another fund-raising project, Caring Christmas Trees, was pronounced a '*Tree*mendous success'. It began in the summer of 2005 when IT manager, Rhoda, had an idea. She was involved as a volunteer in IT database package selection and did an evaluation of furniture collection and distribution for the Bethany shops. She acknowledged that at that time she didn't really have a heart for homeless people, but compassion began to grow in her for what Bethany was doing as her understanding of its mission increased.

Previously, Bethany had appreciated people paying for trees at Bethany Home Farm, but this project was on a whole new scale. The idea of selling Christmas trees for profit came from another source, and Rhoda envisaged a super-sized version that would work for Bethany. She did a feasibility study, and the detail of what would be involved was daunting.

Highly dubious that it could be achieved, let alone make any money from it, the idea floated about for a while. But she persisted, telling Emma Galloway, 'Let's sell trees to raise funds for the Care Shelter'. Funding the Care Shelter had been an issue for as long as it had existed. However, with the expansion of the service in the winter of 2004, the burden weighed heavy (£28,000 in debt-heavy!).

Soon Emma Galloway was on board and she and Rhoda prayed together trusting that this was God's work and He would help them to pull it off. They sat down and listed things that would be needed to make it work, including a free website, sponsorship to pay for promotion, one hundred volunteers, and 2,000 customers. Logistics were difficult but a grower was found who was prepared to be flexible, and so trees could be ordered the week before the pick-up dates. They asked that 2,000 trees would be sold by 30th November and reached that target by 29th. From September to December every target on the list was smashed by God's amazing power. His blessing exceeded every expectation.

Every venue which was approached was willing to allow the use of their site, which was a great relief. Another big ask had been for volunteers. The group was concerned they wouldn't manage the one hundred needed. However, over 230 volunteers, including Scouts, Boys Brigade and Guides, willingly stood in the cold. As one commented. 'I thoroughly enjoyed myself. It was four hours of really good atmosphere between volunteers and customers.'

Local IT designers Whitespace contributed a fabulous design and website. Local housebuilders Applecross gave sponsorship so that money did not have to be spent on promotions; and companies, MPs, MSPs, radio stations, newspapers and magazines all helped to promote the appeal. In the end 3,078 trees were sold, raising £40,000, which was just under half the cost of running the Shelter. For the cost of just one Caring Christmas Tree, the Care Shelter provided a homeless person with a bed for the night.

When 2006 arrived it happened all over again, and this time it included locations in Fife, with the work there also benefiting.

From their comments, customers seemed satisfied too. One said 'having signed up for a tree with trepidation, when we obtained one it was by far the best specimen ever. The needles didn't even think of falling off'.

Strategic planning for Caring Christmas Trees 2007 saw development officer Katerina Hatziioannou-Faulds acquiring a new site in Musselburgh. Her appointment allowed Emma Galloway to concentrate on developing the franchise part of the project. It had been hoped that it would be operational in Glasgow in 2007, but that was not possible. However, we as a 'Berry' family, who always feel seasonal at Christmas time, were even more so last December, as the car park adjoining our house in Dunfermline was a designated collection site.

The organizers of Caring Christmas Trees feel it has been a great privilege to be involved with so many people giving of their time to support homeless people in the city through the Shelter. God has really blessed the project and, just to top it all, it won the Institute of Fundraising Scotland Community Fundraising Award 2006 for the huge success and impact the campaign had on the community. The project will be made available for other organizations to operate on a franchise basis across the UK. Charities from three cities are currently discussing the prospect of operating a Caring Christmas Trees campaign in their communities for Christmas 2008. Orders will be handled centrally by Bethany, and trees delivered locally by franchise partners.

It is good when hard work and dedication are recognized, and in November 2007 Catherine Rawlinson-Watkins, known as 'Cat', who heads up Bethany's Fundraising team, received a coveted award and was proclaimed 'Fundraiser of the Year' for Scotland.

If at the beginning of the Bethany story the trustees had known where the journey would take them, it would probably have seemed too daunting to undertake and the

Catherine Rawlinson-Watkins

responsibility, too heavy. But in the wisdom and goodness of God, He has revealed His plan one step at a time, and through many individuals, organizations, churches and companies has provided what has been necessary to carry out the vision He gave.

Chapter 14

Special Days

Last year our grandson, Oliver, started school. During the year each child in the class had their own 'special day'. The other children were encouraged to think of and then say positive things that made the child 'special'. At the end of the day the child was presented with a certificate which incorporated all the positive comments. It was a way of building the child's confidence and self-esteem, and encouraging the children to think of others. The class thought Oliver was 'very polite and friendly, had lovely brown eyes and was a good boy'. It certainly seemed to work for him because he said the best part of the day was when the class said nice things about him!

For many of the residents who come to the doors of Bethany, it is a long time since they have had a special day or had positive statements made about them. Not only were some of them poor in material terms but for many there was a poverty of good memories or a sense of being valued or loved. Birthdays were an opportunity when at least an effort could be made on their behalf.

In the early days at the Centre we weren't expert in making fancy cakes but it was amazing what could be done with a big packet of sponge mix. Perhaps we were a little ambitious but we tried to make cakes that would appeal to each particular resident. Hence football cakes and one covered with green icing representing a pool table, with coloured marzipan balls, duly appeared and were appreciated and shared.

Later Hilary Wylie lovingly created a celebration cake to mark the birthday of everyone in Supported Housing. This very practical expression of kindness was much appreciated, though as the number of tenants increased it definitely became a labour of love.

But cakes weren't just for residents. The birthdays of members of the Care Van steering committee were not forgotten. Their meetings were brightened by the presentation of a 'Rita Sutherland special'. Rita put a lot of thought and care into each one, and on one occasion in honour of our wonderful egg-laying hens at Broxburn, Alan received a cake decorated with mini eggs extolling his virtues as 'egg-sellent', an 'eggsample' and even 'eggsentric'!' Rita also helped make some of the Bethany anniversary celebrations special with lovely cakes, including one decorated with the original Bethany motif of two hands outstretched to one another. This motif could be understood in a variety of ways – God's hand reaching out to mankind, the hand of staff outstretched to help service users, the hand of those outwith the Trust who wished to offer their support, or even co-operation between Bethany and agencies with whom they networked.

But birthdays can be stressful too. I remember one resident spending his 21st birthday in a drunken stupor, and then later on sitting with him all night as he battled with the agonies and tremors of withdrawal.

And what about Christmas, the time when we celebrate Jesus' birthday, and specially think of God's wonderful Gift, Jesus, whose whole purpose in coming was to die and rise again to save us from our sins and to show us how to live God's way?

Christmas can also be a time when feelings of loneliness and anxiety are heightened. If ties with family have been broken, it can simply reinforce a sense of loss and failure, and be a season of great sadness. When we lived in the flat beside the Centre, we became aware of the reality of this. One Christmas Eve Alan and I sat in the large lounge at the Centre watching the midnight service on TV and comforting a very drunk John Rodgers, who told us 'we were his best friends'. Another resident had been anxiously waiting and watching for the post each morning in the couple of weeks before Christmas. By Christmas morning nothing had arrived for him and, although he was delighted with the cards and gifts from staff and the churches who had kindly remembered each resident, there was no word from his family, and both his heart and ours were sore.

In the early days when the Centre represented all Bethany's work, we tried to recreate a family feeling at Christmas time. A traditional meal with all the trimmings was prepared, gifts were given and games were organized for anyone wanting to participate though, as we realized to our cost, a game of 'twister' is not to be recommended when you're full of turkey! One of the residents had a little boy whose birthday was on Christmas Day, and he came to join us, which added to the fun.

And one particular Christmas Day we had two surprise guests for dinner. As we were pulling out all the stops catering-wise and had the dining room brightly decorated, we asked the residents if they too would consider making a special effort by getting dressed up. Imagine our surprise and delight when Tony and Eddie made a grand entrance completely kitted out in dinner jackets and bow ties which they had hired for the occasion!

New Year could be even more problematic. Looking back can be a daunting task and some residents stayed in their rooms not wanting to talk. However, some did come to appreciate that it could be a positive time and began to see that it was possible to have a great time without drink and, even better, remember that they'd had a good time! The New Year ceildihs in South Leith Baptist and other churches became a feature of Hogmanay. The food, fun and fellowship were greatly appreciated, especially by those residents who had become Christians and were pleased to begin the New Year in God's House in a caring, safe environment.

Other days throughout the year were made special by the opportunity to have fun together and create happy memories. Doing so is an important part of the work and helps redress some of the sadness that may have been experienced. One such occasion involved a Barbecue at South Queensferry, when one of the residents, a Senior Citizen, sat in an old chair on the beach and watched the fun. He was eventually evicted as the chair itself was thrown on to the bonfire. Everyone had to move about a hundred yards down the beach as the pall of acrid smoke graphically demonstrated why such furniture had to comply with fire regulations!

There were other special times at the seaside, when residents who had made a commitment to the Lord, were baptized. With the pollution level in the Forth, candidates might well have felt a little like Naaman when asked to bathe in the Jordan rather than Abana and Pharpar, but these events were a real witness to people who were out for a Sunday afternoon stroll in the summer sunshine at Silverknowes or Cramond. However, those organizing the services had to be mindful of the tide, otherwise a very long praise time might ensue while the water reached the required depth!

The sea featured significantly in a short break when Marion Gemmell and Andrew Gillies took a few residents to the Isle of Colonsay where the Baptist Church manse was made available to them. Marion and husband Bob were no strangers to the island, as they regularly holidayed there. This holiday was nearly longer than anticipated. One of the group would not be hurried, and sailing timetables were of no consequence to her. Eventually they did make it to the boat in time for the return sailing, but by then the whole of the island would have been aware that there had been a Bethany invasion!

Blairvaich cottage in the Loch Ard forest, which at the time belonged to the Scripture Union, was a favourite haunt of Alan's. Sometimes he took a party of two or three residents to work on the outhouses there. Besides helping to keep the place maintained, it gave the men the opportunity of working in a beautiful environment and feeling they were helping someone else.

And Blairvaich featured in recent conversations when Barbara Neale, who had worked at the Centre in the early 1990s, was visiting us while on home leave from Cambodia. We reminisced about our visit to the cottage with a very assorted group of residents; of treating them all to coffee and cakes in a very posh hotel in the Trossachs to get out of incessant rain; of the almost impossibility of trying to play 'Pictionary' and draw objects in a room with dim Calor gas lights; and being warmed by a fire that created dancing shadows. Happy memories!

Donations given especially for recreational purposes helped to make it possible for staff and residents to share fun together, learn more about one another in an informal way and thus strengthen relationships. One trust donated money for group outings, but also encouraged individual residents to take up their own sports and subsidized these activities. Such money also helped with the purchase of games equipment and a video recorder.

A gift which made an immense difference to recreation in the early days was Abbeyhill Baptist Church's old minibus. In 1990 it took residents to Hawick, Ben Lomond, Ben Nevis, Nottingham and the National Trust's Hermitage property at Dunkeld, as well as other local trips.

Such times away became a regular feature of Bethany life. Whithaugh Park Christian retreat centre, in the Scottish Borders, was a favourite where residents were able to participate in swimming, canoeing, hill walking, fishing and mountain biking.

Supported tenants visited the New Lanark World Heritage Centre, while ten people involved in the Training section's activities, went to Dundee to enjoy ten-pin bowling and Laserquest. Sometimes theatre tickets were donated and plays and pantomimes were enjoyed. This was the case in January 2000 when seventeen from Bethany House went to see 'Cinderella'. Volunteer Laura Frost said 'we put on our glad rags and armed with "Oh, yes you Did's" and "Oh no you Didn'ts" went off to the Kings Theatre'. As one resident said, 'It was all very enjoyable, colourful and made me feel like a kid again'.

Possibly one of the funniest plays I have ever seen, and which cost nothing except probably a lot of grey hairs on the part of the producer, was that directed by Rev Ian Paterson in Bethany Hall one Christmas. Certain residents and staff displayed previously hidden and amazing talents. Although many of the 'in-house' jokes would have been lost on an outside audience, the Bethany crowd who gathered greatly appreciated the clever and witty humour and seeing staff as they'd never been seen before. Again a special day for all concerned.

Over the summer of 2000, two very different locations gave Bethany residents the opportunity to use their practical skills to benefit others.

On 6th June, eight people, including Rev Ian Paterson, set off to France on a joint Bethany and South Leith Baptist Church enterprise. They went to help renovate a building which was used for Christian summer camps. Work consisted of painting, floor tiling, installing showers and ground maintenance.

They were only back two weeks, when the Bethany group were off to Skye, this time to clear out a large house. Both ventures were a lot of hard work but they also received much through the fellowship shared, mutual encouragement and the sense of God's presence in everything in which they were involved.

A group of nine residents and three staff, and sufficient supplies to equip and feed an army, were back over to Skye for a holiday the next year. In 2004 residents from Bethany Christian Centre helped fund their own holiday at Arbroath Windmill Christian Centre by organizing a Car Wash day, which made £160. Such different environments helped to enrich experience.

One very different environment was the Palace of Holyrood-house, where on 3rd July 2001 Alan Berry was invited to receive an MBE from the Queen 'for services to Bethany Christian Trust and the homeless of Edinburgh'. If Alan had been in danger of being 'puffed up' because of this honour, the initial incredulity of certain family members, would have been enough to deflate him! Alan had received notice that he had been nominated and had to write confirming his acceptance, but was sworn to secrecy until the Honours List was published at New Year. To be perfectly honest, when he first received notification, he couldn't believe it either. But he felt it was an honour he was receiving on behalf of everyone involved in the Trust and recognition of their commitment to fulfil Bethany's vision.

Investiture day was beautifully sunny. Alan wore his new 'palace suit'. I wore my new outfit; Elizabeth and Stephen were there to share in the occasion; Alan followed all the correct protocol. The Queen, as always, had done her homework and asked intelligent questions, but what Bethany people really wanted to know afterwards was whether Alan had managed to explain 'Seven levels of Care' to Her Majesty in the short time allotted!

Another important milestone was reached at the end of that year. Iain Gordon was appointed as Alan's successor and took up post in early April 2002. Iain originally hails from Aberdeen, studied Engineering at Glasgow University and had experience in research and business management in the oil and gas industry before he and wife Karen joined the Baptist Missionary Society World Mission in 1992. Through them he was seconded to the United Mission for Nepal to provide services for the Nepali Government. He sought to focus on promoting a successful mix of profitability and social responsibility. During his seven years there, Iain had responsibility for business planning and development, and staff training. He had the opportunity to present the Hydroconsult Company's achievements and vision to domestic and foreign commercial, diplomatic and political audiences.

Alan and Iain

Still under the auspices of B.M.S. World Mission, the Gordon family moved in 2000 to Cyprus where Iain was seconded to SAT-7, a Christian satellite television broadcaster transmitting programmes in Arabic for the Christians of the Middle East and North Africa. There he was chief operations officer in Nicosia and acting personnel director. Iain saw it as part of God's plan to be in Cyprus for a time, but also that everything he had been through and the work and experience he had had, was God making him ready for heading up the work of the Trust.

On 27th April Alan handed over to Iain in a special Bethany celebration day held in Charlotte Baptist Chapel. Iain said his

overwhelming feeling to be working at Bethany was one of excite-
ment. When talking to Bethany staff and supporters he sensed
a real note of pride in the growth and development that the Lord
had brought about and of which they had been a part over the
years.

There was an infectious enthusiasm for a shared vision of
moving the work forward in scale, quality and diversity as they
sought to practically demonstrate the love and compassion of
Christ for those pushed out to the margins of society.

Alan was grateful for the privilege he had had of seeing the
work come into being and grow, and for all the enriching experiences that it had brought. He was grateful too for the vision, enthusiasm and gifts of the new chief executive and all God had for
Bethany in the future.

Thinking of Iain's remark about everything that the Lord had
'brought him through', we remembered the particularly difficult
time when Iain became critically ill in Nepal, had to be airlifted to
hospital in Singapore, and family and doctors feared for his life.
Many people around the world, including Bethany staff, prayed
for Iain and God granted a miracle. We were very grateful at the
time that he made a full recovery, but on the special day of his
appointment to Bethany, were again glad that in God's purposes
he had been spared to direct the future work of the Trust.

Whilst in the midst of writing this, the 2007 Bethany annual report was delivered, the theme of which was Relationships,
'which are at the very heart of homelessness'. The report told
how 'throughout the past year Bethany had been building their
own relationships by focusing on the developing of supportive
relationships across all areas; between project staff and those using the services, between supporters and projects, among staff
colleagues and with project partners. Every person and the relationship with them was greatly valued.'

Just as God's mercies and His faithfulness brighten every new
morning, so whether or not there are outings, ceildihs, birthday
cakes, holidays, or just the usual routine, relationships with others
and with Him can and do make each and every day special.

CHAPTER 15

MAKING IT KNOWN

Making known the work of the Trust has been an important aspect in the realization of Bethany's vision. Those who could benefit from Bethany's services, needed to be aware of what was on offer. Those who had found help were in a good position to try to encourage others to use the services. And those who supported the work by their prayers, gifts and interest needed information to make their prayers and giving relevant and effective, and their interest – and in many cases their faith – encouraged, stimulated and challenged.

HEARING ABOUT THE WORK

From the very beginning there were annual open days or celebrations giving opportunity to hear an update of the work and sometimes the opportunity to inspect newly acquired or refurbished premises.

Many churches have been willing to have a speaker from Bethany share about the work. The last Sunday in January was often chosen as this is designated 'Homelessness Sunday', which brings together thousands of churches across the UK to draw attention to the devastating effects of homelessness. There is plenty of prepared material for all ages to participate in an 'interactive' service, such as the prayer printed on a small publicity card which read 'God of justice, Have mercy on those who sleep on the streets or in hostels, on the floor or on a sofa, in storerooms or offices, and those who know their friends' hospitality is at breaking point. Help us to build a fairer society, where having no home does not exclude anyone from work and health and respect. Help us to build a society where all may 'dwell in safety'. In the name of the homeless Saviour Jesus, Amen.

Many women's guilds, men's guilds and Christian coffee clubs have given Bethany an 'annual slot' in their syllabus, and this has been appreciated and encouraging.

When Alan was speaking at such meetings, he took a supply of crafts and cards along. Some had been made in Bethany's craft workshop while others, like Kate's famous butterfly cards, were produced by supporters. Publicity boards displayed photos and statistics relevant to each of the Levels of Care, and often past or present residents have been willing to accompany a speaker and give a word of testimony.

Darren's testimony

One such was Darren who always started his talk 'I have been in Bethany for so many years, months, weeks and days and hours, (giving the exact number) and now have a home, a hope and a future.' He came to Bethany on his seventeenth birthday be-cause he had nowhere to live. After spend-ing time in the Centre he moved to shared  and then single, long-term supported accommodation. He worked for a time in the Homemaker café and now many years later is still attending the same Baptist church, is employed in a caring profes-sion and has a lovely Brazilian wife.

In 1989 groups visited my home church in Nottingham, as well as taking meetings in Larkhall, Livingston, Cowdenbeath, Hay Drive Mission and Tor Christian Nursing Home. On one particular visit to an Edinburgh church, Alan was speaking to the children. He was illustrating the fact that many of the people who came to Bethany felt as if they had fallen into a pit out of which they couldn't climb. He asked them if they were in that position what would be the thing they wanted most. The answer he was looking for was 'a ladder,' because that led on to Bethany's 'seven levels of care', but the children were far more technologically ad-vanced than Alan, and the reply was 'a mobile phone'!!

On occasions our cross-collie dog, Perro, also accompanied Alan to meetings. She behaved beautifully and was often used as an 'object lesson' for a children's talk. Perhaps her finest hour was in Hamilton Baptist Church. Alan was to take the Sunday service but had arranged beforehand that the church secretary would welcome everyone and announce the first hymn, where-upon Alan, dressed as a homeless person who looked as if he had slept on the streets the night before, would enter the church with Perro. No-one else was aware of the plan. Alan announced his ar-rival by walking down the aisle and telling Perro in a loud voice that they would be 'alright for help in here because the place is full of Christians'. The 'drama' had the desired effect – the con-gregation was momentarily stunned until they realized this was the preacher in disguise, but it had proved a very effective way of 'making the work known'.

Part of Fiona Weir's remit in the late 90s was to raise the profile of the Trust within the churches. In the year 2000, twenty-four staff spoke at over one hundred events. But it wasn't only people going 'out' to speak. Fiona and Alan organized lunches at Bethany Hall to which ministers and church leaders were invited. A short presentation of the work was given, as well as opportunity to meet staff members involved in different aspects of the work.

Staff member Graham Findlay was invited to speak to chil-dren in primary schools, and in 2000 Bethany Addiction workers led a seminar at the Operation Mobilization Christian Festival about helping people with alcohol and drug problems. Alan and Gordon Weir had the opportunity of visiting different parts of the country to see work similar to that done by Bethany. They were able to make the work of the Trust known, and see and hear how others addressed similar problems. Members of staff in the Commerce and Training sections also participated in conferences and seminars, sharing their expertise and learning from others.

READING ABOUT THE WORK

Publicity too was a way of spreading the word. Stands at Spring Harvest and the Scottish Resources Exhibition have been an ef-fective way of introducing many people to the work. Newsletters, annual reports and leaflets highlighting different services were produced. Perro the dog, who featured alongside the 'homeless' director, on the cover of the 1999/2000 annual report and various leaflets, was blissfully unaware of having attained international fame! The 1994/5 annual Report, designed by MAK Design, received 1ˢᵗ prize in the Scottish annual Award Scheme[1]. The Amos Trust produced beautiful small cards which had a picture of praying hands and the verse from Jeremiah 29.11 on one side and a list of the 'Seven Levels of Care' on the other. They fitted conveniently into a pocket or diary or could be kept in a Bible as a reminder to pray for the work.

The Christian press such as *Life and Work, The Christian Herald* and *The Scottish Baptist News* all featured the work of Bethany, and Sir Fred Catherwood mentioned it in his book *Jobs & Justice, Homes and Hope,* published in 1997.

But it wasn't simply the Christian press that gave coverage. The *Edinburgh Evening News* reported events, and in 1996 Rosaland Paterson wrote on article in *Scotland on Sunday.* In talking about her visit to Bethany, she said 'one senses an unspoken agenda. Bethany offers not just a stab at a Scotvec but also a sense of belonging. People who have been isolated and uncared for naturally seek to maintain the new security they have found and do so through Christianity. Perhaps in our increasingly individualistic society it falls to faith to bring people together to achieve altruistic ends.'

It was a busy year in 1998 as far as the media were concerned. There were features in the Evangelical Alliance's magazine *Idea, The Independent* newspaper and interviews and reports on the STV 'Eikon' programme and on radio. One of the by-products from this exposure was the number of people from similar organizations who contacted or visited Bethany. It was good to share ideas, encouragements and problems and to hear of what God was doing around the country.

In 2005 the first edition of *The Bugle* newspaper rolled off the press. It was a quarterly magazine (now bi-monthly), written and produced by the Bethany Press team, which is a group of people who have been, or who are currently, homeless. It provides an opportunity for those using Bethany services to share their experience of homelessness.

1. Run jointly by the Scottish Council for Voluntary Organizations and the Institute of Chartered Accountants.

MUSIC SPREADING THE WORD

For a while Bethany had a Praise Band, and their contribution over the years was greatly appreciated. Led by Gordon Weir, it comprised both staff and residents. It was in great demand and was used in both religious and secular events all over Scotland, including prison work. Not only did it tell of the work of Bethany, but more importantly shared the Christian message through word and music. The band produced two tapes which meant that many more people other than those who heard them 'live' were able to be blessed by the music and testimonies.

The attempt of one group from the Centre to be a 'choir' at Carrubers Christian Centre will long be remembered. Unknown to Alan, one of the party had been drinking, and this became apparent, at least to the Bethany contingent, when they stood up on the platform to sing. Two other residents firmly sandwiched the 'offender' between them and they sang! It wasn't perhaps the best advert for the success of the work, but it did show its realistic side.

Definitely more successful and professional were internationally acclaimed guitarists Duo Montes-Kircher who gave a concert in Broxburn at which the work of Bethany Home Farm was highlighted. At the 2006 Prom Praise Celebration in Dunfermline and again at the Male Voice Praise Festival there in 2007, the work of Christian Concern and Bethany at the Toastie Club was featured.

VISUALIZING THE WORK

In 2000 at a Millennium celebration at the Edinburgh Festival Theatre the work of Bethany was highlighted in a video presentation in which three people shared their experiences of homelessness and the faith that had taken them in a new direction.

EVENTS

There were various events too. The 'Amazing Grace' tours around the country were very successful. In 1997 there was a week designated as 'Bethany week' when supporters were encouraged to be involved in making known the work of the Trust. All sorts of enterprising events resulted, such as bread and soup lunches, special prayer times, sponsored silences and a flower festival. One year (it is to be hoped it was a good summer) supporters who were having a barbecue could send for a pack which was full of ideas for making the work known.

For a good many years Leith has celebrated a week of summer festival activities, beginning with a parade of decorated floats. Local businesses, schools, faith groups, etc. all participated. Bethany joined in the fun, with residents, staff and the praise band all aboard a float and helping to make known the work of the Trust as they trundled down Leith Walk. It was an especially exciting time in 1995 because over half a million visitors converged on Leith for four days in July to see the magnificent spectacle of the Tall Ships race. During this time Bethany highlighted the social issues which it sought to address by running a craft stall on Leith Links and entering a float in the Gala Day historical pageant.

When Bethany was the chosen charity to provide a free gift-wrap service for Christmas shoppers in the Ocean Terminal one year, it was a golden opportunity to publicize the work of the Trust

And the Fundraising team continue the good work of 'making it known', co-ordinating the talks which are given at community groups and churches, or highlighting homelessness and addiction issues at conferences and exhibitions. When interviewed for the Bethany Newsletter, Chris McNeil said that telling the outside world about the work of the Trust is the favourite part of his job. He found it encouraging to see individuals moving from apathy to enthusiasm and seeking involvement when they heard how people's lives could be changed for good.

Perhaps the most effective way of making known the work is, as the song says, 'one shall tell another and he shall tell his friend'. This was the experience of one Bethany supporter featured in the 2007 annual report, and I quote, 'I've lived in Edinburgh for almost five years now but one of the first things I learned about was Bethany Christian Trust.

On my first day my new flatmate took me along to the old Bethany Shop in Stockbridge and declared it to be the best charity shop in town. Apparently not only were the shops brilliant but her mum had heard all about the work at church and was really impressed. As time went by I learnt more about the work, snippets of information either through the shops, through my new in-laws who turned out to be supporters and through my own church. I'm not sure what order it all happened, but I now support Bethany through volunteering at the Care Shelter, praying for their work and giving financially. I love the fact that you can see the results of their work so clearly. Everybody involved is so focused on helping vulnerable people. With most charities I support, I feel pretty distant. I give money and trust them to put it to good use. I get so much more out of my relationships with Bethany. I know wholeheartedly that I am making a difference. I meet the people who benefit from their work. I know that every penny is carefully and prayerfully spent. It's a genuine privilege to play a small part in their life-changing work.'

(Well done flatmate for making it known!)

CHAPTER 16

THE CARE OF THE CHURCHES

The Apostle Paul speaks of 'the care of the churches'. He was referring to the burden and responsibility he felt for those, who under God, he had been used to bring to faith. But in a very real sense Bethany has benefited *from* the care of churches who have entered into the vision and become involved in sharing the burden and responsibility of caring for others. It is probably true to say that many residents who have found a new purpose in life and gone on to see that potential realized day in day out, have done so because of the support received from a church community.

In many ways South Leith Baptist Church is a prime example. It gave initial vital support which has been ongoing. Not only has it given financial support such as a monthly offering towards the Care Van and Christmas and Harvest gifts, but made its premises available for open days, ceilidhs, staff training, group sessions, Drop-In games evenings and the Care Shelter. Because some of Bethany's premises used to belong to the church, shared roofs have needed to be maintained and occasionally incidents sorted out when the church premises have been damaged by tenants' carelessness, often involving leaking washing machines. And there have been times when Bethany has had to be reminded to leave the church premises as they would have wished to find them.

In the early days members collected used postage stamps for recycling and donated surplus black rubbish bags. Secretary Bob Souza did printing jobs at home for the Trust, and others volunteered in a Care Van team, at Homemaker and the shops.

But most importantly, others in the congregation put aside prejudices and preconceived ideas regarding homeless people and made a real effort to get to know residents who attended services. They learned to see them as individuals and not just as the 'Bethany boys'. This, you may say, is what church members should do, but it is not always easy, especially if one has been brought up in a Christian context and has no experience of addiction problems or family breakdown. They may not understand how alien a church service may appear to someone who has never, or not for a long time, been in that environment, and whose behaviour in such circumstances may seem 'inappropriate'.

Both the present minister, Rev. Ian Paterson, and the previous pastor, Rev. Ross Brown were employed with Bethany for short periods. They have personally been supportive of the work and spent many hours encouraging and counselling residents, and seeking to make them feel part of the church community.

Giving in kind has always been a feature of the care of the churches. Not long after the Centre was opened a list was made of items that were required. By the end of the same day everything except one item had been supplied by a church in West Lothian. Who told them what to bring so that it matched up with requirements? Surely, it was just another example of the faithfulness of God. We did wonder about the one missing item. Perhaps we didn't really need it, or maybe God was just keeping us from getting too sure of ourselves and reminding us to rely on Him.

In 1995 there were expressions of church generosity. Bristo Baptist Church gifted a fifteen-seater minibus for the use of the Trust. A Leith Church of Scotland offered Bethany a single-bedroom flat for Supported Housing which was to be leased on a peppercorn rent. And the Brethren Assembly in Jane Street, Leith, who no longer required their building, but were anxious it should remain in 'Christian hands,' offered it to the Trust at a most favourable cost. It was already called Bethany Hall and so the hanging sign at the entrance didn't even need to be changed.

Generous donations of church pews were also forthcoming. Listeners to Radio 4's long running soap *The Archers* will be aware of a debate raging there about whether the pews in St Stephen's should be removed to make the building multifunctional. Arguments for and against are probably indicative of those that have been debated in every fellowship that has considered this step. However, some churches who supported Bethany's work had taken the decision to replace pews with seats, and kindly offered their pews to the Trust. Some people reading this account may be the proud possessors of a beautiful yellow pine pew originally from Bellevue Chapel or one of Oregon pitch pine from Queensberry Baptist Church in Nottingham. Brought back to the Trust's workshop they were rubbed down, prepared and then sold on. We have one in our front garden, though not knowing its origin we're not sure whether to sing hymns, psalms or chant when we sit on it.

Handing over the keys (Bethany Hall)

Friends in the Queensberry Baptist Church in Nottingham have been faithful supporters from the beginning of the Trust. It is my home church and, alongside supporting local homelessness initiatives, many individuals have been faithful in prayer and financial support for Bethany. The fellowship as a whole has given of its 'thank-offerings', made a visiting group of residents and staff very welcome, and collected £2,000 for the 'coppers count' appeal.

Christmas has been a time when schools, nurseries, companies and churches have shown overwhelming care. In the early days when resident numbers were not so large, some churches took the trouble to find out residents' names and match Christmas gifts accordingly. Not only residents, but the units themselves benefited from gifts as diverse as turkeys to holly wreaths and Christmas trees. Certainly all these were a practical means of stretching Bethany's budget but, more importantly, residents and staff alike felt and appreciated the warmth and concern that these gifts represented.

Similarly, the months of September and October had the offices in Jane Street looking like a supermarket. Harvest gifts were often delivered to the various units, but when they came to the office in Jane Street there was much delight and a lot of activity. Margaret Rees and I tried to be even-handed with the distribution, making up parcels for people in the supported housing units and making sure the hard-working full-time volunteers felt valued by sending some special 'goodies' to their shared accommodation. The non-perishable goods were great for storing and later distribution. There were some raised eyebrows in the early days at the Centre after the first harvest gifts arrived. Before coming to Bethany, most of the residents had been all too acquainted with the great Scottish 'fry up', and were alarmed when healthy salads and fresh fruit appeared on the menu! The breaking of habits didn't just involve drink and drugs!

In 2006 many churches and twenty-two different schools in the Edinburgh area, as well as individuals, donated over £4,000-worth of goods for the 'Harvest Homemaker Appeal'. Items such as towels, bedding, cutlery, crockery and cleaning/household products were made up into starter packs for the Homemaker service, enabling people to settle more quickly in their new-found tenancies and turn their 'houses into homes'.

With the work expanding, there were more opportunities to give, and more locations at which such gifts were appreciated. Donations of foodstuffs were appreciated by the Women's Group, and toiletries were welcomed by all, especially people using the Drop-Ins in Fife, for some of whom having the opportunity to 'get clean' and use such products was an infrequent luxury.

Then there were the Border Berries! No, they are not long-lost relations of the retired director, but rather the name given to the delicious soft fruit grown by Martin Johnson on Rutherford Farm in the beautiful Borders country. Just as in the Bible the Israelites were commanded to leave 'gleanings' in the field to help those in need, so the Johnsons invited charities, including Bethany, to benefit from their harvest. 'Pick Your Own' took on a whole new meaning. Initially Alan and I were involved in picking fruit; and Alan's raspberry and gooseberry jam became famous and much sought after at the Charities Hypermarket and in the Bethany shops.

Residents became involved too. On one memorable occasion a group had been down picking fruit but hadn't used small containers in which to collect it. Imagine the consternation at our house that evening when the doorbell rang and we were presented with several large black refuse bags all full of extremely squashy fruit. Plans for the evening were rapidly changed, jelly-pans came out, jars were washed and jam-making took priority.

But it's not just the making of the jam that was a labour of love. Jars needed to be collected, washed, sized, weighed, labelled and priced. Several friends began to help with the jam-making, but in later years the folks in the churches in Melrose and Selkirk showed their care for others in very practical ways. Not only did they pick the fruit, but also made the jam, and latterly also sold it in and around the churches, donating the money to Bethany in what has become an enterprise worthy of a military operation. Finding enough jars was always a problem, and we were grateful to folks in Gullane who brought in their empty jars to the Bethany Shop there. The problem was alleviated one year by Alan and myself making a detour on our way back from Newcastle Airport after a holiday. We had intended to drop off the jars at the farm on our way down, but the journey took longer than anticipated. There were a few smiles at the thought that if anyone had broken into our car boot while it was parked at the airport they might have been disappointed at their find.

The Trust owes a great debt to the Johnsons, the local organisers, especially Jane Barley, and the Melrose and Selkirk congregations for their generosity, hard work and commitment. Jane's email after the 2007 season said she certainly intended to carry on the good work for as many years as she could and for as long as the jam would sell. She was even hopeful of still making jam in heaven!

Quoting the December newsletter issued in 2005, 'Homelessness is far less to do with bricks and mortar and far more to do with relationships and the impact breakdowns in these support networks have on individual lives'. So while the care of the churches does involve material things, people giving of their time to visit and befriend residents can have a real impact on lives. Beginning in 1994, such visits were made to Bethany House by Bob Akroyd with volunteers from two local Free Church of Scotland congregations.

Each week Bob spent time going round the hostel, introducing himself to new residents and catching up with others. These visits were eagerly awaited – not least because Bob and his team arrived armed with jam doughnuts. Bob had the opportunity to invite residents along to church and the team were also able to remain in contact with people once they moved on from Bethany House.

Bob and Heather Akroyd

Such important work was officially recognized on 21st Aug 1999 at Buccleuch and Greyfriars Free Church of Scotland, when Rev. Dr Robert Akroyd, alias 'doughnut Bob' was inducted as assistant minister 'with responsibility for the pastoral care of the congregation and to follow up contacts made in the course of his work with Bethany Christian Trust'.

It was good that two previous residents took time to be at his induction. It was an exciting time for Bethany knowing that Bob, who had previously had to balance his work commitment with a demanding course of study, would be able to devote more time to follow up important contacts. It was exciting too for his congregation who, with him, would be able to make a greater impact upon the work of Bethany.

Another project that was brought about by cooperation among caring churches was 'Friday Friends.' Beginning in April 2002 Bethany reached out to the young people in Haddington and East Lothian whose lives were affected by alcohol and drug abuse. During one eighteen-month period they worked with over forty individuals. It was organized in partnership with local churches, and the Bethany Addiction team and volunteers from the churches were involved. Their main motivation was an expression of God's love to all who attended. They provided a welcoming lunch, a listening ear, gave advice on possible drug rehabilitation centres, and aimed at bringing a sense of hope that life could improve and positive change was possible.

The project received £6,500 from East Lothian Drug and Alcohol Action Team, and the work was featured in a 'Songs of Praise' programme when the minister of Haddington's West Church, the Rev. Cameron McKenzie, had the opportunity to share his own testimony.

Alongside 'Friday Friends' there were also monthly meetings called 'Moving Forward Together' when church supporters from Haddington and East Lothian met for praise, prayer, Bible teaching and testimony. They brought together Christians from different churches to look at social action and help churches become more active in their local communities, as well as exploring ways in which they could support new Bethany projects.

For some time Abbeyhill Baptist Church has also been an example of a church that is seeking to build relationships with residents in Bethany House. They began an evening group for clients wishing to explore questions about Christianity. As well as helping them in their spiritual journey, these evenings provided an opportunity for them to increase their self-esteem and social interaction skills. Working with church members who valued them provided a great opportunity for people to build links in a community where they once felt alienated.

PASSING THE BATON

Several years ago John Rodgers, director of Residential Care, was challenged with a vision. John saw an opportunity to continue the Bethany care system further than its current remit: to bring together church communities and people who had just left a supported lifestyle and enable the two groups to learn from and support each other. He saw a future where people who were scared of living within a society of which they didn't feel part were supported by those who wanted to give something to members of the community around them. The vision was given a name – 'Passing the Baton'.

The project was first piloted in January 2005. Its main aim at that time was to support the service users who were moving out of Bethany House into new and unfamiliar areas of Edinburgh, primarily helping them to combat the issues of isolation and loneliness which were recognized as major causes of resettlement breakdowns.

It began with partnering the Niddrie Community Church, which is located in an urban housing estate in the south of Edinburgh and whose members saw the role of the local church as supporting people in the community, particularly people moving on from Bethany who may already have had some spiritual awareness. They began building relationships by visiting, meeting up for coffee, and playing pool, emphasizing the two-way nature of the relationship. By June 2006 this 'Passing the Baton' pilot scheme was going well, supporting five people who had used Bethany's services. The five developed social networks, supported each other and were willing to offer support to others moving into the area. Twelve months into the project, all five still had their tenancies and three had full-time jobs. One former service user was restored to home and community, and had a new baby called Bethany!

The Trust's 2006 annual report stated that plans for the future would 'facilitate active involvement of church and other community groups in the development of social action programmes which would build supportive relationships in their communities'. The pilot scheme had produced such encouraging results and feedback that Passing the Baton developed further partnerships with the City of Edinburgh Council housing department in Craigmillar, YMCA (Pilton & Broomhouse units), Granton Baptist Church, Elder Memorial Free Church, Buccleuch and Greyfriars Free Church, St Paul's & St George's, Bellevue Chapel, St. Mungo's in Balerno, Holy Trinity Church in Wester Hailes and Morningside Baptist Church.

Passing the Baton has worked well for two ex-residents of Bethany House. Eddie and Stewart told their story in the 2007 annual report. Stewart said 'Bethany House was good, friendly and helpful. All I wanted was a place to put my head down but it turned into a lot more than that. It was a place to stay which had very supportive people. I was surprised by how much they would do to help service users.

Eddie and Stewart

'I met Eddie when he was still a resident at Bethany House. Mostly we ate meals together and had nice, relaxing conversations. I suffered a devastating bereavement while I was in the House and Eddie, seeing how distressed I was, talked to me and notified my key worker. It was at that point when I was so emotional that I was glad that everyone was there to help me.'

'Eddie moved out of the House later, was successful living on his own and became a member of Passing the Baton. When it was time for me to leave Bethany House, it was felt that Eddie would be a great person to support me through the new project. We talk on the phone once or twice a week, go to meetings together, and always meet for the free lunch at a local church on Fridays. We sit and relax and talk about the week. He's been there when I needed him. Any problems I am having, I phone him. Any questions I have, he's there to answer. I get a lot from Passing the Baton'.

Eddie says, 'Our Passing the Baton relationship involves lots of give and take and is more of a friendship than anything else. The initiative encourages participants to be independent, while also inviting them to seek out support if they need it. It's a mix of reliance and responsibility. We try to be supportive, and an ear to listen whenever possible.

'At one point, Stewart was having trouble getting furniture. After a little while he phoned me up and I went down to Bethany House with him to see if we could sort something out. That's the great thing about Passing the Baton, not only because Stewart knew he could rely on those involved in it when he needed something, but he saw that there are always other people to talk to or get help from. Eventually we were able to get Stewart all the furniture he needed.'

The concept was seen as so important that Bethany decided to employ a full-time lead facilitator. That post was taken up in November 2007 by Gavin Lawson, who was formerly manager of Bethany House and while in that post was involved in the early stages of Passing the Baton. When a legacy of £80,000 specifically earmarked for the initiative was received shortly afterwards, it was an endorsement that this was indeed the way forward.

The scheme is now developing in Aberdeen in partnership with Aberdeen City Mission and the wider Christian community from the Deeside Christian Fellowship, Vine Church and the Way Trust. It is active in discussions with other agencies in Scotland and hopeful that it will develop its service in partnership with them in their localities. By making Bethany's experience and resources available to other organizations, it is hoped that a significant partnership programme can develop to further demonstrate Christian love in action in Scotland. The project refers to its service users as 'members' and has so far successfully supported over twenty-five members to integrate into their new communities, thereby demonstrating a 96.2% success rate. It is Gavin's hope that through the vision of Passing the Baton becoming a reality, vulnerable people who have previously been homeless, will find a dignified, meaningful and satisfying life with the added bonus of economic savings to society by stopping the 'revolving door' scenario whereby people go out into a community, only to experience a failed tenancy and return again.

CHAPTER 17

WHO CARES FOR THE CARERS?

Caring is expressed in many ways. Sometimes it is shown in the selfless actions of parents who for many years care for a child with disabilities. Or maybe the one cared for is an elderly relative, and the life of the younger generation is put on hold for a while. Care can be shown in the writing of letters or telephoning friends who need encouragement or maybe just noticing when someone needs a cup of tea and giving them the opportunity to talk. Whatever form it takes, caring can be costly.

It is the same for Bethany staff who make themselves vulnerable so that the ministry may be effective in helping to change lives. So who cares for the carers?

PRAYER SUPPORT AND RELATIONSHIPS
As the number of Bethany staff has increased so has the opportunity for fellowship and support among them – most of the time! I say this because although a staff team may be made up of Christians, that does not mean that they will always see eye to eye. Tensions, even serious ones, can and indeed have arisen. Understanding needs to be shown, and sometimes forgiveness and reconciliation need to be sought. However, the blessings of working with so many different people from so many diverse backgrounds, but all seeking to bring hope and a future to homeless and vulnerable people, is very special.

When the Centre was the only area of operation it was easy for the whole staff team to come together each morning for prayer, and these were times of support for one another. At the same time as staff numbers began increasing, so did the demands and regulations from statutory bodies regarding 'care' work and the professionalism that this involved. 'Supervision' sessions were introduced, during which senior staff discussed with project workers the nature of the work, supported them in any difficulties they were facing and encouraged them. This was vital because it is easy in such work to become very tired, and burn-out can be a real possibility without adequate support.

Building on this, in November 1989 the trustees invited Gwen McDowall to become the staff trainer and care adviser for Bethany. Gwen was a qualified social worker and Christian counsellor, and had wide experience in many forms of residential work. She commenced her work with Bethany initially for two hours per week. I well remember Gwen's input in staff meetings. She didn't say anything, just sat and listened and took notes. I think the staff forgot she was there; they were all so busy enthusiastically and passionately putting across their point of view. But then she gave feedback! She had noted how many times different staff members cut across others, not listening to what they said but interrupting with their own opinion. It was quite enlightening, and not a little disconcerting! Hopefully we all learnt some lessons.

It was during one of these staff meetings that there was a phone call to the office and I was called out of the meeting – apparently it was urgent. In one way it certainly was, and was another indication to me of the faithfulness of God. I had been very troubled about a certain family situation and it was difficult because it also involved a Bethany resident. I had lost sleep over it. One of the other residents had actually commented to me that I looked as if I had the cares of the world on my shoulders, and quite honestly that is how I felt for a while. The phone call was from my friend Chrissie, who was the church organist of Cowdenbeath Baptist Church, where Alan had had his first pastorate. She had been a faithful prayer supporter of the family and the Bethany work. She simply said that she had been praying that morning, but every time she tried to move on to pray for someone else, God kept telling her to ring me and tell me that 'it would be alright'. This she did. 'Is there anything particularly wrong?' she asked. I didn't go into detail, but was so grateful to God for His assurance and to Chrissie for being faithful enough to pray for us and obedient to what God said to her. And God was true to His word; the situation was eventually resolved.

I am sure many Bethany staff have been wonderfully upheld over the years, without at times realizing it was because others, who maybe had no knowledge of a given situation, were praying for them. People like those in Newhaven Parish and Duncan Street Baptist, whose representatives phoned the office once a week for prayer requests. One supporter said she used the seven days of the week to pray for a different level of the work each day, while another used the news letters to pray by name for all the staff mentioned. And staff do have needs! One day when Alan had been on duty at the Centre for thirty-six hours I decided to sit in the queue outside the office door and wait my turn. Other residents were bemused – 'I'm just waiting to speak to my husband' I said, 'and this is the only way I can do it!'

I remember an incident at the Centre when a resident presented himself in the office with an open wound. Without giving it a thought I began cleaning it, never taking the precaution of protective gloves. In was in the early days when awareness of HIV/AIDS was only just beginning, but even so I should have automatically followed simple hygiene rules, for his sake as well as mine. We did know of some who had potentially life-threatening conditions but there was no obligation on residents to share their medical history with staff if they did not wish to. I suddenly realized that I had been less than 'professional,' when in walked Eddie Reevie and simply prayed for me asking for God's peace and protection. The timeliness of his concern has stayed with me as an example of what caring is all about.

STAFF MEETINGS
As the work expanded and the different Levels increased, so each section was particularly involved with colleagues in their own department. Prayer breakfasts, lunchtime prayer meetings, fellowship nights and fun nights all helped to make staff feel they

were a part of something bigger, but still a valued individual. During their period of employment with the Trust, the pastoral hearts of Baptist ministers, Ross Brown in Contracts and Ian Paterson in Training were evident in the caring ministry they exercised among those with whom they worked and for whom they were responsible, especially in Ross's case the apprentices.

Staff fellowship night

When the Bethany Hall premises were officially 'dedicated', Ian combined this with a training seminar called 'Caring Enough to Confront'. It was the first of a series of seminars entitled Competent to Counsel and sought to equip Bethany staff members to do the work to which they were called. It addressed such topics as how to deal with a colleague or client who got on your nerves (yes it does happen!), or with whom you were tempted to lose your temper, seeking ways to deal with such situations to the mutual benefit of both.

PERSONAL EXAMPLE

I think of staff who worked at Bethany Hall and whom I regarded as an inspiration and an example as they went about their work, fulfilling their tasks in such a professional way as they dealt with the needs of others, despite having deep sadnesses of their own. Some had family members who had serious medical conditions, others personal problems and, in the wider Trust, two young members of staff lost their life's partner through illness or accident. During my time at Bethany Hall, I personally appreciated and benefited from the care of colleagues. It wasn't always in the context of major issues but could be in such everyday situations as my giving Andy Davis the opportunity to exercise his undoubted gift of patience as he, yet again, tried to get me to want to understand the workings of the computer! Sometimes those who are used to giving out to others find it difficult to receive. However, it is my experience that a climate exists within the Bethany structure whereby staff know that if they wish to share there will be a listening ear and practical help where appropriate and possible.

VOLUNTEERS

Some of the full-time volunteers who served Bethany so well were often a long way from home, and support for them was important. They could face times of crisis, as in the case of Gunilla, from Sweden, whose young brother was seriously injured in a car accident. So many people prayed, and it was wonderful when later in her volunteer year the whole family, including the young brother, came to visit her. It was the practice for the volunteer in the Training section to act as coordinator for all the other volunteers, and Susan and Louise, among others, played important roles in this respect.

Time for God and Careforce encouraged an 'adopt a volunteer' scheme which involved people outside Bethany, often in the local churches, in providing informal support. Sharing accommodation with a group of volunteers could be stressful if everyone didn't pull their weight around the house, but it also provided much fun and encouragement.

Hillary, who worked in the Training section for her volunteer year, reflected on what it had meant to her. She had anticipated that she would be changed, but it was not in big moments that she experienced this, rather she felt she had developed through the mundane, the simple things of daily living. Work in the Training team increased her knowledge of the realities of life, as well as the daily run-ning of a busy office and the many hidden responsibilities that entailed. Settling into life outside the States, away from familiar faces, was difficult but it had been crucial to her personal growth. She had become more independent and flexible through living in a foreign country, and had fun at times trying to understand a Scottish accent. But she had been blessed by discovering the importance of community – at Bethany, at church and with other volunteers throughout the UK, relationships which enriched her life, expanded her mind and strengthened her faith. She had been able to establish a day-to-day support system which had helped when she encountered challenges and had to deal with the home-sickness issue.

This latter is a reality many of the volunteers face and some staff members, being aware of this, have helped in caring for these young carers by inviting volunteers to share in their family life and providing a home from home.

AWAY DAYS

'Away days' were great for meeting other members of staff off duty. Initially everyone met together, but as Bethany grew this wasn't feasible as there was always a need for the residential units and the shops to be manned, and so extra days were organized.

In 1996 the staff met in the beautiful surroundings of Carberry Tower and looked at 'Managing Stress in the light of God's Word'. In 1998 two Wednesdays were set aside at the beginning of November, when staff met in the excellent halls of St Michael's Church, Linlithgow, West Lothian. The fellowship there have been very supportive of Bethany's work and this was another indication of their generosity. This venue had the advantage that during the lunch break, staff could make a quick visit to the beautiful, historic church of St Michael's (definitely the warmer option) or enjoy the autumn colours beside the loch.

On the first Wednesday Rev. Andrew Rollinson, now the Baptist Union of Scotland's Ministry Adviser, used Psalm 84 to challenge staff about the importance of keeping a relationship with God as central to their lives. The second week Eddie Lyle, then of Youth for Christ, addressed the subject 'honesty before God is the catalyst that enables us to grow', basing his thoughts on Psalm 74. The programme also included group discussions, which helped increase staff awareness and appreciation of the jobs, joys and frustrations of other members working in the Trust. Each group independently suggested that this might be further facilitated by staff members exchanging jobs for a week!

There was laughter too as staff tried to find the most innovative way of executing their joint responsibility for promoting the work of the Trust. The prize Kit Kat on the first week went to Keith Johnston (Supported Housing) for his suggestion of parachuting from a plane and distributing annual reports on the descent, but he didn't seem to volunteer to follow it through! One group on the second Wednesday suggested that the director might bungee-jump, and this definitely took the biscuit! All in all it was good to take time out, stand back, refocus and be encouraged to move on.

Writing an article entitled 'The Cost of Caring', one staff member said 'the sheer scale of the needs of the people with whom we work can result in staff becoming drained and overwhelmed. These retreats therefore provide an important opportunity for us to be refreshed. Together we share fun, difficulties, encouragements and vision. At a recent day-away, God reminded us of His great love for us and that we were to love one another in the same way. He showed us how our work with Bethany has many parallels with the story of the Good Samaritan. Just like the victim there, many who come across our path have been beaten; by bereavement, discrimination, bullying, unemployment, rejection and abuse. They have been stripped of dignity and left powerless. They have sought refuge in alcohol, drugs, immoral relationships, food, gambling, fantasy and denial of truth, but God loves them.

'He reminded us that we were not to be like the Priest and Levite. They seemingly embodied all that was good among men and excited expectations of hope but they passed by on the other side. Looking professional and being outwardly religious would not heal the broken-hearted or set captives free. Just as the Good Samaritan used his donkey to carry the man to a place of refuge and healing, so God would have us use faith, hope and love to lead broken people to Him'.

TEAMWORK
Until 1997 Alan as director, carried the sole responsibility for the day-to-day affairs of the Trust. He reported directly to the trustees and was assisted by a team of eight managers. As the work increased so did the pressure, and the trustees followed

the example of Moses' father-in-law, Jethro, in Exodus 18, and suggested that Alan should have some assistance and sharing of the burden. Consequently, the trustees appointed three assistant directors, Gordon Weir, Ewan Foreman and Simon Laidlaw from within the ranks, each with their own area of responsibility seeking to facilitate growth and expansion in the Trust's work of expressing Christian love in action.

As the different aspects of the work increased, it became more difficult for staff to be aware of what was happening in other sections, and so the monthly staff newsletter 'In Touch' fulfilled a useful role in disseminating information. Each section supplied news, items for prayer and praise, along with photographs of new employees.

TRAINING

The 2003/4 annual report explained that Bethany was obtaining accreditation by the Care Commission and had taken steps to ensure that all its policies were clear and in accordance with the best professional practice. It was believed that as a Christian organization, the Trust should do its work as well as it could be done, and in addition demonstrate to those with whom it worked, the example of people who had committed their lives to being followers of Jesus Christ. These developments placed a great burden on the directors of the various divisions and, in response to this, a review of the management structure was undertaken. This led to the splitting of the Care Division into two – residential and non-residential care – as well as some relocation of responsibility to other divisions. The directors of all the divisions and their staff responded nobly to these changes but such burdens demonstrate that caring can be costly in giving of oneself.

Someone who had certainly given of himself was Gordon Weir, who in spring 2004 moved on to a new ministry working with churches to help develop their social action programmes. In his last year Gordon had overseen substantial growth in Bethany's Care Division. He had been with the Trust for thirteen years and his energy, enthusiasm and dedication had been greatly valued

Mike Sherlock, who worked as part of Bethany's team at the 2007 Care Shelter, said he thought 'Bethany was a great company to work for'. It is hoped then that while staff show Christian love in action and care for others they too may know they are valued and cared for.

CHAPTER 18

ONE VOLUNTEER IS WORTH TEN PRESSED MEN

The previous chapter spoke of caring for the staff and Bethany's full-time volunteers. It is arguable that the Trust would be unable to function without the latter and the many part-time volunteers who give of their time and talents to serve Bethany and, through it, homeless and vulnerable people. Mention has already been made of the hundreds who help man the Care Van and the Care Shelter but it seems appropriate that a chapter should be given over to highlighting the contribution of volunteers – the 'unsung heroes'. They have made such a difference to the life of the Trust.

In a very real sense the Trust would never have been formed if the original trustees had not been willing to 'volunteer' their services. Over the years the number of these non-executive Directors, as they are now called, has doubled. Their length of service has varied, but all have freely given of themselves and their expertise in areas such as law, insurance, social work and finance. Les Bell deserves special mention (and a long-service medal), as he was there at the beginning, has served for periods as honorary treasurer and chairman, and is still on the governing council.

In the late 80s and early 90s when staffing levels were still relatively low, the input of people like Philip Hacking was invaluable. Once a week Philip finished his own shift working in a residential care home for the elderly, and then came and provided overnight cover in the Centre. He was also an accomplished musician, and when the Thursday evening praise nights became a regular feature often played the piano there.

For a period too, Rev. Bob Gemmell, a trustee and qualified social worker, volunteered a day shift, and in later years when minister of Portobello Baptist Church, Rev. Don Currie volunteered a regular slot.

Volunteering became a feature of the visits from our wider family. My mum always did baking, and when the new extension part of the Centre was finished, my stepfather, Doug, arrived from Nottingham complete with working clothes and brushes to emulsion the outside of the building.

As the Trust became more widely known, the number of people receiving newsletters and annual reports increased. It was a great help to be able to call on a group of volunteers to assist with the mountain of mailing. Some stayed for hours, patiently filling envelopes, and others, like Mrs Margot MacInnes, not only brought their cheery smile, but also home-baking for the inevitable tea breaks.

THE SHOPS

With the advent of the charity shops, volunteering really came into its own. Some of the work was on the shop floor, serving the public, but there have been many unsung heroes in the stockrooms, usually in the basements of the shops, who have emptied endless black bags, and sorted, ironed and priced goods.

Volunteers in the shops, like the goods they sell, come in all shapes and sizes and span a wide age-range. They have included young people who were using the work experience towards obtaining the Duke of Edinburgh Award, prisoners working under the Training for Freedom scheme, Bethany residents using such placements to gain confidence before re-entering the world of employment, and many retired people.

Bethany has certainly benefited from having such volunteers, but they in turn feel they have been recipients. Bill, a volunteer in the Duke Street shop, called it 'a privilege to work as a volunteer in a happy environment which gave him a sense of purpose and fulfilment in helping such a good cause' and Marion 'thoroughly enjoyed her voluntary work and looked forward to spending time at the Summerhall shop'.

One young man, Steve McComb, who had previously worked with Bethany as a volunteer, returned in 1998 with a team of ten young people from Baptist Churches in Northern Ireland. They gave up a week of their holidays to get involved in practical caring. Summing up their experiences, team member Emma said, 'Each member of the team spent several days in both the commercial and care sections which gave us an overall picture of how different aspects of Bethany's work complement each other. Some spent time working in the charity shops, picking up a few bargains along the way, while the more energetic members were involved moving furniture out on the vans. On the care side, we basically just spent time talking to the residents, getting to know them a little, and providing a listening ear.

'The week was challenging in many respects. We met many who told how the power of Jesus had transformed their lives; we all learned to abandon some of the restraints put on us by society's theories; we realized afresh the universality of God's grace and our responsibility to share that with everyone.

'Being in a situation where we were able to form relationships with some residents was a humbling experience, making us more aware of how we are often guilty of approaching people from a less fortunate background with a hint of awkwardness or condescension. We thank Bethany for teaching us so much.'

Some full-time volunteers came to the Trust independently, having heard of and seen displays of the work at Spring Harvest or a Christian Resources Exhibition, or knew of the work of the Trust through their families and churches. Two such were Beth and Robert Landon, who in the first year of marriage gave voluntary help at the Centre for a year.

Beth says 'I came to Edinburgh in October 1999 because my husband was starting his final year of Chemistry at the university. I heard about Bethany through his family and got a year's voluntary placement at Bethany Christian Centre, while Robert did one sleepover every week'. At the end of the time she looked back over a great year. She said 'we have made many friends and have felt supported by the staff – we've had many fun times. This year has taught me about the nature of addiction, the struggles people go through and what it takes for someone to break free.

'I have been involved in a wide range of activities: administration, key working, cleaning, escorting residents to the doctors, visiting someone in hospital who took an overdose, running an Alpha course and a Mission course, and keeping drunk people away from the door! Robert enjoyed his nights at the Centre too. He appreciated getting to know the guys and escaping from his studies.'

CAREFORCE

Many of the volunteers came to work at Bethany through Careforce. Initially Alan heard of this organization through a fellow minister, Rev. Ian Mundie. The Trust will always be grateful for that initial contact. The organization seeks to be a facilitator for young people wishing to volunteer full-time for a year working in a supportive environment with a church or Christian caring agency. Applicants' preferences are noted, and volunteers and vacancies matched up wherever possible. The young person visits the proposed placement and if both parties are happy with the arrangement then wheels are set in motion.

Full-time volunteers

Initially only one volunteer a year came to Bethany, living in accommodation within the unit, but as the Trust grew there was increased opportunity within the residential units and the shops, and over the years as many as thirteen have been employed simultaneously. This has had the benefit of providing fellowship and friendship for the young people with others of a similar age. Separating 'living' from 'working' was important, and volunteers have been accommodated in two large flats, and a former manse. It was envisaged that the manse would be a short-term lease but the Trust had the benefit of it for approximately ten years, following which another property was offered for their use.

Most of the young people were new graduates and were taking a gap year before commencing their career, but some came prior to university. The arrangement was that they received board and lodging, and pocket money. Some of them had met Careforce workers while they themselves were university students and this had encouraged them to get involved.

TIME FOR GOD

When contact was made with another organization, Time for God, it resulted in more volunteers coming from overseas, and the initial fact-finding visit often wasn't possible. For some volunteers in this position, arriving in Scotland was quite a culture shock, and the climate – a challenge, to say the least. John, from Kenya, initially wore three pairs of trousers to try to keep warm, and Kelly, from Texas, shivered her way through one of the warmest Scottish Septembers on record! Language could also pose a problem. Hearing a broad Scottish accent and local dialect words might have little in common with how some volunteers had learned English at school. Yet for many of them their grasp of English was amazing and a reproach to those of us who can only speak our mother tongue.

REFUGEES

Someone who was definitely not in that category was Rev. Stuart Robertson, the rector of the Episcopal Church in Leith during the 1980s. His volunteering of his considerable linguistic skills was a life-saver, both to the staff and some of the overseas residents who had been referred to Bethany by an organization working with refugees, and were early asylum seekers. At the time the

U.S.S.R. still existed, and there were refugees from Russia and Georgia, of whom one at least had jumped ship in the north of Scotland and had been put in contact with Bethany. There was tension between those from different Soviet states, and this was compounded at times by the presence of others from Romania, Poland and Bulgaria. Added to these were two Africans who had fled persecution in Nigeria and Somalia. This was quite a challenge for the staff, especially when it came to the inevitable form-filling and contact with Social Security officials, never mind food preferences.

Stuart was fluent in an amazing number of Eastern European languages and, although Bulgarian wasn't one of them, he managed to converse with Peter our Bulgarian, through the use of Russian. It was a great comfort for these refugees to find someone who could speak their language. Not only did Stuart ease some of the administrative burden but he and his wife were also generous in their hospitality to the refugees.

Some had heart-rending stories to tell. One such was Peter from Romania, who was a delightful gentleman and always politely stood up when any female member of staff entered the room. Such behaviour was not a normal occurrence in Bethany but after the initial surprise everyone got to appreciate his courtesy. He had fled Romania, leaving behind his wife and a handicapped child, but he had a strong faith and trusted God for the future. He had relatives in Canada and eventually was allowed to go and settle there, where happily his family later joined him.

Peter, from Bulgaria, was full of fun and determined to learn English as fast as he could, even to the extent of using colloquial expressions. He presented himself in the kitchen one day and said very solemnly 'I am not as green as I am cabbage looking'. Whether he just liked the sound of the words or whether he had any idea of what they meant, we were too amused to enquire. Seeing our reaction, he was like a child who, realizing he has said something funny, keeps repeating it, complete with big smile.

When Careforce and Time for God volunteers arrived at Bethany they usually had in mind that they would be there for a year and then move on. However, over the years many have stayed and become full-time paid members of staff. Some have not only found friendship but their life's partner, and others a new sense of direction for their career, returning to study to gain qualifications in social work or other caring professions. For one young man who arrived straight from school in 1991, contact with Bethany was to change his life and ours as a family.

ENTER ANDREW GILLIES

Andrew Gillies came to visit Bethany with a view to volunteering for a year. He was taking a year out before going to university to read English and German. He had been offered a job plus a car in Germany, but on a theatre trip to London he had seen people sleeping rough, and God had prompted him to use his gap year to do something positive about homelessness. At the time of Andrew's initial visit, Alan was working on renovations of bedrooms on the top floor of the Centre. One day in the middle of the job Alan realized he should have been at the railway station to collect Andrew. Obviously never looking in the mirror, he grabbed car keys, shouted to our daughter that if she wanted a lift up the town she was to come 'Now', and raced out the door. Waverley Station in Edinburgh can be a very busy place, and there were plenty of people milling around. Alan had his own preconceived ideas of what a Careforce volunteer would look like – Andrew was to be only Bethany's third, so Alan naively hadn't thought through that there was no such thing as a 'standard volunteer'! Eventually there seemed to be only two people left on the station. Alan diffidently asked the young man with a long black coat, winkle-picker shoes and hair standing straight up (graphically declaring he was an ardent fan of a group called The Cure), if he was Andrew Gillies. Rather bemused, Andrew also asked the vision before him with plaster in his hair, dirty face and definitely not wearing his preaching clothes, if he was Rev. Alan Berry!

However, one person was definitely impressed. Elizabeth had decided that this Careforce volunteer had 'potential'. Later that evening, after Alan told the family about Andrew's arrival, Elizabeth asked me where in the Bible did it speak of 'man looking on the outward appearance but God looking on the heart'. She wrote out the verse and placed it in a prominent position on her dad's desk! Andrew was typical of our full-time volunteers – hard-working and eager to contribute his talents to the work of the Trust, and learn from others. He was particularly good at taking minutes at staff meetings, and through these – though always politely worded and written in such a way that offence could not be taken – he had the uncanny ability of reminding other staff of things they had agreed but failed to do! His example of consistent Christian living had a great effect on Elizabeth. Not only did he help her to make a full commitment to the Lord, but after several years of study also married her! There is, however, no truth in the rumour that Alan managed to get 'Seven Levels of Care' into his 'father-of-the-bride's speech' at the wedding – he had been warned!

Some placements have had outcomes far beyond what the volunteer ever imagined. Helen is someone who comes to my mind in this respect. During her conversion course to become a staff nurse, she had to organize her own placement. Bethany House was suggested as a good place to gain some experience of social problems in the community. The staff agreed that she could work two evenings a week as a volunteer. She completed and passed the course but continued at Bethany for a while longer. She enjoyed the friendly atmosphere of the staff and residents, with her role being mainly that of a befriender.

During this time she went to a Stauros meeting with some of the residents. She was not a Christian and had no idea what the group was about, but she went and joined in the singing, and listened to people speaking of how God had changed their lives. She was really moved and saw in the others a faith and compassion that she did not have. She began reading the Bible and eventually committed her life to God. She and her husband started attending Penicuik South Church, and were baptized and joined the fellowship there.

Due to working commitments and family bereavements, she had to give up her time in Bethany. Her hospital work continued to become increasingly stressful, so she resigned and decided to have a complete break from work. She then started to ask God to show her what He wanted her to do. She eventually rang Bethany House again and was delighted that she was able to go back three mornings a week as a volunteer.

She helped with household chores, cleaned and prepared the rooms for new residents, cooked lunch and helped residents with their kitchen duties. The variety of tasks made the job interesting and enjoyable. The residents were encouraged to develop skills to help them cope better in their own homes in the future. Working with them helped to build up good relationships and the residents' self-confidence. Being a volunteer, she found that residents saw her slightly differently from regular staff and that made it easier to be a friend. She did not have the barriers that come with the role of enforcing house rules. Going back to Bethany was a joyful experience. She was so glad she made that call and knew that she was giving back a little of what Bethany had given her.

Other residents and tenants have volunteered outwith Bethany. One such is John who for six years has helped at the Cyrenians Fareshare Project, which goes to supermarkets to collect good-quality food which isn't going to be sold and distributes it to homeless hostels. The enterprise takes orders for fruit, vegetables and other food from the hostels, and John makes up the orders in trays and sends them out on the vans. The project has grown so much that it now delivers to forty-three venues across Edinburgh and the Lothians, with about eight tonnes of food every week.

Carol-Anne, of Cyrenians, says as well as distributing healthy food to those who need it, and at the same time preventing this food going to waste, the project provides supported volunteering opportunities. This helps people like John have a purpose, and being able to make a contribution to society makes a huge difference. About 80 per cent of their volunteers have homelessness issues in their lives. John has supported other volunteers through their problems and his enthusiasm and total reliability have been of real value to the project. John himself says that, having been hungry and homeless himself, even to the extent of sleeping rough for two years in Dumfries, his heart is really in his voluntary work.

From time to time Bethany has joined with Volunteer Development Scotland and other organizations nationwide to participate in 'Volunteer Week,' which aims to recognize and reward the contribution and achievements of volunteers, and raise the profile of volunteering in the community. Probably a good many people who read this will have volunteered within Bethany in some capacity or other. If not, why not try it? You will find that you are not only giving, but receiving much as well.

CHAPTER 19

GIVING HOPE AND A FUTURE

The previous chapters have shown how, in the grace of God, it is possible for men and women to find hope and a future. They have shown too that 'breaking free' from cycles of homelessness, addiction, unemployment and despair is not easy and may take a long time, with stops, starts and falls along the way, and how loving, caring support is vital for those who are brave enough to try.

In the April 2007 Bethany newsletter there was a challenging article entitled 'Repeats'. It reminded me of a certain ex-resident who, having had a drink, would periodically arrive at reception in Bethany Hall. His usual greeting was 'Once a Bethany boy, always a Bethany boy'. This statement can be understood in different ways. Certainly if people have been helped by Bethany, it is encouraging for staff to feel the services rendered have been appreciated and therefore that the ex-client will always to some extent feel 'a Bethany boy'. Some have experienced support through several of the Levels of Care, and others have even been involved with all seven. But one of Bethany's aims is to offer a level of support which does not encourage a dependency syndrome. Rather, service-users are urged to take responsibility for their own choices, move forward and become their own person – or even better, God's person To change their thinking, so that the 'revolving door' scenario (coming to Bethany, leaving Bethany and then repeating this), which sees no escape from being a 'Bethany boy' is not inevitable. There is a world of difference between accepting 'once an alcoholic, always an alcoholic' and equating this with having no hope or future.

Below I have quoted the article verbatim because, although in one sense it is distressing, it sums up what the Trust believes and is seeking to do, and in the will of God will continue to do. This does not mean that the Trust has never made mistakes, in its structures, plans or day-to-day dealings with individuals. Christian trusts may be run by Christians, but they too are only sinners saved by grace. But God does not make mistakes, and in Jeremiah 29:11, in the context of the first exile of the Jews into Babylon, God was assuring the people through the prophet that He had plans for them, 'plans to give them hope and a future'. The article reads as follows:-

'Have you ever checked the TV Guide to find out which programmes you would like to watch, only to discover it's all repeats you've seen many times before? Do the same old reruns make you fed up and wish for something new?

Yet while we get excited about new things, many of us are creatures of habit who take comfort from the familiar and our known routines. To some, though we may not like to admit it, the repeats are the highlight of our TV viewing. Even if it's a dreadful film, there's a sense of comfort in knowing what will happen. For whatever reason, we re-watch TV programmes or reread books we have read a hundred times before, no matter how bad.

Sometimes trudging dreary paths of familiarity is more appealing than facing uncharted open waters. If a loved one were to become homeless, or fall foul to an addiction, it is difficult to imagine the impact that would have. Yet were they to turn their back on these ways and return to the fold, most of us would welcome them with open arms. Imagine the euphoria. The father ran to welcome back the prodigal son, so great was his relief that his son had returned. Picture the celebration. Now consider this.

The same person strays again. They return to their old ways. Your hopes are dashed. If they return again, how do you react? Do you forgive so easily? The third time? The sixth time? People regularly fall back into old ways, no matter how bad. How many times can we forgive and have faith that the renewed life is permanent this time?'

Nationally one third of tenancies fail in the first six months. One third of people who have been homeless before and have worked to acquire a new home, lose it just after they have moved in. It seems crazy.

Research done at Bethany House shows that 21% of service users were readmitted within a two-year period. That means that one in five residents have been there before.

There are a myriad of reasons for this, practical and emotional. Bethany has a range of services specially designed to combat this, and an exceptional success rate when compared to other agencies. This still doesn't make it easy though.

How do staff feel when a service user who has been reunited with their family, found a new home, released from their addictions, returns again? The practical and emotional price of falling backwards is high for everyone involved. When does a parent give up on their child? When do we as individuals stop forgiving and having hope? Should Bethany ever turn people away?

Service users often have little faith in themselves. They have little faith in services to genuinely care for them and they presume that forgiveness is out of the question. Hope is a foreign word. Hope is our secret weapon. Moving on positively and permanently is our ultimate goal. We can only succeed through hope and forgiveness. There is a hope and a new future for all.'

One who found this to be true in her own experience was my dear friend, Margaret, to whose memory this book is dedicated. For years Margaret had her own struggles with addiction, yet her last years were ones of release in which she fulfilled a role as a loving wife and a valued colleague in the administration office in Bethany Hall. Dressed in her smart black suit and with her briefcase, she delighted to accompany Alan and others to meetings at which she willingly and humbly gave testimony to the power of God in her life. But it had not always been the case. She was indeed an elegant lady but when bound by her addiction, was anything but – sleeping rough in car parks in central Edinburgh, and drinking from puddles. She was grateful for all the love and care she had received, initially from the staff at Bethany House where she had arrived dirty and alone and was greeted with a hug, and later from her support worker Marion Gemmell. As Margaret said, Marion had faith in her when she had none in herself. And yet she wanted to move on, not always wanting to be seen as 'a Bethany girl.' Confident in her renewed faith in God, it was important to her to move from 'Supported' housing to her own home, to make friends outwith the Trust and to undertake a course of study which would enable her to help others.

During her final months as she battled with a new enemy, cancer, her courage and faith were an inspiration and, although physical healing was not granted, the evidence of inner healing was evident to all. The ex-resident who felt that 'once a Bethany boy, always a Bethany boy' was at her funeral – a funeral where there weren't enough seats in the church for all the people who wanted to give thanks to God for the life of someone who only a few years before had been isolated and alone. Maybe it gave him cause to re-evaluate his own position and trust God for new hope and a future himself.

CHAPTER 20

WHAT'S IN A NAME?

And finally, back to where we started – the name 'Bethany'. Over the years many people have asked how it was chosen. In Chapter 1 the suggestion was made that it was probably chosen because the name of the village in the Bible meant 'A Place of Quiet Rest'. Bethany may not always have been such, but years ago when Alan was asked to speak about the work of the Trust, he looked up the references to Bethany in the Bible and found the implications of the name were far-reaching, and were particularly relevant to the work of the Trust.

For instance, it was a village where *Jesus stayed* during the most traumatic week of His earthly life, beginning with Palm Sunday and ending with the crucifixion. He preached in the Temple in Jerusalem during the day and went out to Bethany in the evening. It must therefore have been a place where he felt welcome and at home. (Mark 11:11) The residential units operated by Bethany Christian Trust are also places where people come to stay, often at traumatic times in their lives and where hopefully they will feel welcome and able to find peace. It is important too that they operate in such a way that Jesus Himself would feel comfortable staying there.

It was in the home of Mary, Martha and Lazarus at Bethany that Jesus *was fed*. (Luke 10:28) Over these twenty-five years there has been an amazing amount of food supplied by Bethany, ranging from full catering in the residential units, soup and rolls served at the Care Van, new culinary skills shared by staff and tenants in supported housing, and special celebration meals.

In the Biblical Bethany home, Jesus had *kindness* and love shown to Him. (John 12:1-8) It costs to be kind, and the anointing of Jesus at Bethany was with expensive ointment. There are many ways to be kind and a dose of TLC to someone who has been hurting may cost, but it has often been the beginning of healing for service users in our modern-day Bethany.

Jesus showed *emotion* at Bethany. (John 11) He wept at the grave of Lazarus, and any real involvement with people will quickly affect the emotions. So too over the years, staff have been deeply moved as they have empathized with people.

But it was also the place of *resurrection* where Jesus brought Lazarus back from the dead. Many who have had contact with the Trust feel they have had their lives given back to them, not just physically but spiritually as they have received new life in Jesus.

The vicinity of Bethany was also the place from which *Jesus ascended* into heaven (Luke 24:50), and those who have trusted in Jesus through the ministry of Bethany will also be ready whether He comes again or calls them home first.

And Bethany was a *place of contrasts*. There was a beautiful anointing, but also the accusation that Judas was a thief. Mary was worshipping, Martha was worrying and fussing. Jesus expected fruit from the tree, but on finding none it was cursed. (Mark 11:20) In our Bethany too there are always contrasts of joy and sorrow, successes and failures.

Bethany is undoubtedly a good name. One has to draw a line and halt the story somewhere, although maybe the final 'news bite' should be that Bethany will move into a new head office at 65 Bonnington Road, Leith, during 2008. The new premises will allow for teams now in different locations to operate out of one building and will provide much-needed space for expansion. If the Lord doesn't return during the next twenty-five years, someone else can write the Bethany sequel. That will certainly not be my task! By then the world at large and the community of Leith will be a very different place. Far-reaching plans have been announced that would change the face of Leith. But people's hearts and aspirations will not have fundamentally changed. People will still need to be fed, loved, released and to find hope and a future in Christ Jesus. It is good to know that God will not change and His faithfulness will still be new every morning.

Seven Levels of Care

Bethany provides a variety of services that can work together or separately. Each one meets people where they are at, and helps them move forwards towards independent living.

Level 1 **Street Work**
Nightly food, blankets and clothing
Drop-Ins providing basic support, addiction and housing advice

Level 2 **Emergency Accommodation**
Basic accommodation, hot meals and advice (from November-April)
Resettlement hostel

Level 3 **Specialist Units**
Residential addictions unit for men
Supported hostel for young men
Supported hostel for young women

Level 4 **Supported Housing**
Accommodation for individuals and families
Support vulnerable people to maintain their homes

Level 5 **Social Furniture Provision**
Furniture for people on low incomes

Level 6 **Community Education**
Learning sessions bridging the gap between homeless services and formal education
Support for vulnerable people through formal education
Facilitating volunteering and employment opportunities

Level 7 **Community Integration**
Providing networks and skills to prevent homelessness
Employment, apprenticeships and volunteering placements

BETHANY TIMELINE

EVENT	DATE
Realization of the need	1979 – 1981
Formation of Bethany Christian Trust	Late 1982
Opening of 1st building, Bethany Christian Centre, 6 Casselbank Street, Leith	4 April 1983
Verbal agreement to purchase derelict Caley Club next door to Bethany Christian Centre	May 1984
Actual purchase, renovation, which included flat at 48 Kirk Street, and official opening	Jan 1985 – May 1986
Purchase of Hope House, 5 Casselbank Street, for Supported Housing	December 1988
Development of Housing Management. Gordon Weir supported people moving on from BCC	1989
Gordon Weir takes over from Alan Berry as officer in charge of Bethany Christian Centre	1990
Continued expansion of Supported Housing work	Throughout 90s
Care Van investigation and start of joint work with Edinburgh City Mission	1990
Joe Kirkhouse full-time support worker	1991
Homemaker, managed by Ewan Foreman, opens in Pilton	1992
1st Bethany Shop, Hamilton Place, Edinburgh	1993
Purchase and renovation of Bethany House	1993-4
Purchase of Bethany Hall for Admin and Training	1994
First official BETAN course	Feb 1995

2nd Bethany Shop, Summerhall Place, Edinburgh	1995
Bethany Home Farm purchase	1996
First 'pilot' Christmas Night Shelter	1996
Three Assistant Directors appointed	Sept 1997
3rd Bethany Shop, Gullane, East Lothian	Jan 1998
New Hub leased in Leith	March 1998
New Homemaker developed in Haddington Place Shop	May 1998
Specialist Addiction Support workers appointed	Dec 1998
Fife expansion work (forerunner of Toastie Club)	1999
Bethany Shop, Morningside, Edinburgh	2000
Dumfries expansion begins	2001/2
New Lease in Haddington Place for Referrals Section	2001
Bethany Shop in Corstorphine, Edinburgh	2001
Bethany Shop, Dalry, Edinburgh	2001
Bethany becomes a Charitable Company Ltd, by Guarantee	2002
Alan Berry retires, Iain Gordon appointed as CEO	2002
1st Bethany shop in Hamilton Place closed	2002
Bethany Shop in Duke Street, Leith, opened	2002
Matthew/Martha Houses, West Lothian, purchased as young people's units	2003
Floating Support to vulnerable households in Fife	2003
New Bethany Shop relocated in Hamilton Place	2003
Leven, Fife Drop-In opened	2005
Bethany Shop in Kirkcaldy, Fife	2007

Christian Focus Publications
publishes books for all ages

Our mission statement:

STAYING FAITHFUL
In dependence upon God we seek to help make His infallible Word, the Bible, relevant. Our aim is to ensure that the Lord Jesus Christ is presented as the only hope to obtain forgiveness of sin, live a useful life and look forward to heaven with Him.

REACHING OUT
Christ's last command requires us to reach out to our world with His gospel. We seek to help fulfil that by publishing books that point people towards Jesus and help them develop a Christ-like maturity. We aim to equip all levels of readers for life, work, ministry and mission.

Books in our adult range are published in three imprints.
Christian Focus contains popular works including biographies, commentaries, basic doctrine and Christian living. Our children's books are also published in this imprint.
Mentor focuses on books written at a level suitable for Bible College and seminary students, pastors, and other serious readers. The imprint includes commentaries, doctrinal studies, examination of current issues and church history.
Christian Heritage contains classic writings from the past.

Christian Focus Publications, Ltd
Geanies House, Fearn, Ross-shire,
IV20 1TW, Scotland, United Kingdom
info@christianfocus.com

For details of our titles visit us on our website
www.christianfocus.com